The Undercover Police Scandal

The story of the spycops network by the
women who uncovered the shocking truth

'Alison', 'Belinda', Helen Steel, 'Lisa' and 'Naomi'

With Veronica Clark

EBURY
SPOTLIGHT

5 7 9 10 8 6 4

Ebury Spotlight, an imprint of Ebury Publishing
20 Vauxhall Bridge Road
London SW1V 2SA

Ebury Spotlight is part of the Penguin Random House group of companies
whose addresses can be found at global.penguinrandomhouse.com

First published with the title *Deep Deception* by Ebury Spotlight in 2022

This paperback edition is published in 2025.

www.penguin.co.uk

A CIP catalogue record for this book is available from the British Library

ISBN 9781529108323

Printed and bound in Great Britain by Clays Ltd, Elcograf S.p.A.
The authorised representative in the EEA is Penguin Random House Ireland,
Morrison Chambers, 32 Nassau Street, Dublin D02 YH68

Penguin Random House is committed to a sustainable future
for our business, our readers and our planet. This book is
made from Forest Stewardship Council® certified paper.

Five women.

Five true stories.

Twenty-four years of deception.

Thousands of police lies.

Just the tip of the iceberg.

Who can you trust?

To Rosa and her children, in the hope that one day
your story will also be truly heard ...

To Kate and Ruth, who also fought the case with us, and to
all other survivors of deceitful relationships whose lives have
been intruded upon by such state spying operations ...

And to Harriet Wistrich for enabling us,
with her patience, commitment and tenacity,
to start out on the long road to justice.

Prologue

In 1968, a shadowy undercover police unit was established in Britain – the Special Demonstration Squad (SDS) – to spy on protesters in mainly left-wing and progressive groups. This police unit along with its successor – the National Public Order Intelligence Unit (NPOIU), formed in 1999 – targeted anyone with a desire to protest the status quo. That included anyone expressing a dissenting voice, or attempting to hold the government or big business to account. Only a handful of far-right groups were infiltrated among the many hundreds of left-wing ones.

Officers from the SDS and NPOIU secretly infiltrated organisations by 'any means necessary', including forming long-term, intimate sexual and emotional relationships with women activists like us, having children with some and robbing others of the chance of motherhood. More than twenty undercover officers have so far been identified as having deceived women into intimate relationships. We had no idea we were involved with men who were police spies. Some of these officers had relationships with more than one woman during their missions. There are undoubtedly many more such stories to be uncovered.

We discovered the truth about these men's identities and tactics through our own research and shared experiences. It was those efforts that led to the public exposure of the officers and subsequent widespread outcry about the activities of these units. If it wasn't for our hard work and that of other activists who were spied upon, it is likely that this kind of tactic would still be in operation without scrutiny. Since these initial discoveries, the tactics of the SDS and NPOIU have become one of the biggest policing scandals of our time. The revelations led in part to the announcement of a public inquiry, which began taking evidence in November 2020. The fight for truth and justice is far from over.

For those targeted, the betrayal and the Orwellian surveillance that was behind it have devastated lives.

Here, in our own words, five of us tell our stories.

The Women and the Spies

The five women when they met 'their' spies (1987–2010):

'Belinda', 24, non-activist, worked as an accounts assistant with the Central Electricity Generating Board.

Helen Steel, 22, gardener and environmental and social justice activist with London Greenpeace, later one half of 'the McLibel Two'.

'Alison', 29, English and media studies teacher and political activist with the Colin Roach Centre.

'Lisa', 29, student, climbing and mountaineering enthusiast and environmental and social justice activist with groups including Earth First!

'Naomi', 32, gardener, social justice campaigner and environmental activist with Earth First!

The four undercover police spies who targeted the women:

Bob Robinson, 29 (real name **Bob Lambert**, 35)

John Barker, 27 (real name **John Dines**, 32)

Mark Cassidy, 27 (real name **Mark Jenner**, 31)

Mark Stone, 34 (real name **Mark Kennedy**, 34)

Given the intrusion we were subjected to, four of us wish to remain anonymous – so are identified only by first names, some of which are pseudonyms. Other names in the book have also been changed to protect privacy. Those spied on have a right to anonymity in a way that was never afforded to them by the police. We do not accept that any of the police officers who have perpetrated the kinds of abuses described in this book are entitled to anonymity. Those who commit such serious abuses should have to answer for their actions.

Belinda

(Officer: Bob Robinson)

East End, London, April 1987

I didn't want to go to the party – it was a Monday night and I had to be up early for work the next day. But my old university friend Simon persuaded me to go.

'Just because you want to get with that girl!' I teased.

Simon looked up, smirked and shrugged his shoulders as though he'd been caught out.

'Okay, Belinda, but when do you ever say no to a party?'

I grinned; it was true.

The party was being held at a shared house in East London and by the time we'd arrived it was already in full swing. There were around a hundred people crammed inside an impressive Victorian townhouse, spread across three floors. People had spilled into the garden and street outside as music thudded from within.

Unfortunately, the target of Simon's affections seemed to be the target of everyone else's too. Although I didn't know her myself, she'd gone to the same university as us and he'd already told me on the way over that she was involved in animal rights. I was a vegetarian, so I understood the sentiments and supported the ideology. However, I was more interested in other issues like world inequalities, women's and children's rights myself.

I'd met Simon in my first year at uni and we'd been firm friends ever since. He was extremely well-read and great fun to be around. Once we'd graduated, we moved into a shared house in London with six other university friends to try to seek our fortune. We knew that living in London would help us to secure professional jobs, something so much harder to come by up north.

None of us were remotely involved in political activism, other than attending the odd student demo and having a shared dislike for Margaret Thatcher's policies.

We'd graduated a few years earlier from the University of Lancaster, and I had recently started a new job as an accounts assistant with the Central Electricity Generating Board (CEGB).

We'd arrived at the party around nine o'clock, armed with cans of Stella. The living room was thick with smoke and the conversation was loud. People were desperately trying to be heard above the sound of The Smiths' 'This Charming Man' as it boomed out of speakers in the corner of the room.

I felt a bit of an outsider at the party because this wasn't my usual crowd. There seemed to be a lot of political types there so I decided that, if the subject arose, I'd keep my job to myself. To me, my job was a means to an end in that it paid the bills and enabled me to further my career. Some of the people there looked pretty hardcore, and I thought they may have disapproved of me working for the CEGB because of its association with nuclear power.

A crush of people had congregated in the kitchen, coats had been draped over the back of the sofa and an ashtray had accidentally tipped over, carpeting a patch of the floor in grey ash. A bottle of wine had also been spilt; claret red splattered across the floor.

Simon left me alone almost immediately to try to find the girl he fancied, but she was far too busy chatting to her friends so he didn't get much of a look-in and soon returned to me. Besides the girl, neither of us knew another soul there. Everyone was really friendly though, so Simon and I stood around and chatted happily to each other and some of our fellow partygoers for a while. We were still sipping our lukewarm lager when people began to drift off and the room thinned.

'Shall we call it a night then?' Simon asked.

I glanced at my watch.

'Yeah, we'll catch the last bus if we're quick.'

My eyes drifted around the room, and that's when I saw him – a dark-haired guy who was standing over in the corner; he was staring straight at me. He was tall, slim and so good-looking that I felt a spark as our eyes locked and we smiled at one another. I didn't want to make it too easy for him so I turned away. When I glanced over again he was still staring. He looked older than me – in his late twenties – and was standing with five other people. But he seemed distracted.

'I think I'm going to go and find her, you know, to say goodbye.'

It was Simon; his voice snapped me back into the moment.

'I think she might be downstairs,' he continued, nodding over towards the door. 'Anyway, I won't be long.'

'Right,' I mumbled, taking another sip of lager.

Running for the bus now was the last thing on my mind. Things were looking up and I didn't want to leave, at least not until I'd spoken to this guy. With Simon gone, I was all alone; I peered awkwardly down at the can in my hands – my fingers tapping against the tin. I was just wondering what to do when the stranger crossed the room to speak to me.

'Hi, I'm Bob. Bob Robinson.'

'Belinda.' I smiled.

He nodded.

'So,' he said, gesturing around the room. 'Who do you know here?'

I took a too-big gulp of lager and shook my head.

'Oh, no one. I don't know anyone, really. I've come with my friend, Simon. He's just nipped downstairs to say goodbye to someone.'

We started chatting. I very much hoped that Simon wouldn't reappear immediately because it would cut my conversation short with Bob.

The more we spoke, the more at ease I felt. Bob was both charismatic and charming and by the time Simon eventually resurfaced fifteen minutes later, we were deeply engrossed in conversation. I spotted him hovering behind Bob, so I shot him a warning glance: push off and leave us alone. Simon took his cue and tactfully disappeared. It was blatantly obvious from our body language that Bob and I were interested in each other. Half an hour later, when Simon returned again, I felt my heart sink a little. However, I couldn't stop smiling when Bob offered to give us both a lift home.

'My van's parked outside; it's no problem,' he insisted.

'Are you sure?'

'Absolutely!'

I was still beaming as we left the party and followed Bob outside; I'd already decided to ask him for his phone number. As his white van trundled off down the road, we chatted some more and Bob told me he was twenty-nine years old – five years older than me. He explained he was a vegan who was passionate about animal rights. I thought maybe I'd found someone who I could not only have an intelligent and interesting conversation with but, potentially, a relationship too. I'd recently had my heart broken and was still hung up on my last boyfriend, who had decided to end things. So Bob could be just the tonic I needed.

We pulled up outside our shared house in Forest Gate. For a split second, I felt tempted to ask him inside, but thought better of it. After all, I'd only met him an hour before. Bob wasn't even my usual type; but there was something about him that had piqued my interest and I could almost feel a ripple of electricity as it passed between us. Although it was clear he was also extremely interested, I decided to tread carefully and give myself space to think.

With Simon already at our front door, I turned to Bob and we shared a quick kiss.

'Could I ring you?' he asked enthusiastically.

I hurriedly scribbled my phone number down on a piece of paper. He folded it and slipped it into his back pocket. I couldn't stop grinning as I got out of his van and slammed the door behind me. I turned to give him a final wave as the van jolted forward and pulled away. I stood there, watching the tail-lights as they became two small red dots before disappearing into the night.

By the time I'd walked inside the house, Simon was waiting for me.

'He seemed really keen,' he said.

'Yeah, I was going to invite him in, but I don't really know him, and I've got work tomorrow.'

Simon nodded.

'Yeah, better to get to know him a bit first. I mean, he could be anyone.'

The following evening, I felt exhausted as I walked in after a long day at work. I'd just turned the key in the lock and pushed open the door when Simon walked past.

'There's a letter for you. It's on the side. Someone put it through the door.'

I ripped open the envelope to reveal a piece of card; it had been crudely trimmed with a pair of scissors. On one side was a colourful illustration of a fox, a dog, a fish and a bird. On the other was a handwritten note from Bob. In it he said he'd been thinking about me a lot and that he'd ring me shortly to organise a date! I was absolutely thrilled because my instincts had been right; Bob liked me as much as I liked him.

True to his word, he called and we arranged to meet for a proper date. He told me he lived in Hackney, which wasn't too far from my place, so we decided on a meal in Stoke Newington. The vegetarian restaurant was packed out and the food was delicious. At the end of it, I insisted on paying half.

'No,' Bob said, putting his hand over mine. 'Let me get this.'

But I was adamant.

'Bob, I don't like any man paying for me – I always pay my own way, and I want to pay half.'

'Okay,' he reluctantly agreed, resting back in his chair.

I had my principles too, which were important to me. I wanted him to understand that.

Bob was genuine, romantic and attentive towards me at all times. He was also a member of London Greenpeace, a supporter of the Animal Liberation Front (ALF) and a vegan; he had all the credentials of a committed activist. I picked up my drink and sipped it, trying to swallow my discomfort as I remembered I needed to tell him about my job at the electricity board. Surely, he would much prefer a girlfriend with similar political motivations and a lifestyle more like his own.

I wasn't ashamed of my job in the slightest – people need electricity, after all, and I worked hard with my team in the payroll department. I just thought he might disapprove. There was a chance it could effectively end things before they'd even had a chance to begin.

'Penny for your thoughts?'

It was Bob.

'Oh, nothing.' I smiled.

'Good. Listen, do you want to come back to my place? It's not much, it's …'

'Yes,' I answered a little too quickly.

We stepped out into the mild London spring evening; the smell and anticipation of a warm summer ahead had filled the air with hope. I felt Bob's hand slip into mine and allowed any initial doubts to disperse. It had been a long time since I'd felt so buoyant with happiness.

Somewhere above our heads, U2's 'With or Without You' blared out of a half-opened window and drifted down to the street below. I knew it right then – I could feel it in my bones – I was falling for Bob already.

Bob's flat, Graham Road, Hackney, London, April 1987

The first-floor flat was above a barber's shop and was really grotty inside. There was a single mattress on the floor, a small bedside table, a bookcase, and a few clothes and personal possessions scattered around. Other than that, there was very little else. In some ways, the sparse furniture gave the impression of someone who didn't plan to stick around for long. But this was Bob – he was anti-capitalist, so it totally fitted that he wouldn't have many possessions.

In spite of this, somehow, I'd expected more. I swallowed down my disappointment and turned to face the windows. They overlooked the street outside and were thick with grime, both inside and out. There was no living room or other space to speak of apart from a small, draughty shared kitchen and toilet. I tried to hide my shock and instead wandered over to the bookcase. There was a pile of leaflets stacked on it, so I plucked one from the top. Printed across it were the words: *What's Wrong with McDonald's?* I glanced down at the rest of the leaflets – there were around 500 of them stacked in a neat pile. Anti-McDonald's pamphlets didn't surprise me in the least. After all, I knew he was a committed vegan campaigner.

'Told you it's not much,' Bob said, gesturing to the room.

But I didn't care; it was a small fault in a good man, and Bob was definitely a good man who shunned capitalist values. I also thought he might think I was a bit of a fraud because I wasn't an activist.

'I've been on a CND march,' I offered, even though it had just been the one.

I felt guilty that I wasn't as committed to my own political values as Bob; his priorities seemed so far removed from my own. I wasn't even bothered that he didn't have a proper job – it wasn't important to me because I had money of my own. I was an independent woman, and I didn't need a man to keep me. I always had and always would pay my own way.

'I drive a taxi as well,' Bob explained as we settled down with our drinks. 'It's mainly nights, but I share it with another guy. It helps pay for all this,' he said looking around the room.

I knew then that he must have a very limited income.

Belinda's diary entry, London, May 1987

I'm writing this at a good point in my life. Living in a house with eight people in it … no problems to report except minor insecurities. That is, of course, until I met Bob recently, which has brought all kinds of questions for me to worry about. It's the first time for ages I've started seeing someone I could really get to like. A recent party introduced me to Bob, the cab-driving, gardening vegan, who seems to be an active member of Greenpeace. The most obvious problem is that I have slightly covered up the fact that I work for the dreaded CEGB, which I get intermittent pangs of guilt about. I'm toying with the idea of coming clean and telling him about it tomorrow.

I've only seen Bob three times, and am already developing tell-tale signs such as boredom with time between seeing him, irritability and downright neurosis about me, him, what will/won't or should/ could be.

I needed to tell Bob and come clean about my job before he found out. Honesty was the best policy, especially if we were to have a proper, loving relationship. There couldn't be any secrets between us – what was developing between us was far too good to mess up.

A few days later, we were sitting together in Bob's dingy flat.

Tell him now!

'There's something I need to say. I haven't been quite straight with you ...' I began, casting my eyes towards the floor. I wasn't sure where to even begin. By nature, I'd always been an honest person, so it had to be done.

'What is it?' Bob asked, propping himself up on the mattress. His eyes searched mine, trying to second-guess what bombshell I was about to drop.

'... I work for the Central Electricity Generating Board,' I said, blurting the words out.

They hung heavily in the air as I waited for Bob's reaction. I expected him to be thoroughly pissed off that I'd not been straight with him from the beginning. But instead, he began to laugh.

'Is that it? For a minute, I didn't know what you were going to tell me!' he said, roaring with laughter.

I was absolutely dumbstruck.

'But don't you mind? Aren't you annoyed with me?'

But Bob was only half-listening because he was still busy chuckling away to himself.

'No, of course not. I wouldn't do it myself, but I'm not angry with you. How could I be?'

His reaction surprised me, but in a good way. It also confirmed that he really did like me regardless. If he hadn't, surely he would have used my job as an excuse to finish it then.

However, moments later, he revealed a secret of his own.

'I've got something to tell you too,' he said. 'I've got a son.'

Bob explained how a former girlfriend had fallen pregnant.

'But you'll have to meet him, Belinda,' he said, his eyes lighting up at the thought. 'He's such a great kid.'

I felt happy he'd told me about his son, also that he'd suggested I meet him; it reinforced the possibility I could be part of Bob's future – our future.

Even though he didn't earn a regular income, Bob explained that he got by doing cash-in-hand gardening jobs in well-heeled areas around London, such as Hampstead; he also illegally touted for cab pick-ups and customers at Heathrow to top up his money.

We were both busy with work but still managed to spend most evenings together. Usually, he'd come over to my place because it was more comfortable and sociable. Bob seemed very well-read and was a great conversationalist. He'd often get into deep debates with my housemates, usually Simon. The two of them would spend hours sitting on the floor in front of the gas fire, drinking Stella, having intense and meaningful discussions about animal rights and politics in general. I knew Bob was involved in the Animal Liberation Front (ALF), but I didn't know much about it and wasn't interested in that. By now, I was smitten; I couldn't believe how easily this wonderful man had slotted into my life. He was genuine, passionate and committed and everyone liked him.

Hackney, London, June 1987

One day, Bob and I were strolling around Hackney when he suggested we nip into a nearby café. As we took our seats, he told me there was something urgent that he needed to speak to me about. His face looked so solemn that I expected the worst; my heart felt like a lead weight. We'd been seeing each other for over a month and I was as blissfully in love with him as he seemed to be with me.

'What is it?' I asked, slumping down into the chair opposite his.

'It's important, Belinda.'

He looked so serious that I convinced myself it must be bad news. 'Just say it; whatever it is, just tell me!'

'Belinda,' he said, holding my hands in the space he'd created between us. 'I want you to promise to be faithful to me and not sleep with anyone else.'

The nervous breath I'd been holding came flooding out of my lungs as a sigh of relief.

Was that all?

'Of course,' I insisted. However, Bob didn't give me a chance to reply because he hadn't finished.

'I don't want to get HIV,' he added bluntly, not even looking me in the eye.

'What?' I gasped.

I waited for him to laugh and say it'd been a joke, only he didn't – he was deadly serious.

'I … I … I don't know what to say. I can't believe you've even said that. I'd never do that to you,' I said, trying to hide my disbelief. 'Listen, this is the real thing for me, Bob. I love you.'

He smiled and returned the sentiment. We'd never said that to each other before. But I felt hurt that he could ever think I'd be interested in anyone else when we were both so passionate about each other. I just wouldn't do something like that to him.

How could he even ask such a thing?

I felt disconcerted and also a little insulted, but I was madly in love so I made excuses for him. I put his sudden sombre mood down to all the doom-and-gloom government HIV public health adverts being screened on TV – one with a volcano ominously erupting and John Hurt's voice booming as a tombstone fell. Government leaf-lets had also been pushed through doors up and down the country, warning us: *Don't Die of Ignorance.* Luckily for me and Bob, we'd found each other now and, since our conversation, I knew neither of us were going to take any risks.

Earl's Court, London, Peter Gabriel gig, 27 June 1987

As we approached the distinctive white art deco building of Earl's Court, I turned and squeezed Bob's hand.

'Thanks for buying me the ticket. I can't wait to see him.'

We walked inside the venue, my hand still wrapped inside his. The place was packed with people of varying ages. I bought some drinks and we found somewhere to stand where we could see the stage. The noise from the crowd gathered momentum; the lights dimmed into blackness and a huge cheer rose up from the back. Then Peter Gabriel walked onto the stage bathed in a pure single white light.

Bob turned to me, his eyes glinting with excitement as he pulled me close. This was our first gig together, and it was amazing. When Peter Gabriel started to sing 'Games Without Frontiers', I looked at Bob; he was busy facing the stage, singing along.

I realised then just how happy and lucky I was to have met him at that party.

Forest Gate, London, July 1987

Bob had often talked about direct action on behalf of the ALF, including damaging a random butcher's shop front with graffiti. It sounded more like vandalism to me, and I couldn't even see what he thought he was going to achieve.

'Why do you have to do it?' I asked one afternoon as we walked in a nearby park.

'Because it's who I am – it's what I do.'

I wasn't convinced. It felt more like bravado on his part, as though he was trying to prove to his friends that he was the most serious activist they had. I could tell he was desperate for me to show an interest and get involved. I hoped it meant he saw me as his soul-mate. However, secretly, I wanted him to grow up a bit.

I assumed that now he'd met me, he'd stop whatever he was up to, and he did seem to be going in that direction. He seemed to be getting more and more uncomfortable about going on demos and being an activist, whatever that involved, and something was definitely bothering him.

'Well, I think it all sounds very ill-advised,' I remarked.

It was at that moment he mentioned the anti-McDonald's leaflet – the one I'd picked up from the pile on his bookcase, back at the flat.

'The police are looking for me, you know,' he told me as we strolled around the park.

'Why?'

'It's those leaflets …' he replied, before starting to laugh.

But I didn't get the joke.

'What's funny?'

He was laughing so hard that he found it difficult to finish off his sentence.

'… It was me; *I* wrote them.'

By now, Bob was creased over with laughter, but I still didn't get it. I waited for him to elaborate, but he didn't say anything else. Instead, I stood there looking at him in total confusion.

What did he find so funny about him writing anti-McDonald's leaflets?

Bob discussed the ALF with me. Even though I knew it was a big part of his life, I really didn't want to know what he got up to in case he dragged me down with him. However, in the weeks that followed, I noticed cracks in his armour, as though he'd had enough himself.

'Why don't you back off a bit? Give it up for a while?' I suggested.

He thought for a moment and then shook his head.

'No, I'm in too deep, Belinda. I'm involved in stuff I can't get out of now.'

He looked at me as though there was so much more he wanted to say but he couldn't explain why.

In spite of his reservations, he remained on the activist scene and once even managed to drag me along to a London Greenpeace meeting. I found the meeting to be boring beyond belief but fortunately it was nearly over when we'd arrived.

When Bob had first walked into the room, I'd noticed how everyone turned to look at him. Their eyes seemed to follow him because he oozed confidence, and everyone wanted a piece. He owned every room he entered and when he spoke they all seemed to listen. At first, I couldn't fathom it. Then I realised that he had a special kind of confidence and presence that was uncommon among other activists. Instead, he carried himself in the same way a professional person or a manager would. Somehow, his body language didn't match a largely unemployed animal-rights campaigner. I couldn't put my finger on it, but Bob commanded respect, and people gave it to him.

You certainly are an enigma, I thought as he mingled with other activists after the meeting. He could have had a great career in something but he'd forgone all that for his principles. In some ways, it made me proud to be his girlfriend, but I'd much have preferred it if he used his personable nature and energy to get a proper job.

'People love you, don't they?' I remarked later as we cuddled up in bed.

Bob shrugged in his usual self-deprecating way.

'What can I say? I love what I do.'

However, no matter how hard I tried, I just wasn't interested in his politics. So, following the activists' meeting experience, I arranged to meet Bob and his mates down the pub instead. Our whirlwind relationship had taken me by surprise because he'd absolutely swept me off my feet. Bob was handsome, funny and engaging. Somehow, his sheer passion for activism, his personality and charisma injected an excitement into my life that working for the electricity board just couldn't. I found him an irresistible mixture of security and danger and he brightened life in so many ways. If only he'd sort out his priorities, he'd be my perfect man.

It soon became clear to me that I hadn't been Bob's only serious relationship. I wanted to find out more but I knew I should tread gently in case he wasn't ready to share it with me.

'So, have there been any significant others?' I asked casually one day as we lay in bed. 'Apart from the mother of your child?' I was dying to know, but I also knew he was a deeply private person.

'There was an ex-girlfriend, but she moved to go and live in Ireland,' he said after a few moments. He showed me a photo of them planting a tree together when they parted.

I tried to press him further, but Bob was a closed book. In fact, he never seemed to like talking about himself or any of his past relationships. His only interests were politics and the here and now.

Forest Gate, August 1987

Bob had been busy delivering the anti-McDonald's leaflets.

'Do you want to come and help me?' he asked one morning as we awoke with a start to the sound of the early alarm.

'But it's such a waste of time,' I complained.

Bob laughed, peeled the duvet away and crossed the room to get dressed. I didn't budge; it was the weekend – my only days off. The thought of standing in shop doorways, handing out leaflets, left me cold.

'No, I'm all right, thanks,' I said, burying myself back beneath the duvet.

I had better things to do; I found it hard to be enthusiastic about causes that mattered to him because I felt they'd taken over his life. I wanted to do other things with Bob – not just sit there passively, listening to his beliefs. Meanwhile, he thought it quaint that I prioritised family life and a good job over politics. I remained quiet; I didn't tell him what I was really thinking – that I wanted and was planning for a future with him and a family of our own. *Surely he must want that too?*

Forest Gate, September 1987

Bob told me he had a big gardening job lined up in King's Lynn, in Norfolk.

'I won't be gone long, only a few weeks.'

He held me tight and told me what agony it would be to be apart. 'But I'll write,' he promised.

I knew I'd miss him, but I also knew he had to earn some money. Even anti-capitalists needed enough to live on.

Belinda's diary entry, London, September 1987

Bob. I <u>could</u> cope without him, couldn't I?

... Sameness, boredom, no challenges at all except to keep Bob, who I wish was already in the bag.

I absentmindedly began to doodle at the bottom of the page. I drew a stick version of myself and wrote: *'To Bob, love an admirer'* and scribbled a heart with an arrow, with the words: *'Bob loves Ann R Kist'*. I even signed off: *'By a nee mal rights'*. It was childish, but I didn't care because even though I was bored with the routine of my life, I was with Bob. He'd made me feel happy and carefree.

A few days later, he left for King's Lynn. True to his word, I received a letter through the post. I couldn't hide my excitement as my eyes scoured his words. He wrote, 'nothing but thoughts of you once I'm lying down in the back of the van resting my aching body!' and he said he couldn't wait to see me again. 'One thing I keep thinking about – okay, two things I keep thinking about, but I'll stick to writing about one – is our expedition next weekend. I'm so excited about it. Bob and Belinda go camping ...'

Underneath his note, he'd drawn a map of King's Lynn with dotted lines above the town and the words: *'Old Roman wall to keep Northerners out'*. I laughed because I knew he was referring to me. Holding the letter to my face, I inhaled, trying to smell him – trying to detect an ounce of his scent – but there was nothing. No trace.

He'd written that the area reminded him of the setting of *The Go-Between* by L. P. Hartley, so I searched it out and read the opening line, which seemed particularly poignant: *'The past is a foreign country: they do things differently there.'*

Soon Bob returned home and we settled into a routine. I'd see him several nights a week, depending on whether he was driving the cab or not.

REM gig, Hammersmith Odeon, London, 30 September 1987

We were driving to Hammersmith Odeon in his van when Bob decided to take a sudden detour.

'I just need to check out this bloke's house,' he told me. 'Wait there, I won't be long.'

'Can't you go another time?' I complained, but he took no notice.

I watched bewildered as he pushed open a gate and went into a garden opposite. A small dog appeared from nowhere and sank its teeth into his leg. I was just about to climb out and go to his aid when he managed to free himself and stagger back over.

Bob cursed as he eased himself back into the driver's seat. He turned the key in the ignition and the van fired into life.

'What the hell, Bob? The thing's just bitten you! Aren't you at least going to have a word with the owner?'

He indicated and the van pulled away from the kerb.

'No,' he said, shaking his head. 'I shouldn't have been there. He's something to do with one of the hunts and he knows I'm a hunt sab [i.e. saboteur]. He probably let the dog out on purpose.'

Bob did agree that he should go to hospital for a tetanus jab. However, when the nurse asked his name, he gave her a false one. After the nurse had gone, I twisted in my plastic seat to look at him.

'It's the police – they're after me, aren't they?' He shrugged by way of explanation.

'What for? Why are the police after you?' I demanded.

Bob shifted uneasily.

'Parking fines. I've loads of them. I can't let them catch me, otherwise I'll have to pay.'

It didn't make any sense but then less and less was beginning to make sense when it came to Bob. Giving a false name in a hospital felt very wrong to me and almost unfathomable, but I was young and in love so I shrugged off my feelings of unease.

Later, at the REM gig, Michael Stipe sang 'The One I Love'

I looked up at Bob and thought, *how appropriate*.

Stoke Newington, London, autumn 1987

There was a party in a squat next to a pub called The Cricketers that we drank in. Bob, a few others and I had been invited along. The squat – a disused social club – was a real dive, even by Bob's standards. At one point, we had to sit on the floor. The building was packed out, with people standing all around. A guy who'd been sniffing poppers accidentally dropped the phial he'd been holding and a bit spilled onto Bob's hair. It'd been an accident, but Bob went absolutely crackers.

'That's it,' he said, standing up, looking really upset. 'I'm going to have to go home now and wash my hair!'

I couldn't understand why he was being such a drama queen. It had been a few drops of amyl nitrate, which would have evaporated almost immediately. However, he refused to discuss it and practically sprinted off.

Connah's Quay, North Wales, 29 December 1987

It was just after Christmas when I took Bob to meet my mum and dad in Wales. I'd already told them I'd met a nice guy, so they were really looking forward to finally meeting him. We drove up and as soon as we'd stepped out of the van, Mum was waiting to greet us. The drinks were already being poured as we walked through the door. Bob wasn't a big drinker, but my dad handed him a whisky while I sipped a beer. It felt like a party atmosphere as Dad walked over to the turntable and put on some trad jazz music. My parents knew I really liked Bob, so they welcomed him with open arms. He was middle class, well-spoken and had a real presence. He oozed confidence but, unlike previous ex-university boyfriends, had no job prospects whatsoever.

'We've heard a lot about you, Bob,' Mum said, making conversation.

I felt myself blush.

She passed Bob a bowl of vegetable soup she'd rustled up for our arrival. I'd warned her in advance to make something vegan.

It was a lovely weekend and, by the end of our visit, Bob had won them both over, even though Dad seemed troubled by his lack of a 'proper' job.

'But what does he do?' he asked.

'He's a gardener, oh, and he drives a cab.'

I tried to make him sound like the hard worker my parents expected me to settle down with. However, I failed to mention his activism or lack of possessions. I could just imagine my dad thinking: *Who the hell have you just brought into our home?*

Helen
(Officer: John Barker)

I first began campaigning as a teenager, while still at school. Unusually, my comprehensive school had an agriculture department: the boys were enrolled in rural science, woodwork and metalwork, while the girls were directed to cookery, needlework and secretarial skills. My best friend and I were keen on animals, so we asked to join the rural science class. Initially we were refused and told it was for 'boys only' but eventually, after finding a couple of lads to swap with us for cookery, we got to study agriculture. We usually cleaned out the pigsty on Fridays and the pigs almost became friends. They had piglets, which were adorable, and we loved looking after them. One day, the piglets were rounded up and the whole class went on a trip to the local slaughterhouse. My best friend was a lifelong vegetarian and, after watching a whole line of other pigs being killed, I was so upset, I became vegetarian too. During a parents' evening we handed out leaflets against factory farming and asked the adults to sign a petition against veal crates.

As I learnt about other forms of injustice I campaigned on a wide range of issues – against racism and apartheid; against poverty and police repression; for women's equal rights; for lesbian and gay rights; for environmental sustainability; and for freedom to roam. At seventeen I took part in the huge 'Embrace the Base' demonstration when women surrounded Greenham Common airbase to oppose nuclear weapons, and at eighteen I stayed in a mining village and joined picket lines in support of striking miners in the dispute of 1984–85.

From these experiences I learnt that the police would protect the status quo and often use violence against people protesting, but I also learnt the strength of people joining together to achieve change, even if they weren't always successful. The feminist groups I joined taught me that when women came together and shared experiences, we could start to see patterns of male dominance, male feelings of entitlement to women's bodies and women's socialisation to defer to men's wants. Armed with that knowledge we could then see the importance of overturning sexist values.

London Greenpeace, spring 1987

I became involved with London Greenpeace after the group hosted a talk by an Australian Aboriginal speaker. He was in the UK to campaign in support of Aboriginal land rights during a re-enactment of the first fleet sailing to and colonising Australia 200 years before. I liked the fact that the group was directed at both environmental and social justice issues. People there seemed friendly and weren't too dogmatic. I also liked that the philosophy was about people taking action to improve the world ourselves rather than appealing to politicians to do it for us.

We'd arrange protests on various social and environmental issues. An activist called Bob Robinson was part of the group and, at some point, he introduced his girlfriend Belinda. She wasn't involved in campaigning but was friendly and easy to chat to.

London Greenpeace, late 1987

A guy called John Barker started coming to the weekly meetings on a regular basis. Although we always began with everyone introducing themselves, I can't recall exactly when John first turned up. My first clear recollection was of him giving people a lift home from the meetings. Unlike most others in the group, he had a vehicle. It didn't take long before he was nicknamed 'John the Van'. Following the meeting, we'd usually go to a nearby pub and afterwards would all pile into the back of his van. Most of my friends lived in Hackney, so John would drop them off first and then take me to Tottenham. As I was usually the last to get out, I'd often sit up front with him. He was friendly and easy to talk to; we'd chat about anything and everything. He'd told me a bit about his background, that he'd lived in New Zealand for part of his childhood and that his parents were still there. He'd returned to the UK a couple of years before, and had been living in a campervan on the South Bank. He was now working as a kitchen fitter.

Slowly, we became closer.

Belinda

(Officer: Bob Robinson)

Forest Gate, London, January 1988

The contract on my shared house was up for renewal but I didn't want to tie myself down for another year because, secretly, I hoped Bob and I might move in together.

'I'm not sure what to do,' I sighed after explaining my predicament to him.

I thought he might suggest that we move in somewhere but instead he came up with another solution.

'Some of my mates live in a flat in Hackney and they have a spare room; you could move in there.'

I was a bit gutted as he obviously hadn't taken the hint.

Seaton Point tower block, Nightingale Estate, Hackney, London, 7 February 1988

I was finally leaving Simon and all my other friends, but it was time for a change. Bob suggested the flat; it was less rent and also much closer to his place. I couldn't believe how much my life had changed in the eleven months since we'd first met at that party – the one I'd almost not bothered going to.

The flat would be a new start for me. I'd be living with two of Bob's friends – a Swedish girl called Greta and another guy called Brian.

We drove over to Hackney and began to lift my stuff out of the van. The flat was on the eighth floor of a tower block on the Nightingale Estate – the roughest place I'd ever lived.

But the flat was actually quite nice inside – much better than the estate itself.

Bristol, 19 February 1988

We travelled to Bristol to visit my sister, Maria. I hoped she'd love Bob as much as I did, but for some reason she didn't seem quite as enamoured as everyone else. Maria never said anything, but she didn't have to – I could just tell. My suspicions were confirmed when, a short while later, she came to stay with us in London. We visited an art gallery and, at the end of the weekend, Bob and I gave her a lift to the train station. They were busy chatting about something in the front seat when the discussion suddenly became heated. Soon, it had developed into a full-blown row even though I wasn't sure what it'd originally been about. As I hugged her goodbye, Maria made a remark about Bob being 'far too jolly'.

'What do you mean?' I asked, holding her away from me at arm's length.

'I don't know; there's just something about him – something a bit … false.'

I was gobsmacked and more than a little hurt.

'Well, it's just my opinion,' Maria said as she turned to leave.

I wanted to ask what she'd meant by false, but the moment had gone.

Afterwards, I couldn't stop thinking about what she'd said.

Was Bob false?

I shook my head.

No, Bob was lovely.

Everyone liked Bob, everyone apart from my sister.

Connah's Quay, North Wales, 3 April 1988

Mum and Dad had invited us up to stay for Easter, and I was really looking forward to it. They'd all met just after Christmas and had got on famously, even if it was obvious Dad didn't approve of, or understand, Bob's employment status.

'Hi, Bob,' Mum said, leaning in for a hug.

I tried not to laugh. He'd pretty much been ambushed by her.

We'd been staying a day or so when we decided to go and visit my 99-year-old still sharp and intelligent grandmother who lived in a care home nearby. She'd emigrated from Cork to Bradford as a child along with her parents and most of her eleven siblings.

'I'll just peg yours and Bob's washing out before we go,' Mum said.

She'd taken one look at us when we'd arrived and offered to wash our clothes. I knew it was mainly directed at Bob, whose clothes looked permanently grimy. He laughed it off. We jumped in Dad's car then headed over to see my granny. I was keen for Bob to meet her and wondered what she'd make of him. 'He has a good heart,' she whispered to me as we left. When we came back, it looked like it might rain so Mum went into the back garden to bring the washing in.

'Belinda, Belinda ...' I heard her cry.

I ran to see what was wrong, and found her standing there, totally flummoxed.

'The clothes, look – they've all gone!'

I told Bob: 'All our clothes! Someone's stolen them.' I'd expected him to go mad, but weirdly he just burst out laughing.

I was absolutely livid and I found it utterly infuriating that Bob didn't seem to care.

Why wasn't he bothered?

And why would someone steal second-hand clothes?

It just didn't make sense.

There was something else that didn't make sense – something else that had been playing on my mind. Though Bob was an anti-capitalist with sporadic cash-in-hand work, he never, ever seemed to be short of money. He was mad keen on going to gigs and we went frequently but he would never accept any money from me for my tickets.

'Don't worry,' he'd tell me. 'It's what I choose to spend my money on and I've got a close friend who works in the music industry and gets me all the tickets for a fraction of the usual price.'

London Greenpeace office, London, spring 1988

Bob had wanted to nip into the London Greenpeace offices to see someone, but I was desperate for a cup of tea so I popped across the road to see my friend in the Peace Meal café.

Afterwards, as I walked into the Greenpeace office, I spotted a girl with long dark hair. She was called Helen Steel. We'd briefly met before and I'd seen her at a party recently, having a laugh with some of the others.

Helen's eyes rested on the cup of tea in my hand.

'I hope that's not from McDonald's,' she said, smiling warmly.

'Oh no,' I insisted, defensively. 'I'd never go to McDonald's. It's from Peace Meal, over the road.'

'That's okay then,' she teased. We both laughed as I realised she was pulling my leg.

Bob's flat, Graham Road, Hackney, London, April 1988

A few days earlier, I'd brought up the idea of Bob and I living together, but Bob had seemed horrified. No doubt he'd thought it was a counter-revolutionary idea. But to me our relationship was dominated not by politics but by love and passion.

I wanted to have children and, with Bob, I felt I'd found my soulmate. However, he already had a son who, he said, he could barely support. So, I guessed having another child wasn't exactly at the top of his agenda.

'Okay, I get it, but I still don't understand why we can't live together.'

Bob looked up from what he was doing.

'I'm not good enough for you, Belinda – I never have been. I really don't deserve you.'

His words upset me so much that I began to cry. He'd always behaved as though I was the one for him, so why was he saying these things now? It was not what I was expecting.

'Don't say that, Bob.'

'But it's true; you deserve so much better ...'

I loved him so deeply but trying to get him to commit seemed like an impossible task. Instead, I sobbed quietly into my sleeve as Bob insisted his main interests in life were politics and direct action.

'They take up so much of my life – I don't have time for anything else.'

But I was going through a monumental shift in my own life and I'd decided I didn't want to waste time sitting around doing nothing. I wanted to continue to build my career and see my friends but, most of all, I wanted to settle down and start a family, and I wanted to do all that with Bob. Maybe he just needed a bit more time.

Belinda's diary entry, the flat, Seaton Point, 24 April 1988

Bob's away working on the motorway. I've decided to accept the fact that I like living with other people and get bored on my own. Specifically, I want to get married and have kids – how dare I harbour such thoughts? There are alternatives on how to fill my life (and none of them are in the slightest bit political). Politics – what does it all mean? What good can anything really do as far as changing the world? I see it almost as a hobby – other things in life are definitely more important to me.

I think this year will see some kind of decision on the Bob situation. I know what I want and, if he won't give me it, I'll go elsewhere. It's easy to say this, though no doubt more difficult to actually do.

I put my diary away and went through to the front room to see my flatmates. The flat was very bohemian to me. Greta, the girl who lived there, thought nothing of walking around stark naked, not caring who saw or what they thought. She also flirted with Bob whenever he called to see me, which really got on my nerves. The novelty of living there soon wore thin. The council estate was grim and rundown, a scar on the London skyline. The whole area had a feeling of tension and foreboding, as though something terrible might kick off at any moment.

One morning, I was leaving for work early when I spotted a rabbit's head. It had been positioned intentionally at eye level right outside the entrance to my tower block. It was totally shocking and I thought I should move it in case any children came out and saw it but I would have missed my train and been late for work. I couldn't shake the horrible vision from my mind all day and wondered why someone would want to make living on the estate feel even worse

than it already was. I was so relieved to find it had gone by the time
I came home from work.

The flat, Seaton Point, May 1988

My job had been going well and I'd finally got a promotion. I was
still in the payroll team but I was now a senior administrator and
a manager of a small team, which meant more money. I'd already
saved up quite a lot and nearly had enough for a 10 per cent deposit
to buy a flat – something of my own. I'd hoped having my own
place might help give my relationship with Bob more security – a
solid base.

In the meantime, Bob knocked me for six when he announced
– totally out of the blue – that he wanted to move into the flat with
me. For the first time in ages, I began to feel really excited.

Belinda's diary entry, the flat, Seaton Point, May 1988

*I have this nagging feeling Bob isn't good for me (not at the moment,
but in the future). I think maybe we're too different – what hell is it
going to be like when we do part? I'm going to see what it's like when
he moves in here at the end of the week … but I want a home and I'm
not sure he does.*

The flat, Seaton Point, May 1988

Bob was heading over to an activist meeting so I decided to go over
with him because I wanted to nip in and see a friend who lived in a
squat over there, someone Bob had originally introduced me to. As
we approached, I spotted a man unloading some stuff from the back
of a flatback van.

'John!' Bob called out, his eyes lighting up as the two of them
threw their arms around each other like long-lost friends.

'Belinda, this is John,' he said by way of introduction.

'Hi.' I smiled.

His name was John Barker, and Bob told me he was a great
personal friend and fellow activist. I met John various times after

that, usually at parties. He was a nice guy and we got on really well. Bob and John seemed to have a special bond. A couple of years later, the same John became the partner of Helen Steel – the girl I'd met at London Greenpeace.

The flat, Seaton Point, May 1988

Bob had finally decided to move into my flat. I went to help him but, as we moved what few boxes he had from his grotty place into my flat, I found one that contained some photographs. Knowing so little about him or his past, I was curious and flicked through them. To my utter surprise, they were mainly photographs of police in uniform at various protest marches.

'I've found all these pictures,' I said, showing him.

Why does he have photographs of police officers?

Bob stopped, took one from my hand, then shook his head.

'They're not mine,' he insisted, quick as a flash. 'They must be someone else's.'

I knew with 100 per cent certainty that they were from his flat but Bob was adamant he'd never seen them before. How odd. I supposed somebody else must have left them there and then forgotten them.

The flat, Seaton Point, mid-June 1988

Bob had been spending a lot of his time at the Old Bailey. Two of his more radical ALF friends – Andrew Clarke and Geoff Sheppard – had been accused of planting incendiary devices inside three Debenhams stores, and had gone on trial. Bob would set off for the Old Bailey just after I'd left for work. He told me he would go, sit at the back of the court, and listen. I knew he was really worried about them and about what was going to happen. But if I'm honest I was beginning to find Bob's friendship with them a bit weird.

Bob would go almost dewy-eyed every time he spoke of Geoff. I couldn't put my finger on it, but I found his obsession with Geoff and his interest in the trial a bit creepy. Certain things about Bob just didn't add up: not only his unexplained income but also his attachment to Geoff.

Where was he getting all this unexplained money from? Why did he hold Geoff in such high regard?

The Old Bailey, London, 17 June 1988

Andrew Clarke and Geoff Sheppard were found guilty. The Debenhams stores were targeted by the ALF because they sold fur. Andrew Clarke was sentenced to more than three years, while Geoff Sheppard got four years and four months.

Belinda's diary entry, the flat, Seaton Point, 20 June 1988

With Bob living with me, I'd begun to feel different – more settled somehow. I picked up a pen and added notes around a previous downbeat diary entry.

I've completely changed my mind about my comments before.
P.S. If you read this, Bob, what's written here was when I was feeling really negative! (Kiss, kiss.)

I turned the page and carried on.

Bob – I'm madly in love still.
I think I'm feeling more positive because he's living here with me (at least for the time being) and it's really nice.

The flat, Seaton Point, late June 1988

'I've got to go away, for work,' Bob announced one evening.

We'd just finished dinner. I'd cooked a delicious butter bean casserole with mashed potatoes and this was unexpected.

'For how long?' I asked, sitting up straight in my chair.

He glanced down at his plate as though he couldn't look me in the eye.

'Two or three weeks, I reckon.'

After he'd left, a few days later, I found myself feeling uncharacteristically lonely. Two or three weeks felt like a lifetime. When he returned, Bob promised he'd find more local gardening work. Suddenly, things had started to feel a little mixed between us – I couldn't explain it, but his working away had even made me consider if I'd be better off without him. All his toing and froing and non-commitment felt like death by a thousand cuts.

The flat, Seaton Point, late July 1988

While he'd been away, I'd kept myself busy, viewing different flats. I'd found one in Dalston, East London, and I thought it would be perfect. I couldn't wait to show it to him. I hoped he'd love it as much as I did and would decide to move in there with me. However, when I arranged to borrow the key from the estate agent and we went to look at it together, his reaction shocked me.

'Just look at it, Belinda, and tell me what's wrong.'

The flat was absolutely gorgeous; it was set away from the road, which meant less noise, and it was a very good size for the price.

'I don't know. I can't see anything wrong with it.'

Finally, after I'd given in, Bob pointed it out to me.

'It's above a fried chicken shop, Belinda. Do you think it's right for an animal rights activist to live above a shop like that?'

I put my hand up to my mouth in horror. The thought hadn't even entered my head.

'No, I suppose not,' I replied meekly, feeling my excitement flush away.

The more I thought about it, the more disappointed I felt; apart from the shop, the flat had been absolutely perfect.

Just my luck, I thought, *to have my future scuppered by a fried chicken shop*.

Whatever my feelings, I listened to Bob and immediately withdrew my offer.

The flat, Seaton Point, 30 October 1988

Bob couldn't seem to get over his friend Geoff being imprisoned, so he'd gone to visit him again in prison. On his return, he seemed sullen and refused to say much about it but I could tell it'd left him feeling really down.

The flat, Seaton Point, 31 October 1988

Halloween day and, for me, the stuff of nightmares.

Bob had been deep in thought, so I asked what was wrong.

'I'm going to have to be able to leave at short notice, Belinda,' he said, blurting out the words.

I felt each one stab me.

'Why would you need to leave?' I asked, falling down into a chair, trying to absorb the shock.

'I think the police are onto me; I might need to go on the run.'

It was obvious by the look on his face that he was really worried – but he wouldn't or couldn't tell me anything about it.

New digs, Upper Clapton, London, November 1988

I left the flat and moved into a nearby house with some other friends of Bob's. I didn't want any problems at work so we both thought it'd be better if Bob and I didn't live together – as a temporary measure, just in case something did happen, which seemed fairly unlikely to me.

I'd still stay over with him at the flat in Seaton Point, and he'd come over to my new place. It was hardly perfect, but at least he wasn't talking about definitely leaving and I just couldn't imagine it could actually come to that. Moving out felt like the best of a bad situation.

The flat, Seaton Point, mid-November 1988

One evening, I called over there after work, as I often did. Only this time I found Greta shaking – she looked absolutely terrified.

'The flat's been raided!' she announced dramatically, her eyes wide with horror.

'Raided? By who?'

'Special Branch.'

I was so stunned that I felt my legs fold beneath me.

She lit a roll-up cigarette; I noticed that her hands were still trembling as she held up her lighter. I felt equally terrified; I didn't know much, but I knew that Special Branch didn't call for a social visit. They were anti-terrorist police. My job flashed through my mind and I wondered what my manager would say if he knew. It wouldn't exactly be good for my promotion prospects.

'But why, what did they want?' I asked, desperate to know.

'They said they were looking for Bob.'

'But didn't they say why? Did they say anything else?'

'No, but they looked through some of your stuff. In fact, one of them picked up a pair of your shoes and asked who they belonged to.'

I suddenly felt desperately scared.

'And what did you say?'

'They asked if they were mine, but I said no, those belong to Belinda.'

'You gave them my name?' I gasped.

'It's okay. I didn't give your surname or anything.'

But I was petrified.

What the hell had Bob been up to?

When I later relayed the news to him, he seemed equally scared.

'I'm going to have to disappear,' he said.

My breath caught inside my chest and I felt the room closing in on me. I was utterly terrified; terrified I'd never see Bob again.

London, late November 1988

A week or so later, I received a very strange letter from Bob. I hadn't seen him at all since we had spoken about the raid and as I read his note, I felt a sense of unease grow inside the pit of my stomach. He wrote that he was feeling 'dazed and confused' and that he hoped I'd been able to carry on with my life as usual. He said he loved me, but didn't seem to be able to see me at all. 'Please take care. I love you. Let me know if there's anything you want me to do – or not to do. Bob xx'

Something was horribly wrong.

Greenwich, London, late November and December 1988

Simon had moved and was living in another place in Greenwich. One day, he rang to tell me that Bob was staying there with him. I felt relieved but I also desperately wanted to see him.

'I don't want to say too much over the phone,' I said, cautiously.

I was utterly convinced Bob was being watched and I didn't want to be the one who led the police directly to his door.

'I'll come over to yours,' I told Simon.

I grabbed my coat and headed over to Bob's new hiding place. Despite everything, I still loved him and was excited to see him.

'Are you okay?' I asked, wrapping both arms around him.

Bob seemed unnaturally calm.

'Yes, I'm fine here. Don't worry. This is a safe house.'

Afterwards, I regularly met him at Simon's new place. We'd gone through the motions of parting time and time again yet neither of us seemed to be willing or able to let go. For the rest of the month, we continued to meet until, one night, Bob seemed freaked out.

'The police have been looking for me again, Belinda. They've finally caught up with me. I'll have to go – this time for good.'

I felt my heart clench inside my chest like a tightened fist.

No! I screamed silently inside my head.

'But where will you go? You'll be safe here at Simon's. You said so yourself ...'

Bob shook his head.

'No, this time I *have* to disappear.'

'Disappear where?'

Tears pricked at the back of my eyes before blurring my vision.

'Spain. I'll go on the run to Spain.'

Bob nodded and turned away. He could barely look at me.

'Well, I won't lose you! It won't happen. I'll come with you,' I declared.

Right then, at that very moment, I didn't care about anything – work, money or possessions – all I cared about was Bob. I was so devoted that I knew I'd give up anything just to be with him.

'No,' he insisted, looking me in the eye for the very first time. 'You can't, I won't let you. It's too dangerous.'

I was feeling more and more upset.

'But I don't care!' I sobbed. 'I want to go with you. Please don't leave me. Please!' I didn't care about me, I didn't care about anything, only Bob.

But he was adamant. He insisted he'd go alone, and he refused to change his mind.

I felt my heart freeze before shattering into a thousand tiny pieces.

Dorset, late December 1988

Bob and I travelled to Dorset for a farewell trip. Simon had offered to let us stay at his mother's house near Lulworth Cove while she was away on holiday. On the way there in the van, I poured my heart out, insisting that I'd pack in my job and travel to Spain with him.

'No, Belinda. I'm not having you waste your life for me,' he said, focusing his eyes on the road ahead.

The thought of him leaving for good sickened me. I couldn't bear to lose him. But the more I wept and begged, the more his resolve seemed to crumble.

'Okay, I'll tell you what,' he decided, turning sideways in the driver's seat to look at me. 'I'll go to Valencia and when I know it's safe, I'll write to you, and you can come and join me when I'm settled.'

I dabbed the corner of my eyes with a soggy bit of tissue that had all but disintegrated between my fingers. 'And I'll come over and join you?'

'Yes, I promise.'

'You'll definitely send for me?'

'Definitely. I can't imagine life without you either.'

Finsbury Park, London, January 1989

A few weeks after the trip to Dorset, Bob and I met again before he finally left for Valencia. My heart felt raw and exposed, like a stripped wire.

'You'll send for me, won't you?' I asked again for the hundredth time.

Bob nodded.

'I love you,' I said, as we kissed goodbye. I couldn't believe this was happening.

After he'd gone, I gave up my job and started temping. After all, I'd need to be free if I planned to move to Spain at the drop of a hat to be with Bob when the opportunity arose.

Finsbury Park, London, March 1989

I waited over a month before the penny finally dropped that Bob might not send for me. Two months later, I received a letter. The envelope had been stamped with a Valencia postmark and I ripped it open. I was so desperate to hear from him that my heart was hammering as I began to read.

He wrote that he thought about me all the time, but that he couldn't let me give up everything I had for an idiot like him. 'Thank you with all my heart for being the kindest person in the world to me. Please forgive me and please be strong. I love you. Bob.' He didn't give an address so that I could reply.

I never heard from him again.

Helen
(Officer: John Barker)

North Yorkshire Moors, August 1988

John had offered to drive a group of us to Yorkshire to disrupt a grouse shoot on the Glorious Twelfth, the start of the grouse shooting season. We kipped in sleeping bags on someone's floor in Leeds then rose at 4am and travelled to Gunnerside on the North Yorkshire Moors to reach the moorland before the shoot began. The idea was to occupy the shooting butts and prevent the shoot taking place. We arrived at 6.30am and, to save our legs, John decided to drive us all in his van onto the moor up a rough track only really suitable for Land Rovers. It was positively hair-raising in places; there were parts where the track was so steep that we had to get out and push, and others with a sheer drop to the side. We were relieved to reach the grouse butts, and people praised John for his driving. It was a bit too scary for my liking but I was impressed he'd kept his cool. We succeeded in stopping the shoot going ahead so it was worth it in the end. However, as we came down off the moors, we were met by a police roadblock that stopped us leaving for three hours. It transpired the moor was owned by Lord Peel, a descendent of Robert Peel, who founded both the police and the Conservative Party.

London, Christmas 1988

By this time, Bob Robinson, Belinda's boyfriend, had completely disappeared from London Greenpeace. He had told a few people he was going on the run to Spain, after the police had raided Belinda's old flat looking for him.

I didn't celebrate Christmas because I wasn't keen on the commercialisation and I wasn't at all religious, but when the London Greenpeace people decided to go for Christmas drinks in a pub in

Hackney, I tagged along. There were a few of us standing around chatting and playing pool. After my game had ended, I sat down to grab my drink and John sat opposite me.

'How's it going, Helen?'

'Yeah, good. You?'

I took a swig of my Guinness and blackcurrant.

'Yeah, I'm okay, I guess …' John replied, casting his eyes downwards, '… though my dad's just died.'

His words took me by surprise and I was unsure what to say. I was only twenty-three years old, and it was my first adult experience of loss. I glanced down at the drink in my hands; I felt awkward and didn't want to say the wrong thing in case it upset him further.

I knew John had been born in England but had emigrated to New Zealand as a teenager; he'd only returned a few years before. We had a lot in common, especially when it came to politics. But he was only twenty-eight – five years older than me – so I was shocked to hear about the death of his father.

'I'm so sorry,' I said, trying to find the right words.

It was a horrible situation to be in at such a young age, and I couldn't begin to imagine what he must be going through. There wasn't much else I could say to comfort him. All I could do was be there as a friend.

My place, Tottenham, London, March 1989

'That's it; I'm all finished in here,' John said, collecting his tools together in the kitchen of my shared house.

I nipped through to have a look at what he'd done, although I knew anything had to be an improvement. The small housing co-op property was great in many ways, but the kitchen was so basic there was no worktop covering the washing machine, which meant we couldn't use it as a surface. John, who said he worked as a kitchen fitter, had offered to fix it.

We wanted to pay him for the work, but John refused.

'No,' he insisted. 'I told you, you're mates.'

My place, Tottenham, London, August 1989

Among my birthday cards was a bright yellow one with an inked image of a small house among trees and mountains. Inside was a message written in an unfamiliar language:

> *Hari huritai*
> *ki he pai hoa*
> *i aroha Hone*
> *x*

I didn't know what it meant, but placed it alongside my other cards on the mantelpiece in the living room. I shared the house with five others and one was an ex-boyfriend I'd recently split up with. He spotted the card and quizzed me on who it was from.

'I don't know. I can't read it and I'm not even sure what language it is.'

My ex nodded knowingly.

'I reckon it's Maori ... and I think it says love ... I bet it's from John,' he remarked pointedly.

To be honest, I was a little taken aback. Not by my ex, but the fact John might have written me a love message in Maori.

Did he fancy me?

I shook my head.

No, of course he didn't!

Instead, I decided my ex had either got it wrong or had read far too much into it.

The day after, I was having a lie-in after a late night of birthday celebrations, when a housemate called up to say John was on his way. I remembered all too late that we were supposed to be travelling to Heathrow to hand out leaflets in solidarity with Polish activists, before heading north for the annual grouse shoot sab. I leapt out of bed and packed a sleeping bag and hiking gear into my rucksack.

Following a couple of days' sabbing, John suggested we head to South Yorkshire to see a couple of friends, Pete and Sue, who had once been involved in London Greenpeace, and who had invited us to stay. They'd bought a small patch of land not far from Barnsley, had set up a small animal sanctuary and were always welcoming volunteers. We arrived on a day of glorious sunshine and I fell in love with the place. John was enjoying it too. We helped out, looking after the animals and weeding the vegetable plot, before we had to set off back to London. As we left, our enthusiasm for the place must have been obvious; Pete and Sue invited us again, insisting we were welcome any time.

McDonald's head office, East Finchley, London, 16 October 1989

As part of an anti-McDonald's campaign, London Greenpeace decided to call for a national day of action every year on 16 October, to coincide with the annual United Nations World Food Day. The idea was to highlight some of the harms caused to society and the environment by the size and dominance of major corporations like McDonald's, whose advertising budgets were so huge they were able to have massive influence on people's diets and were increasingly encouraging children to adopt an unhealthy diet.

Around thirty people turned up at the protest. A few I didn't know performed some street theatre with a pantomime cow and a juggling clown, while the rest of us looked on, holding banners or distributing leaflets. McDonald's security staff were standing nearby, chatting to each other, intermittently videoing and taking photos of the protest. At one point, I looked over and recognised one of the men as a police officer I'd encountered previously. He wasn't in uniform so I approached and asked what he was doing there. I don't recall his answer, which was evasive. John saw me talking to him and asked who he was. I explained and he fell silent.

A short while later, John asked: 'Helen, why do you talk to the police?'

I sensed his disapproval.

'I don't know, you're right, I shouldn't.'

The conversation ended there.

Holborn, London, 21 October 1989

London Greenpeace held an 'anti-McDonald's fayre' in Conway Hall, London. It featured a range of meetings, films and speakers on environmental issues and animal rights, workers' rights and the harm caused by the dominance of capitalist values over our society. There was a hall with stalls from a range of campaigns in the UK. It was an opportunity for people to learn more about the issues and get involved. Hundreds turned up and John was on the welcome stall to greet people. I took a less public role, helping to set up tables and chairs before doing a long shift in the creche. At the end of a successful day, it was all hands on deck to clear up and then John and I took boxes of leaflets and toys back to the London Greenpeace office. He offered me a lift home and we sat chatting for a while in the van outside my house.

'Fancy a drink, Helen?'

'Yeah, sure, why not?'

We walked to a local pub and had just sat down with our drinks when he leaned in towards me.

'Helen,' he said, looking me directly in the eye.

'John,' I mimicked, trying to disperse the awkward atmosphere between us.

He shook his head in mock annoyance.

'No, listen, I'm being serious! Helen, will you go out with me?'

I glanced anxiously at my pint, lifted it up and took a huge gulp for courage, wondering what on earth I should say. I felt nervous so I decided to make a bit of a joke.

'No,' I replied bluntly.

I'd put my drink down in such a rush that the Guinness rose up and sloshed over the side of the glass. I stared as it rested inside a ring-shaped black puddle on the table.

John slumped forward, looking slightly dejected, which made me feel guilty.

'No,' I replied a little too quickly. 'What I mean is, I never go out with someone the first time they ask.'

The answer had poured from my mouth without any thought and, as soon as I'd said it, I realised there was no going back – I'd just given him the green light to ask me out again.

Trip to Yorkshire, early January 1990

I went on a four-day break in the New Year with John and a couple of friends, to stay at Pete and Sue's in Barnsley. We went for lots of long walks over the moors and sat around an open fire in the living room. It was blissful because John was so easy to get on with. Every time we went back to London, I felt deflated at having to leave nature behind and return to a world hemmed in by walls.

London Greenpeace meeting, February 1990

There had been a few new faces turning up at the weekly meetings, and a couple of them had left me uneasy. Their politics didn't seem genuine; I felt a little suspicious.

One guy turned up and introduced himself as Anthony. Although I couldn't put my finger on exactly why, he just didn't seem to fit in. Some of us joked about whether he might be a policeman, but it wasn't like we were planning anything exciting so we couldn't see why the police would want to infiltrate the group. It didn't make sense. I mentioned it to my friend and fellow campaigner Dave Morris, who told me not to worry.

'Stuff like that only ever happens in books,' he remarked.

I felt a bit daft, but I had an uneasy feeling I just couldn't shake.

London, mid-February 1990

John had asked a couple of us to give him a hand moving. He'd rented a place in Stamford Hill, about two miles from where I lived. Around this time he told me his mum had just died, over in New Zealand. I felt sad for him, losing both his parents in such a short space of time. John was desperate to go to her funeral but didn't have enough money. I told him I had some savings and would be happy to lend him enough for the flight. I knew he felt uncomfortable about it and he argued that he couldn't take a penny from me, but I was insistent and determined he could and would go. He couldn't miss his own mother's funeral. In the end, I lent him £300.

When we helped John move, I was struck by how few possessions he had.

Afterwards, he came to my place and we stayed up chatting till late. He slept on the couch while I went upstairs to bed. After nowhere near enough sleep, we got up at six o'clock in the morning and walked to Turnpike Lane, where I saw him off onto the Tube to Heathrow, to fly to New Zealand.

'I hope it goes well,' I said, giving him a hug.

John gripped the tops of my arms and smiled back.

'Thanks, Helen … for everything. I really appreciate it.'

'No problem. Just make sure you look after yourself out there.'

I watched as he waved and slowly disappeared down into the Tube station. The top of his head bobbed down each step until he'd disappeared.

A week later, I received the first of many letters from John; the envelope had a New Zealand stamp and postmark. John wrote that he was feeling 'wiped out and in something of a haze' following the death of his mum. He described the funeral service and said it had been hard to put on a brave face for everyone, but said that Aunt Dorothy and a few old friends had been 'magic – like someone else I remember!' I felt so sorry for him, but was touched by his kind words and that he'd signed off 'miss you heaps'.

London Greenpeace meeting, 15 March 1990

John was back from New Zealand. I'd seen him briefly at an anti-poll tax march the week before, but we'd been separated by police clearing the road, so we didn't get to catch up properly until the next London Greenpeace meeting. As usual, we all went to the pub afterwards. I chatted to John, asking how he was and what he'd got up to in New Zealand after the funeral, before we all dispersed. Shortly afterwards, he called me at home.

'Helen, did you notice anything funny on the way home from the meeting?'

'No, why?'

'Because I was followed home by a guy who I saw talking to Anthony in the pub.'

London Greenpeace meeting, 22 March 1990

Given what had happened the previous week, this time, John and I travelled home together.

'See him?' John whispered, as I tried to look over my shoulder discreetly.

'Is that him? Is it the same man?'

He nodded.

It was dark so I couldn't see the stranger properly but he'd tailed us from Seven Sisters Tube station onto a nearby housing estate. He was dressed casually and was quite tall – much taller than us. We decided to stop and hide around the corner from him. As he approached, I jumped out and snapped a photograph of him with my camera. The man put his arm up to cover his face.

'Leave me alone, I'm drunk,' he said, pretending to slur, only it was obvious he wasn't from the speed at which he'd been following us.

As we walked away, I turned to John.

'Who do you think he is? Do you think it's the police? Why would they be following us? We're not even up to anything!'

John seemed shocked.

'Nah,' he said suddenly, dismissing my concerns. 'I don't think it's the police, I reckon it's a company, you know, someone like McDonald's.'

We'd been campaigning against McDonald's but I was still surprised. *Why would they be following us?* I didn't argue the point much because I couldn't think of any good reason for the police to follow us either.

Everyone had always joked there would be plain clothes police at big meetings and demonstrations, but not at regular meetings attended by fewer than a dozen people, and they wouldn't be following people home.

The following week, I didn't go to our usual meeting. Instead, I followed Anthony. His contact with the man who'd followed John had piqued my long-running suspicions. He seemed out of place; he had been very interested in the anti-McDonald's campaign, but his politics didn't seem to match the interest. In order to disguise myself, I wore a long, dark curly wig and applied some bright red lipstick – I never wore make-up so it was quite a change for me. I waited patiently outside for the meeting to end and, once Anthony had appeared, I followed him along the street to King's Cross Tube station and down onto the Piccadilly Line. He disembarked after just one stop, at Russell Square, then jumped into a crowded lift. I followed, keeping my face turned away from him, hoping he wouldn't recognise me. Once through the ticket barriers, he crossed the road and headed straight on, then around the back, side and front of a hotel. As I came around the corner, he turned left beyond the reception and disappeared from sight. I carried on and discovered he'd gone into an underground car park.

I'm not following him down there.

I wondered if he'd spotted me, but it didn't really matter; I'd done what I'd come to do. There was definitely something suspicious about Anthony. Later, I relayed my story to John, and we both decided to keep an eye on him.

Anti-poll tax demonstration, London, 31 March 1990

A national anti-poll tax demonstration had been planned, from Kennington Park to central London. Margaret Thatcher's government had replaced domestic rates – to raise revenue for local councils – with a new thing called the Community Charge, or Poll Tax, as it had become known. Previously, the rates had been based on the size of your home, so those living in a mansion would pay more than those living in a small terrace house. But the new charge was levied on people, rather than the size of the property, which meant the rich were paying less and the poor paying more. As a result, the tax was widely despised.

I was heavily involved with my local anti-poll tax group, Tottenham Against the Poll Tax, and we all travelled to the march together. Arriving at Kennington, we could see the protest was going to be huge. Hundreds of thousands of people had turned up and there were banners from all over the UK. We marched in the spring sunshine towards Trafalgar Square but, by the time we'd reached Whitehall, all movement forward had been blocked. I was quite a way back so it wasn't clear whether the police had stopped people or whether people had halted outside Downing Street to vent their anger at the Tory government. The police were making baton charges into the crowd every so often and, whenever it happened, people reacted with fear and tried to escape, although there was nowhere to run to. I ended up beside some grass plots outside the Ministry of Defence that were surrounded by chains at shin height. I'd just begun to uncouple the chains from their posts when John appeared and asked what I was doing.

'I'm uncoupling them, otherwise people will trip over them when running away from the police charges.'

I'd learnt from experience that when you're in a crowd that's been charged, it's impossible to look where you're going. You are pushed forward by those behind trying to avoid being truncheoned and there are others in front of you. If one person trips, usually many others fall.

'That's a good idea,' he agreed.

Within a short space of time there was another police charge and I lost John in the throng.

My place, Tottenham, London, 1 April 1990

I was heading to my allotment when John called round. He suggested giving me a hand with the digging. We talked through the events of the day before. He explained he'd been arrested in Whitehall, trying to protect someone from police violence. He also said he'd been badly assaulted by the police; they'd put a boot on the back of his neck to keep him on the ground before handcuffing his arms tightly behind his back. They'd further assaulted him as they bundled him into a van.

'Shit! Are you okay?'

'Yeah,' he explained. 'I gave them a false name, didn't I?'

I was worried he might be hurt, although I wasn't shocked by the false name part; if you stepped in to help someone being assaulted by the police, you'd often end up getting truncheoned or fitted up yourself. As a result, it wasn't unusual for people to give false details to protect themselves, their job, or their future.

Over 300 people had been arrested on the protest. The Trafalgar Square Defendants Campaign was set up to provide court support to them, so people didn't feel isolated and intimidated facing the legal system on their own. I volunteered to help with the court monitoring. We tried to cover all the central London courts to spot those arrested in connection with the demo. I would take notes of who had appeared in court, what had happened, and try to put them in contact with a good solicitor if they didn't already have one. Sure enough, John was due to appear at Bow Street Magistrates Court; however, he'd given his name as Wayne Cadogan, had jumped bail and so didn't show. I listened as the magistrate issued a warrant for his arrest.

My place, Tottenham, London, April 1990

John turned up on my doorstep but he seemed a little edgy.

'What's the matter?'

He looked both tired and stressed.

'My flat was raided by the police. I need you to do me a favour. I need you to call my boss and tell him I won't be in to work today.'

'But what should I say?'

John walked past me into the front room and shrugged as though he didn't know.

'Tell him I'm sick or something.'

He said the company was called Kingswood Kitchens, and gave me the number.

'I need time to think,' he sighed as he flopped down onto the couch.

I nodded, picked up the phone, and dialled the number.

'Hi, I'm ringing on behalf of John Barker. He's not feeling very well and he asked me to call to say he can't make it in today ...'

The man on the other end of the line stopped me dead in my tracks.

'Tell him the police have been here this morning. They're looking for him.'

'Right ...' I mumbled, unsure what to say next. 'Thank you.'

Placing the receiver in its cradle, I looked over at John, who was staring straight back at me, as if trying to guess what was wrong from the worried expression on my face.

'What did he say? Was he okay?'

I sat down.

'He says the police have been there – at your workplace – this morning. They're looking for you ...'

John frowned and twisted forwards on the couch; he rested both elbows on his knees as though trying to think.

'That's it, then. I'm going to have to go on the run.'

He rose up from the sofa and gathered his things to leave.

'But where will you go?'

I suddenly felt very protective of this kind and gentle man.

'I'm not sure. I'll think of something. I'll write, I promise.'

And then he was gone.

London, 16 April 1990

A week or so later I received a letter from John. He talked about visiting Derby then Scotland and said he'd have plenty of time for lots of long walks, but it seemed clear he was worried. He alluded to handing himself into the police but then said he couldn't face the 'inevitable'. He recounted the sadness of having to leave friends behind when he left England as a child for New Zealand and it felt like he was being forced to do the same thing all over again. He said he was feeling tormented, and I felt touched that he said he missed me loads and wished he could see me again. He signed off saying that he loved me and wanted me to have a jade pendant that had been gifted to him when he first arrived in New Zealand as a child. 'I know you're not into such things, but I've worn it every day until now, it's worth little, but it's real valuable to me. It's all I have to give and I'd like you to have it; you're something else I became attached to ... Love you for always, J x'

I peered inside the envelope; there was a greenstone pendant about six centimetres long in an elongated teardrop shape. It was attached to a cord through a small hole at the top. I liked the stone but I hadn't worn jewellery in years; it wasn't my thing. I left the pendant in the envelope and read John's letter again. A wave of concern washed over me.

Would John be all right? Would I see him again? Should I go on the run with him?

Although we weren't officially in a relationship, without really noticing, we'd been spending more time together and I was starting to have feelings for him. Clearly, he had feelings for me too. I opened the envelope again, took out the pendant and put it on.

A couple of days later, I received a job offer in the post for the role of gardener with Islington Council, which I'd applied for back in January. I was excited to be offered the job – it was a permanent, full-time post rather than my present part-time casual driving work – but, thinking of John and reading his letter again, I turned it down. I didn't want to be tied down if I needed to up sticks and move to be with him – something that was looking increasingly likely.

My place, Tottenham, London, May 1990

A few weeks later, I received a phone call late on a Saturday night.

'Hello, is that Helen Steel?' a gruff-sounding man on the other end of the line asked.

'Yes, why, who is that?'

'I am John Barker's solicitor. Please don't say anything that will get him into trouble.'

I was stunned into silence.

'John has been arrested and is being held at Paddington Green police station,' he informed me, before bidding goodbye and putting the phone down abruptly.

I was flabbergasted.

Why was John's solicitor ringing me? What was this about?

I woke early the following morning, which was just as well, because despite it being Sunday, the phone rang at 7.30am.

'Hi, it's John. Can you come to Paddington Green police station to meet me? They're letting me out soon.'

I made my way to Paddington by Tube and walked to the police station. I'd been inside the cells a couple of times before, after being arrested on protests, so it brought back a few unpleasant memories. However, this time my thoughts were mostly about John and what on earth was going on. Just as I'd reached the front door of the station, I spotted him walking towards the door from the other side. I felt relieved to see him. As far as I could tell, he looked okay. As he came out through the doors, he held a hand up to shield his eyes as he blinked against the bright sunlight. Clutched in his left hand was a Met Police property bag with a label still tied round the neck. John reached out and gave me a big hug as I began to bombard him with questions.

'How are you? Are you okay? Have you been charged? Where's your car?'

I realised I'd asked too much, too quickly.

'Let's get away from this place,' I suggested.

As we reached the corner of the next street, John explained how he'd been surrounded by police as he'd driven back into London.

'They hauled me off the road and arrested me. I had to leave my car by the roadside so I need to go back and get it.'

I nodded.

I asked what the arrest was about but, besides confirming he hadn't been charged, all John would say was that he'd had a rough time and wasn't ready to talk about it yet.

Why wouldn't he tell me?

He swiftly changed the subject and told me how the officers had found a card I'd sent him which was hand-drawn and expressed my love and concern for him.

'They all laughed at it and took the piss out of me.'

I felt embarrassed but I also felt sorry for him, and suggested he come back to my house to relax in the garden for a while. John deftly avoided questions from my housemates, including where he'd been for the last month or so. He needed to collect his car so he rang our mutual friend Mike, who called round in the afternoon so they could drive to Finchley. A couple of hours later, they returned and we sat out in the back garden chatting. John seemed exhausted so after supper I invited him up to my room where we lay on the bed talking until he fell asleep. I didn't have the heart to wake him up and kick him out, so I pulled the duvet over him and squeezed in my single bed beside him.

The following day, we had a late start but went for a walk up to Alexandra Palace.

I glanced over at him as we strolled around the grounds.

'I'm worried about you,' I said.

John just didn't seem himself but shrugged off my concerns. Instead, he wrapped his arm around my shoulders and smiled.

'Don't worry, I'll be fine.'

London, May 1990

The inevitable happened and we became a couple. Somehow, and in spite of myself, John had found a chink in my armour and he'd convinced me that we were meant to be. In fact, we'd only been going out together just over a week when he said he had something to tell me. We were sitting upstairs on a red London bus when he turned to face me.

'I love you, Helen.'

His words took me by surprise; I'd never met a man so open about his feelings, never mind one who could voice those same feelings out loud and so early on. It was a good sign. Slowly but surely, I let my guard down and allowed myself to fall in love.

Camber Sands, East Sussex, May 1990

A fortnight after I'd met him from the police station, John suggested we take a trip to the seaside. We spent the day on the beach at Camber Sands, swimming and soaking up the sun, before returning home exhausted. John stayed over at mine again.

The following morning, he woke up to go to work only to discover his car had been stolen. The next day, the police rang to say it had been found in woods near Broxbourne in Hertfordshire. We caught the train over there, followed by a long walk, expecting to be able to drive the car home. However, when we reached it, we discovered that all four wheels had been removed. We faced another long walk back until a woman kindly offered us a lift to the railway station. John's favourite jacket had been in the back of the car but I persuaded him to take it with him even though it was a warm day. The following day, after I finished work, Mike picked me up. John was already waiting in the passenger seat of the car as we drove to a garage to buy four new wheels. We travelled back to Broxbourne, intent on bringing his car back. However, on arrival we discovered a burnt-out wreck. His car had been torched the evening before. I felt so sorry for John; he was having such a run of bad luck.

'I'm so sorry,' I gasped as we stared at the charred remains.

He looked gutted.

I felt for him. He was such a lovely guy and didn't deserve this. I was only glad I'd managed to persuade him to take his jacket.

London, early June 1990

John asked me to go with him to his solicitor's office, near Victoria. The police had taken his passport when he'd been arrested. Somehow, it had gone missing, but the police had arranged a replacement passport, which John needed to pick up from the lawyers. The firm was based in a big, flash building near New Scotland Yard, and they seemed very corporate compared to all the solicitor's offices I'd ever visited.

'How come you chose these solicitors instead of using Birnbergs or Bindmans?'

Those were the firms protestors usually used. John brushed off my questions.

'One of the guys I used to work with recommended them; he said they'd been really great.'

I accepted his explanation – it seemed plausible enough. When John pulled out his passport to check it on the Tube, I grabbed it so I could see his photograph.

'Look at you!' I teased, as John mockingly rolled his eyes and laughed along.

Barra, Outer Hebrides, Scotland, June 1990

We caught the train to Oban and the ferry to Barra, where we stayed in a cottage by ourselves for ten days. I was in heaven; we were surrounded by the most stunning scenery, with beautiful walks in all directions and an abundance of wildlife, including seals. By now I was head over heels in love and, although the temperature was chilly compared to London, we kept ourselves warm by cuddling up and spending lots of time in bed.

I became captivated by John's face, taking several photographs as if trying to capture the moment and freeze it in time forever. I took a picture of John sitting on a rock with the sea behind. Then I set up the self-timer on my camera and dashed round to get in the picture. The photo of us together became one of my most treasured memories. At the end of the holiday, we returned to London. I was beginning to hate the 'back to London' feeling and longed for open skies and contact with nature. I felt trapped every time I returned home. However, this time it was more bearable because I had John.

Harringay, London, early July 1990

John told me he'd found a bedsit only half a mile away from mine and I was delighted. His new flat was a bit grotty so I suggested we decorate it and helped him choose some paint. One afternoon, I'd been painting most of the day when John came in from work. He stepped back to admire my handiwork.

'Helen, you've really made this place into a home.'

I felt a glow of happiness. I'd never felt so connected to one human being.

I managed to spruce it up into something half-decent. Although it was a London bedsit, it had more than one room, with a separate kitchen and toilet. The shared bathroom was up a flight of stairs, which was annoying, but John had sole use of the garden which was a real bonus in warm weather.

Within a couple of weeks, I was spending more and more time at his. It was cosy having a space to ourselves; we got on so well, sharing many of the same interests and never having arguments. It felt different to my previous relationships. Life with John was idyllic.

He mentioned he'd secured some casual work as a roofer on a site in Oldham – the Daily Mirror printworks – and it was intermittent so it meant he'd disappear for days at a time. I missed him whenever he was gone but, while he was away, we'd write silly love notes to each other and, when he returned, we made up for it.

During the summer we made several trips together to the seaside or countryside for walks. In late August, we went camping for a few nights in the New Forest and had a magical experience, sitting up late under the stars.

John's flat, London, August 1990

I decided to call round to see John with an old friend. He wanted to collect some books John had stored for him. Normally, I'd let John know I was on my way, but it'd been such a spur-of-the-moment decision that I decided to surprise him. I rang the buzzer, but there was no reply.

'That's strange,' I said, turning to my mate. 'I'm sure he said he'd be in.'

I had a key, so we went inside but John wasn't there. A niggle of doubt burrowed inside my brain; it was only small, but it was a niggle all the same.

Surely John would've told me if he was going out? Why hasn't he mentioned it?

I shook my head to try and rid myself of the thought.

He's allowed to go out. It doesn't mean anything. Stop making such a big deal of it!

A day or so later, when I finally did see him, I mentioned we'd called round.

'But you weren't in ...' I paused.

I expected some sort of explanation but John mumbled something about going for a walk to clear his head. I couldn't explain why, but a sense of unease crept over me.

Cornwall, September 1990

I was asked to drive for a local Asian women's group, who had arranged a week's holiday in Cornwall. We stayed in a cottage near the coast but as beautiful as the scenery was, I really missed John. Still, we wrote to each other most days to pass the time.

Before I'd left, John had told me he'd also be away for a few days because his aunt Dorothy was over from New Zealand to visit old friends and he wanted to spend some time with her. He also needed to sort out the sale of his mum's house in New Zealand. Dorothy had been dealing with the estate agent so he needed to liaise with her. He told me he hoped the money from the sale would enable us to buy somewhere to live together in the countryside at some point in the future.

After we'd returned from our respective trips, John told me he had some surprising news.

'Dorothy told me I really am a bastard. Apparently, my dad wasn't my real father, my mum had an affair with one of his workmates on the railways.'

It seemed pretty shocking news, so I was relieved John didn't seem too upset by it, more curious to find out about his real dad.

McDonald's serves libel writ, London, 21 September 1990

I was spending much more time at John's bedsit in Harringay, but I still lived in the housing co-op in Tottenham. One day, a friend had given me a lift home but as soon as I'd stepped through the door, I was confronted by my housemates asking if I'd noticed the dodgy-looking men outside. They were worried. They explained the men had been hanging around outside all day.

A short while later, Paul Gravett from London Greenpeace unexpectedly turned up. He told us he'd been served with a libel writ from McDonald's and that I'd also been named in the writ. I stepped over to the window and looked out; the dodgy men were still loitering in the street outside and we guessed they were there to serve a writ on me.

A little while later, John turned up in his van.

'Are they still outside?' I asked as he came in.

'Who?'

'The dodgy-looking men.'

'I didn't notice anyone.'

I peered through the window again and couldn't see any sign of them. I explained what had happened to John, who suggested I should come over to his place and stay the night. I didn't need much persuading.

We parked up in John's road, a little uphill from his flat. There was a large tree on the pavement and it prevented me from opening the van door fully. I twisted round but as I climbed down, a man I'd never seen before stepped forward.

'Helen?'

I looked up but didn't reply. I didn't know who he was. The stranger didn't say anything else; instead, he threw an envelope at my feet and walked away. My name was written on the front of it. I picked it up and went inside John's bedsit, where I opened the envelope. It was a libel writ from McDonald's and a letter that said there would be a court case unless we apologised for the London Greenpeace *What's Wrong with McDonald's?* leaflet.

John seemed shocked and angry that we'd been followed to his address.

'I can't believe they did that. That's such an invasion of our privacy!' he said angrily.

He was worried what might happen to me and asked what I was going to do.

'I've no idea. I need to talk to the others before making any decisions.'

The following day I went to a meeting of the Trafalgar Square Defendants Campaign, in Tottenham. A solicitor I knew, Timothy Greene from Birnberg solicitors, was there along with Dave Morris, who had also been served with a writ. Together, we seized the chance to ask Tim's advice on what to do about the libel writs. He told us libel was a specialised field of law and he had no experience in that area so he couldn't advise us. However, Tim kindly offered to ask a lawyer friend who, he said, owed him a favour. He thought he might be able to help and introduced us to a young barrister.

His name was Keir Starmer.

Keir was based at Doughty Street Chambers – a recently established group of radical lawyers. The five of us who had received the writs met up with Ben Birnberg and Keir and asked for their advice. None of us had ever encountered anyone being sued for libel before. Under the 'Green Form' legal advice scheme available at the time, we were able to get one hour's free legal advice. The advice turned out to be that basically, libel cases were hard to fight at the best of times but, with no legal aid, no resources and up against a wealthy multinational corporation, we would likely be on a hiding to nothing and could well end up bankrupt. They advised us we'd probably be better off apologising and moving on to the next campaign.

Originally, five of us were sued and in a meeting several weeks later, one by one we were asked what we wanted to do. Three people said that, in light of the advice, they would reluctantly agree to apologise. Dave said he would go with the flow. But by the time it got to me, I was feeling so angry at the idea of a huge corporation demanding we apologise to them. If anything, I felt *they* were the ones who should be apologising to the public for their impact on the environment and society. At that point I didn't know if I would fight the case in court or just ignore it – and risk being jailed for contempt of court, but my gut instinct told me they didn't deserve an apology. Fortunately, Dave agreed and said he'd join me.

Keir offered to help us. He agreed to draft our defence, which was a good job as we had absolutely no idea how to do it. However, he also warned we would need to find primary evidence to back up all the statements in the leaflet. People who had central involvement in writing the leaflets were no longer around so we couldn't go to them for help with the source of the information. One of the authors was Belinda's ex-partner, Bob Robinson, who was now on the run.

We set up the McLibel Support Campaign to publicise the case and raise money for the costs of fighting the action. John was really supportive throughout it all; he came along to meetings and offered to help with some of the research and fundraising. But he also seemed worried.

'Listen, why don't you just join the others and apologise? You don't want to risk your future,' he suggested.

But I couldn't.

'I can't, John. That would go against everything I believe in.'

I knew he was only asking the question so many had already asked, but I was surprised he was trying to persuade me to give in to McDonald's.

London, autumn 1990

For a change, instead of walking around our local park, John drove us over to Regent's Park, where we fed the ducks and sat around on the grass. After a while he suggested we go back to the van and he took me on a tour round Paddington, where he pointed out his old schools, streets and hangouts. He pulled out a grainy photo of a kids' football team and asked if I could pick him out. I wasn't sure, but managed to get it right the second time. John also showed me a few pictures of him walking in the countryside with old friends. It was a key thing we had in common – our love of nature. We'd travel in John's van to different nature reserves in Hertfordshire and Sussex, or take a trip down to the beach at Hastings.

Although we were blissfully happy and spent every moment we could together, John's job often took him away for a week at a time. With the McDonald's case brewing, I decided to train as a legal secretary. I figured, if nothing else, it would help me with the ongoing case.

Seven Sisters, London, December 1990

We loved each other so much that we decided to move in together. We rented a downstairs flat that John had found, in a converted Victorian house. It had a tiny triangular back garden, like a slice of cake, but it was big enough to sit in. I was so happy to be living with John and my allotment wasn't far away, so that was an added bonus.

We visited our friends Pete and Sue again in Yorkshire over Christmas. While we were there, John said he was going to Derby to visit some relatives, including his aunt, that he hadn't seen in a while. It all seemed a bit sudden, and I offered to go with him.

'No,' he insisted. 'We're not that close; it might be awkward.'

I tried not to feel put out as I knew he'd have good reasons for wanting to go alone. I also knew, from John's passport, that he'd been born in Derby, so didn't question it.

I missed him, but John returned a couple of days later and then we set off for home.

'How was it then?' I asked as we trundled along in the van.

'How was what?'

'Derby, your relatives? Was it good to see them?'

John half-smiled and then shrugged as though he didn't know what to say.

'Yeah,' he replied, refusing to be drawn any more on the subject.

It was obvious he didn't want to talk. I thought it odd but decided to leave it.

New Year's Day, London, 1991

John and I brought in the New Year at a friend's party before walking home in the early hours, making plans for the future year. After a late start, we got up and went to the allotment to dig up the last of the parsnips.

We'd talked about moving out of London as soon as we could. We'd previously visited estate agents in Yorkshire to get a feel for what was available, although we'd been a bit dispirited on seeing the prices for even a small piece of land with a home. John talked again about money he would inherit when his mum's old house in New Zealand sold. He'd suggested we could manage to buy somewhere with the funds from that. I didn't care about the money; I just wanted to be with him. As one of our favourite pastimes was feeding the ducks, John joked that he would dig a duck pond for me if we managed to buy some land. This helped cement the feeling that our love was mutual.

One day, not long afterwards, John surprised me when he discussed having a family together. I was only twenty-five and, if truth be told, the thought of settling down with kids hadn't even entered my head. However, he seemed so keen that I didn't like to argue.

'As an only child I've felt on my own all my life,' he began, 'so I want lots of kids.'

I was a little startled and asked how many he had in mind.

'Six.'

I did a double-take.

'Well, I'm not sure about that many,' I said, laughing.

Although I wasn't ready for that stage of my life, I wanted to be with John. I was reassured and happy that he felt the same and wanted us to have a future together.

Our new flat, Tottenham, London, summer 1991

Although we'd had a few small arguments, overall, John and I had been blissfully happy.

By this time, he was working as a builder, so he was often away but would always come home at weekends. Usually, when he came in from work, his clothes would be grubby and covered with splashes of paint.

At the end of May, he wrote to me from Oldham, telling me anecdotes about what had been going on at work. He signed off suggesting a walking holiday in France at the end of the summer and saying that he loved and missed me. 'I feel that I'd like to spend the rest of my life with you, Hels.'

The trip to France didn't materialise, but we stayed with our friends in Yorkshire again, this time for a week in August. While we were there, we visited estate agents to see what was available and talked again about our plans for the future.

Five days after we got back, I came home to our flat and called out to John.

'Hi!' I said, closing the door. 'It's me.'

But the flat was silent. It was strange: I'd expected to find John in. I wandered through to the living room, and noticed a folded piece of paper on the table.

Maybe he's just left me a note to say where he's gone.

But it wasn't that kind of note. As soon as I opened it, I felt my heart begin to pound. John's distinctive writing was stained and blotchy where it'd been watered by his tears. The words had bled into small blue pools of ghostly scribble. His letter announced that he was leaving home, he couldn't carry on. It was filled with a sense of hopelessness and despair and he said he was too wrecked to write much; he felt angry with himself for letting me down. 'Keep being Helen, she's magic'. He said he loved me but that he couldn't stop running away. He asked me not to hate him forever and promised to phone when he got himself together.

I stared down at the letter.

Where was he? Why had he written this? We were happy, weren't we?

It was too much; so much that my senses felt overloaded. I tried to focus, but my eyes filled with tears and the words jumbled into one.

He'd gone – upped and left without speaking a word and I had no way of contacting him to ask him to explain.

The pain was raw.

He'd gone; John had left. My head kept replaying the events of the last week, trying to work out if I had missed something. It was such a sudden change between us planning our future together and his disappearance.

I felt lost – utterly bereft – and I didn't know what to do or who to tell. I began writing a letter to John, not knowing if I would ever be able to send it to him, but in desperate need of an outlet for my feelings. After a restless night I returned to the letter in the morning.

Dear John, it's morning now, but instead of things seeming better, they seem worse. I got about two hours' sleep last night, the rest I spent tossing and turning, trying to understand what's wrong and whether there's any hope for the future.

… It all seems so strange that only eight days ago we were looking at places to live. What were you feeling then? If you felt the same as you do now why didn't you say something? If you didn't feel the same, how can things change so much in one week that you're sure it's the end? If you're not sure then why not talk before writing / doing something that's left me gutted?

I was still curled up on the sofa, exhausted and numb, when the phone rang a few hours later.

'Hello,' I answered, holding my breath, hoping against hope.

'Hi, Hels, it's me,' he replied.

My heart thumped against my ribcage.

'John, thank God. Where are you?'

'I'm sorry, Hels, I had to go. My head was exploding and I couldn't cope with it any more. I needed to create some space between us.'

'Why? What's wrong? Why didn't you tell me, talk to me? We could have tried to sort it out.'

'I don't know, Hels. It's not you, it's me. I've lost my faith in people. I can't believe we're going to last, and I can't take the heartbreak if you leave me.'

'But you left me!' I replied, a little exasperated. 'This doesn't make any sense. I thought you still loved me. I'm not going to leave you. Come back, let's talk about it.'

John sighed.

'I can't, Hels, I need some time to sort my head out.'

'John, I'm worried about you. I've got no way of contacting you, no idea if you are okay. Please come back.'

But John was adamant.

'I can't just yet, Hels, but I promise I'll phone so you know I'm safe. Listen, I'm in a call box and I've run out of change, but I'll call again. Look after yourself.'

John rang off, but he did call back a few times over the course of the next few days. I tried to keep myself distracted. I was relieved he was safe, but I was still desperate for answers.

What had changed so suddenly and why?

Our flat, Tottenham, 28 August 1991

Another letter arrived from John. He seemed in a state again, but said he'd try to explain why he left, although he wasn't sure it would make sense. He blamed a hangover for his messy writing and said he had the shakes. I worried he was turning to alcohol rather than talking things through. I had blamed myself when he disappeared, wondering what I'd done or missed, so I was relieved that his letter said it wasn't my fault. He said that when his head wasn't all over the place that working at our relationship was the 'single most important' thing to him and that he couldn't feel more strongly about me: 'When I say "all the love I have is yours" I mean just that. I mean I don't think it's possible to feel any stronger about someone than I do for you.'

He was right, it didn't make much sense, but I was relieved to read that he still cared for and loved me, even though he seemed so scared of commitment. He signed off, in capital letters, 'ALL THE LOVE I HAVE IS YOURS xxxxxxxx'

Later that day John rang at 8.30pm and said he was on his way round. I quickly made a meal, but by the time he arrived I felt so anxious that I couldn't face eating. When he came through the door I burst into tears of relief and we embraced in a massive hug. I wanted the hug to last forever, but he broke away and went to the bedroom to unpack.

I tried not to bombard him with questions, but he said very little and after a while I started to feel resentful that he was just carrying on as normal, acting as though nothing had happened, when I'd just had the most horrendous week worrying about him. He didn't give much away, instead just repeating that he needed to clear his head. He insisted that he still loved me but he needed space, adding that he was leaving again the next day. He'd decided to go to Ireland to try to track down his real father. I asked if I could come with him to help with the search, but he said no, he wanted some headspace and would be gone for three or four weeks.

I tried to console myself that at least this time I knew where he was and maybe if he managed to find his real father he might start to feel less insecure and alone in the world. John left early the next morning, but he rang me every couple of days, sometimes more than once in a day.

After he'd been gone a week, we spoke on the phone again. In a moment when I was really missing him, I asked if I could come over to join him. I regretted it immediately; the call felt really awkward after he said no. But four days later, he said he'd be happy for me to come over in a week's time. I was so relieved, and began to count down the days until I would see him again.

Our flat, Tottenham, 12 September 1991

Three days before I was due to leave for Ireland, a letter turned up from our friends in Yorkshire, inviting us to come and stay there until we found a place of our own. I felt the happiest I had been in a while, and hoped John would be pleased we had an easy route out of the stresses of living in London. It felt like it could be the start of a new future together.

Dublin, 15 September 1991

I left home early on Sunday morning and got the train to Holyhead. It was mid-afternoon as the ferry left the harbour, the sun was shining and I sat on deck enjoying the view. But as we got closer to Ireland, anxiety kicked in as I thought about seeing John again. I started to feel sick with worry, not knowing how he was or whether he would want to continue our relationship or not. I went down to the bar and had a few drinks to calm my nerves. By the time the ferry docked I felt pretty tipsy, but managed to find a train to Dublin where John was waiting. He'd booked a B&B and we hit the sack fairly soon after I arrived, chatting about where he'd been until I dropped off.

The next morning we visited the registry office and searched through the records. There was no trace of anyone who fitted the details we had of John's father. I was gutted for John because I wanted him to find some peace. In the afternoon we travelled to the coast and found a quiet field to pitch our tent. Then we spent the next few days walking along the coast and swimming in the sea. It was so good to be back together. John told me more about his search for his dad, and how upset he was not to be able to find anything.

A week later, we packed up the tent in the pouring rain and caught the overnight ferry to Holyhead. We were back in London by 9am and John went off to the launderette. He returned a couple of hours later and announced that he was leaving shortly, this time to get a bus to Carlisle. He needed space. Again.

Our flat, Tottenham, 25 September 1991

Three days later he sent another letter, full of apologies for his behaviour, talking about how messed up he felt in his head and reminding me of all the good times we had. 'I have lots of little snaps of you in my mind – swimming in Poole, struggling up the hills in Barra, letting your hair out of your hair tie (so often) – they are all beautiful memories of you. Funny, but none of them are in London or involving political things. I think you are beautiful. I suppose I must love you.'

He explained he'd been feeling stuck, trying to sort out in his head where he wanted to be in ten years' time. He apologised again for taking out his frustrations on me and said he thought it better if he didn't phone again until he left. I felt confused. He was sending such mixed messages. On one hand, he said how much he loved and missed me but on the other hand, how strong he felt being on his own. His letter ended with 'I LOVE YOU STILL. I hope you can handle it.'

Our flat, Tottenham, autumn 1991

A week later, John was back, but I was still on edge. My confidence had been badly dented by the uncertainty, but I was still in love and cared deeply for him. I didn't want to give up on the relationship if it could be sorted out. I had never felt this intensity of love for some-one before. If John had said he no longer had feelings for me I would have been upset, but could have understood and come to terms with that. Instead, he repeatedly reassured me that he still loved me and wanted to be with me, yet his actions seemed designed to put distance between us. I couldn't understand what was going on.

'It's not that I don't love you,' he explained as we sat together in the flat. 'That's the problem; I still really love you. It's just … it's just …'

Tears snaked down my face. The stress of the uncertainty was too much.

'What is it, then?'

I was desperate.

What's going on? How can we even begin to fix this if I don't know?

John bowed his head and stared at the carpet.

'It's just I feel so alone in the world. Both my parents are dead and the only other woman who once said she loved me went on to desert me. I can't believe my luck with you will last.'

I sat up straight and faced him.

'But I'm not her, John, am I?'

He refused to meet my eye. Instead, he shook his head sadly.

'I know, it's just I feel so insecure … I'm worried you'll leave me.'

I'd heard it countless times but I couldn't make sense of it or of him. Wasn't it obvious I loved him to bits?

I took his hand in mine and held it.

'But I won't leave. I love you.'

I meant it – every single word.

I constantly tried to get John to open up and talk about his feelings, but he always seemed reticent. Yet there was one thing he seemed certain about.

'I love you, and I want us to have a family together.'

He said it so often that it seemed inconceivable it wasn't true. And if it was true then surely it had to be worth working through our difficulties together?

We'd both long dreamed of leaving London, so we discussed our friends' offer to move into the caravan on their land in Yorkshire. Although we still planned to move to Scotland when the money came through from John's mum's will, this felt like a good stepping stone.

'Shall we?' I asked John. 'We could see if we liked living in the countryside or not.'

John grinned. He seemed enthusiastic, almost rejuvenated by the idea. Secretly, I hoped it would help lift his depression and grief.

In mid-October, we spent a long weekend at Pete and Sue's to discuss their offer and see if the move was feasible.

I could barely contain my eagerness. It felt like this could be the answer to everything. With the McDonald's libel case rumbling on in the background, I was desperate to escape London, the trial, and the stress it brought with it.

John said he felt the same.

'Go on then, let's do it!' he agreed.

I was so happy that I flung my arms around him in excitement. It was perfect; we both loved the countryside and I couldn't think of a better place to live than Yorkshire.

Our flat tenancy ran out in mid-November, so we planned our move to coincide with that. But there was a lot to sort out.

McDonald's had summonsed Dave and me to a hearing on 6 November. The company had applied to get our defence of the libel case struck out, and we and the support campaign had arranged a 'March Against McDonald's' on 9 November to raise public awareness of the court case. To prevent the case being struck out we worked flat out to assemble the evidence needed for Keir to draw up the 'further and better particulars' of our defence. I spent days in science reference libraries finding key papers on the links between diet, heart disease and cancer. There were long phone calls to Costa Rica and other parts of Central and South America to speak with witnesses who could give evidence of deforestation to make way for cattle ranching. Dave was busy contacting ex-McDonald's workers and trade unions to assemble reports about the company's pay, working conditions and hostility to trade unions. It was exhausting. We also had to make and distribute leaflets and posters to publicise the march, arrange for a van and stewards on the day, and liaise with police over the planned route.

Our flat, Tottenham, early November 1991

In the week before the court hearing, John's behaviour grew even more erratic and alarming.

One evening when I'd been expecting him home, he rang at midnight to say he was drunk and wouldn't be back that night. He refused to tell me where he was, and I went to bed feeling really worried and distressed.

I had important meetings the following morning and when I returned home, there was a note from John saying he'd gone to the London Greenpeace office. I rang him there; it was obvious something was wrong, but he wouldn't tell me until he got home. I put down the phone and broke down in tears with the stress of it all. John arrived a short while later and told me he had been sacked the previous day and said it was for getting pissed the day before. He had been plagued by the same old concerns about feeling alone in the world but afraid to carry on with the relationship, and he'd tried to drown his feelings in alcohol. I felt at my wit's end and agreed we should end the relationship. We were both really upset. My brain felt in a state of collapse trying to understand what was going on. John stayed but slept in the front room.

The following day, when John returned in the early evening, he told me he'd burnt all his old letters. Then two days after that, he told me that he'd been to Regent's Park, his childhood park, and thrown all his mum's jewellery into the lake – he said he felt she never really loved him. I was really upset and worried for him, but also felt out of my depth and I didn't know what to do or say for the best. John then left to stay at a B&B in Shepherd's Bush for a couple of nights; he said he didn't want to stay with me at home.

With the flat empty, I busied myself preparing for the court hearing and the march, not least as a distraction from the overwhelming worry and grief I felt at John's behaviour and the death of our relationship.

Our flat, Tottenham, 6 November 1991

On the day of the hearing, John returned and began making placards on the floor. I cleared away some of the mess but John took this as criticism; he blew it up into a massive row. The stress was all too much and I broke down crying and trembling, with pins and needles shooting down my arms and legs. Eventually, after telling John that I was scared I was going mad, he gave me a hug and things calmed down a bit.

I really didn't want to leave the flat and face the world, but the McDonald's strike out hearing was on at 2pm at the Royal Courts of Justice, so I had no choice. If I didn't go, the case might be thrown out immediately with us being held liable for damages to McDonald's. I met Dave at the Tube station and headed down to Keir Starmer's legal chambers. By a stroke of luck, a case Keir was presenting had cancelled at the last minute, so he was now free to speak for us in court. It was just as well. Given the state I was in, I doubted I could have held myself together to argue in person if

Keir hadn't been there. McDonald's weren't happy to see him, but they had their own barrister, so it evened things up slightly. For once, the hearing went really well and the judge refused to strike out anything. I felt momentarily elated.

Back at home, John told me he was going to stay at a youth hostel in Highgate and I came back down to earth with a bump. I woke the following day feeling really depressed, not wanting to get up. I lay crying in bed, despairing of ever understanding what was going on or being able to see a way out of the heartbreak. Eventually, I forced myself to get up and went out to go to the printers to sort out placards and leaflets. When I got back much later, John hadn't returned as expected and I started getting worried. I eventually rang the Youth Hostel Association (YHA) to find out if John was there; they told me he hadn't stayed there at all. I got really wound up and worried that he'd lied. By the time he rang at 8.30pm I was in a real state. John told me he was now staying at another hostel in Earl's Court, and managed to reassure me he was okay.

The following day I returned home from training to find John was at home and I asked why he'd lied to me that first night. He said he didn't want me to worry. He'd stayed out for the night, walking, and hadn't slept. I wasn't sure I believed him, but I felt mentally exhausted and had run out of ideas. I had other things to think about too: the march against McDonald's was the following day and I had to rush off to attend a meeting at Scotland Yard with the police that afternoon about the demo. When I returned home later, I found a note from John saying he would ring later. He didn't call as promised so I rang the London Greenpeace office, hoping I might catch him there. But there was no reply and I had a restless night worrying about him. It was really cold that night and I had visions of him freezing to death out in the open.

London, 9 November 1991

On the morning of the march, I awoke about 5.30am and couldn't get back to sleep, my concerns about John still buzzing around my head.

He showed up a few hours later and said he'd had problems collecting the megaphone for the march. We headed off down to Euston, where the protest was starting from; it set off in the early afternoon with nearly 400 people. We made our way through central London, stopping briefly outside each McDonald's en route to hand out leaflets about the McLibel case, then made our way down Whitehall into Victoria Street. The march ended beside McDonald's in Victoria and some people handed out free vegetarian food to passers-by, while others handed out more leaflets. It was a relief that it was finally over and had been a success, despite all the hurdles. John and I returned to our flat with a couple of friends who were staying the night.

The following day, John left early to take stuff back to the London Greenpeace office and I went out with the friends who were staying over. I returned home in the early evening to find a note saying he'd gone for a stroll. While I was trying to pack our stuff for moving out of the flat, he rang a couple of times. The second time I pleaded with him not to stay out in the cold overnight. But he refused and told me to 'stop it', then put the phone down on me. I went to bed feeling really down.

He rang early the next morning and said he had spent the night walking. After I told him again how worried I was, John said he would stay at the office in the remaining days before moving. He returned home the night before the move.

Penistone, South Yorkshire, 14 November 1991

We finished packing everything into a hired Luton van, then set off in the afternoon, sharing the driving between us. After arriving in Yorkshire in the early evening, we had a quick cuppa then unloaded the van. The caravan was jam-packed full of boxes and it was absolutely freezing. We cuddled up with a hot-water bottle to keep warm, but it split just half an hour after going to bed.

The following day, John left at 5.45am to drive the van back to London. I spent the day unpacking. John called later in the day to say he'd got the van back safely and the deposit from the landlady.

Then he dropped a bombshell – he'd decided not to come back just yet. He was going to France instead, to sort his head out.

A few weeks later I received a letter, postmarked Charente, 3 December 1991. John addressed me as his 'dearest darling' but he still sounded confused, saying he wanted to see me but that it was best he didn't. He said he was annoyed and angry with himself for hurting me 'again and again' then asked me to wait a couple of months for him to try to sort himself out. He continued, 'I missed you loads and loads. I want you to love "forever". I want to dig a duck pond for you. I'd really like us to have children. Really, I want all these things with you, but I need a lot more confidence in myself'. He said that he had 'been trying "something" in the past few months, which may or may not help'. He didn't reveal what that was but asked me to believe that he was trying so hard. I really hoped that he might be turning a corner. I so desperately wanted our relationship to work. The intensity of feeling between us was so much stronger than anything I'd experienced before.

A few days later, John phoned and announced he was back in the UK, but was staying in Dover trying to get a job on the Channel Tunnel, which was being constructed at that time. He said the job would help us to save up more money towards buying a house together.

Penistone, South Yorkshire, mid-December 1991

Soon afterwards, a letter arrived from New Zealand addressed to John from his aunt Dorothy. I told John about the letter during a phone call and he told me to open it and read it to him. The letter confirmed that his mum's house was going up for sale on 9 December, at an asking price of $169,000. John was pleased to hear that news and I was too. She also asked him to get in touch about the final disposal of his mother's will.

Canterbury, Kent, just before Christmas 1991

John told me he'd secured work on the Channel Tunnel, and a couple of weeks later, when I had to travel to London in connection with the McLibel case, he suggested that we could meet up at Canterbury Station.

'Wow! You look different,' I gasped as I came through the ticket barriers.

John was clean-shaven with short hair and it took me totally by surprise. In all the years I'd known him, he'd always worn his hair in a long, dark mullet.

'I just fancied a haircut …'

Although I knew it was him standing in front of me, it seemed odd; he looked so drastically different to the John I knew and loved. We headed to a B&B and then spent the next couple of days together, walking and talking. John made it plain he wasn't ready to talk about the future of our relationship yet, so I just tried to make the most of being together again.

As we packed up to leave the B&B I gave him a couple of books on bereavement that I'd come across. I'd wondered whether his recent depression might be down to grief from losing both his parents. As I handed them over, John looked at me, but his face was difficult to read. 'I promise I am trying to sort things out, Hels. I will read them and I do want us to be together. I just can't handle the long term yet.'

John's birthday, Penistone, South Yorkshire, early January 1992

A few days into the New Year, John rang and said he wanted to come up to stay for his birthday in the second week of January. I drove to Barnsley Station to collect him. I had tried to talk myself into accepting what felt like the inevitable, that actually John wasn't coming back, despite his promises, but when he arrived he told me he had been thinking things through and he wanted to come back for good. I was so happy and relieved. Although he was going to carry on working until the money came through from the will, I felt a few more months apart didn't matter if we had a future together.

After a huge birthday meal in the house, we went back to the caravan to be alone. Lying in bed, John told me he was feeling a lot better and we talked about our relationship and plans for the future. John also told me that he had discovered that his real dad lived in London and he was planning to visit him as soon as he got back from seeing me in Yorkshire.

But on the day of his departure, the old doubts resurfaced again.

'It's not that I don't want us to be together ... I really do; it's just that I'm frightened. Frightened you'll leave me.'

This seemed so ridiculous. The only person who'd been doing all the leaving had been John. I suggested we go to relationship counselling but he point-blank refused.

We continued talking as I drove him to Barnsley Station and then went onto the platform with him.

I felt desperate – desperate to make him feel loved and secure. But I had run out of ideas. As a feminist I had long rejected the idea of marriage, the vows that required women to obey their husbands, and as the law stood back then, once a woman was married, her husband was legally allowed to have sex with her whether she wanted to or not. Rape in marriage was not a crime. Marriage seemed like an appallingly sexist and regressive tradition.

But standing on the platform with John expressing his fears and his train due to take him away any minute, I was surprised to hear myself say that while I didn't believe in marriage, if it helped him to feel that I wasn't about to run off and leave him, I would be willing to marry him.

'Do you mean it?' he asked, sounding surprised.

I nodded. But even that wasn't enough to calm the unrest in him.

As I drove home, I felt in turmoil at how desperate I had become and how much I had changed. I wasn't even sure I knew who I was any more. I felt bad that I had said something against my principles. But equally, the relationship with John in its good days had brought me out of my shell and shown me how enjoyable it was to love and be loved, and I didn't want to lose that.

Penistone, South Yorkshire, mid-January 1992

In the next couple of weeks, I received two conflicting letters from John, where he described meeting his biological father. The first presented the meeting as positive although awkward, especially as he'd had to tell his father that his mother was dead. He described his father and his family in some detail. The second said the meeting actually hadn't gone so smoothly, he'd been putting on a brave face, and in fact his dad had been angry that John had made contact and visited his home. John said he'd had a torrid week, he hadn't liked his father and felt 'disappointed that this was the man who "loved" my mother'. This letter ran for several pages and was covered in tear stains and my heart went out to him. He was clearly feeling alone in the world. He wrote that he still loved me but couldn't face any more disappointment in life, that he had decided to leave London and that he 'couldn't risk our love'. 'I'm just meant to roam around Hels. I've decided that's what I have to come to terms with.' He said he had 'lost hope in life'.

I broke down reading this letter, grieving for him and for us, yet again. I felt like I was on a roller-coaster ride, down in the pits after the high of his visit on his birthday. The pain was so intense that I no longer wanted to be alive. It seemed ridiculous that only nine days earlier we were talking about buying a house and living together. Now I didn't know if I would ever see him again.

London, 25 January 1992

Two days later I had to go to London for a meeting with Dave and our lawyers about an appeal to the European Court of Human Rights, over the denial of legal aid to fight McLibel. While there I went on a demonstration. John had mentioned cancelling his intended plans to meet me there, so I hoped we might run into each other all the same. When I didn't see him, I felt so down that I couldn't face talking to my friends. I walked to Regent's Park, where I wandered around in the vain hope I might run into him. But no such luck.

The following day I called Directory Enquiries from a call box and got hold of all the numbers for any Wabernoths in Auckland –

the surname of John's Aunt Dorothy. I then systematically rang them one by one. As luck would have it the third person to answer was a relative and gave me the number of another relative who then gave me Dorothy's number back in Tauranga. I rang her and gave her a message to tell John I loved him still and to ask him to please ring. I wasn't sure what to say as I didn't want to worry her. I returned to Yorkshire and continued to fret about whether John was okay; his letter had sounded so desperate.

Three days later, a new letter arrived from John. He addressed me as 'my love' then said he wasn't sure if he was allowed to call me that any more, but that I was the only person he felt close to. He said he missed me desperately. He had tried but failed to not let the meeting with his father have an effect on our relationship. 'So much for this emotionless, hard, macho, distant John'.

His letter implied he'd been sleeping rough again and I worried about what might happen to him, alone and cold at night, although more recently he said he'd stayed in a B&B and was trying to get road building work in Hertfordshire. He said he'd be jealous if I had a relationship with someone else.

He rang a few days later. It was difficult talking at first but got better and afterwards I rang Dorothy to let her know he was okay.

A few days later, another letter arrived. It was much the same, with more mixed messages, again implying that he'd been sleeping rough but also reminiscing about the good times we'd had. He said he thought of me all the time, that I had given him his 'happiest year' and that he felt 'crap' about how he'd treated me. He signed off, 'I still feel as much for you as I wrote a few weeks ago. Love you desperately. J.'

When John next called, I suggested again that we go to couples' counselling together to see if we might be able to resolve some of the difficulties that way. John refused, but insisted he did want to make it work.

Eventually we agreed to go back to Barra to spend some time together and talk things through. We'd both loved the place and there was a good chance the cottage wouldn't be booked up at this time of year.

Barra, Scotland, February 1992

John met me off the train in Edinburgh and then we travelled together to Barra by train and ferry. The scenery on the journey was stunning and it was so good to be together again. Much of the stress of recent months seemed to melt away while we stood watching the horizon, John stood behind with his arms wrapped around me.

That lasted just one day. On the second day there, after a walk around the peninsula, getting a soaking in the rain, we sat in the kitchen trying to dry out and warm up. I was sitting on John's lap, our arms round each other, when he asked yet again if we could just be friends. As much as he loved me, he was having the same doubts about me walking out on him, and he couldn't handle the thought. I pulled away and broke down into tears.

'What's going on, John? I can't cope with this any more. You keep telling me you love me, but then you keep running away. It doesn't make any sense.'

'I do love you. But I just can't handle the thought of losing you,' John replied. 'I feel like if we part now I won't be with you, but I can keep your love inside a little bottle and have it with me for always.'

I knew there was no logic in this and something, somewhere inside was ringing alarm bells, but I couldn't put my finger on it. My memory flashed back to the time when I had rung the hostel where John had said he was staying and they told me he hadn't stayed there.

'John, please be honest with me, because my fears when you keep going missing are far worse than the reality.'

For the first time, he looked directly at me.

'Why, what are your fears?'

I gulped the words down because I could feel them – right there – dancing on the tip of my tongue. I wanted to say them out loud, but they seemed so utterly ludicrous and potentially dangerous that I just couldn't. I couldn't say what I was really thinking.

That you're an undercover police officer.

The thought had flitted through my head once before, when John lied to me about staying at the hostel, but I had dismissed it when he explained that he hadn't wanted to worry me by saying he was wandering the streets, rather than safely asleep in bed. But now, it came back with a vengeance. It felt like a very real threat, all the more so because I was on my own with him, but at the same time it seemed so ridiculous and disloyal too, to accuse the man I loved of being an undercover cop. I couldn't do it, I couldn't allow it to escape my mouth.

He was still waiting.

'What? What are your fears?' he repeated.

It was such an outrageous accusation; it would surely spell the end of our relationship and ability to trust each other, to accuse the man I loved of being a policeman. I couldn't do it.

'That you are having an affair,' I blurted out. It wasn't what I thought at all, but I had to give some sort of answer to fill the silence.

'There is no one else, Hels, and I promise there won't be, not after what I've put you through.'

I heard the answer, but I felt numb to it.

Edinburgh, 13 February 1992

We left Barra early for Edinburgh and stayed the night in a B&B there. John planned to leave me the following day and return to Tring, working on the roads. That was it. We could remain friends, but our relationship had no future. So when we awoke in the morning and he initiated sex, although I wanted to be close I pushed him away. I couldn't explain it, but I was beginning to feel used.

'What's wrong? Why don't you want to have sex?'

'You're doing my head in,' I blurted out without thought or filter. 'I can't cope.'

As I waved him off on the train, to go back to his work down south, I was broken – my heart splintered into thousands of tiny, sharp pieces. I knew without a doubt that I was losing him.

John wrote again a week later, but although he signed off with love, his words seemed much more distant. He told me that Dorothy was unwell, 'she really didn't sound too good', but that the house sale was still on course to go through and he hoped it would because he didn't want it to be a burden on her, given the state of her health.

I was staying with my parents for my grandmother's eighty-fourth birthday party, when the next letter arrived from John at the end of February. In it, he said that Dorothy had ranted to him about having to deal with his personal life, 'something to do with you phoning her a few weeks back. Don't worry, my fault. Apart from being brassed off at me she didn't sound too well either, so just had to let her go on a bit'. I felt really bad for having troubled her, but it was so hard having no means of contacting John and worrying if he was alive or dead. He could contact me whenever he wanted, but I was stuck waiting for him to call or write.

John said he was only just getting over seeing me in Scotland and was trying to be positive and sort himself out. He knew what a dark place I was in. 'Take care Helen please. Don't do anything rash,' he wrote once, signing off with lots of love.

I headed back to London from my parents' place and met up with Dave and then Keir to discuss the next steps for the McLibel case. That evening, staying at a friend's, John rang and chatted about how the case was going, then suggested that we meet up at the weekend.

On Saturday night he came over for supper, then we stayed up late chatting till he left to get the Tube.

London, 8 March 1992

In the very early hours of Sunday, John wrote a note which he handed to me when we saw each other later in the day. He said how much he had enjoyed spending the previous evening with me, and how he hadn't wanted it to end. He talked again about the confusion of his feelings towards me.

He came over at midday and we went over to Alexandra Palace, an old haunt when we lived together, where we sat beside the lake chatting and watching the ducks. I asked him about his feelings about our relationship and whether he saw us having a future together, but felt none the wiser at the end of it.

My brain felt muddled; I needed John to be completely honest with me. Something was wrong – I couldn't see or touch it – and it couldn't be fixed. I'd tried to be patient – I'd tried everything, but nothing had worked.

We talked long into the afternoon about John's anxieties and what he might do to sort himself out, but he seemed reluctant to try anything new and I ran out of suggestions. We walked back to Turnpike Lane underground station, where I went down to the platform with him and, when the Tube arrived, gave him a goodbye hug.

Postmark Hemel Hempstead, 12 March 1992

A few days later a card arrived from John; the picture showed a small cutesy child cuddling a dog with a long sad face. In his note John remarked that the weekend we'd spent together had done him good, 'little by little – maybe'. John had now been blowing hot and cold for about seven months. I'd pleaded with him to see a counsellor, either together with me or on his own to try to resolve this. I'd also given him books that I thought might help him process his emotions, but his note said he hadn't read them either; 'thought I'd leave it till I needed to'.

The note hit me at a bad moment and I felt angry at the implication that there was no urgency, his problems might just resolve themselves 'little by little' while I was kept hanging on.

I wrote back expressing my frustration. John might feel no sense of urgency at resolving our problems, but the toll on me had been immense and I didn't know how long I could carry on like this. Throughout his various disappearances, I had often felt a sense that I could no longer bear to live through the pain and uncertainty, but although this time I was really feeling I'd had enough, I didn't want to trap him into coming back because he thought I might be suicidal. So instead, I toned it down and just asked him to be aware of the impact it was having on me and that it felt heartless that he didn't see resolving the situation as an urgent priority. I walked across the fields into town and posted the letter.

Almost immediately I was struck by a sense of panic. What if he decided to call it a day? I couldn't bear the thought of that either, so I rushed back to the caravan and began another letter, explaining how desperate I had been feeling but apologising for taking it out on him. I posted the second letter later in the day, but it was after the last post had gone and I spent days worrying intensely about him.

That worry continued to haunt me, as John's next two letters both said he hadn't made it to the post office yet to collect any letters from me. I hoped that at least meant he would see my more positive thoughts at the same time when he finally went, but still I worried about the potential impact of my angry note. John said that contracts had at last been exchanged for the sale of his mum's house and that he should receive the long-awaited money at the end of June. He confirmed our plans to meet up in a couple of weeks when I was going to London and he said he'd ring next week to arrange the details. He signed off saying he felt the same about me now as he did when we started the relationship two years before.

The second note said he'd had a 'grim few days' but was now feeling really good that the house contract had been exchanged and that in ninety days he'd be rich. He mentioned Dorothy was in hospital again. He said he was looking forward to seeing me, but had to cut the letter short as he was about to get a lift to his job in Tring.

London, early April 1992

I'd arranged to stay with a friend, Sinead, in London, and John had promised to ring me there. When his call didn't come, I started to feel anxious. His mental state had been fragile for so long that I had a real fear he might do something stupid. Frantic with worry, I borrowed my friend's car and drove to Tring, where John had said he was working on a road building site. I passed a site just out of town and saw a man who was the spitting image of John from behind. I was so happy

I pulled over and rushed up to him. At the last minute I realised it wasn't him. I showed the man a photo of John, but he said he didn't recognise him, nor did anyone else on the site. I trawled around other sites in the town looking for John, but met a blank. None of the builders I spoke to knew or even recognised him.

'Can you take another look?' I begged one builder, pointing down at John's face. 'His name is John Barker. Have you heard of him? It's really important; he's my partner and I really need to speak to him ...'

The man shook his head, as did everyone else. He suggested that I come back at 6pm, as that was when everyone knocked off, so I might have more chance of spotting him. In the meantime I phoned all the construction companies listed nearby, but he wasn't on the books of any of them. I called Sinead's and the babysitter answered. She told me John had just called moments before and would call back later, so I left a message asking him to tell me where he was in Tring so we could meet up there.

I hung around until 6pm, then went back to the building site and watched the builders stream out of the work entrance – there was no sign of John, and eventually someone told me everyone had left, so there was no point in waiting any more.

I searched for a phone box to call Sinead, but then discovered I had no credit left on my phone card. By the time I'd got more credit it was 7.30pm. I rang to let her know the trip had been a failure.

'Helen,' she said, as soon as she picked up the phone. 'John called here a short while ago.'

Relief flooded through me.

Thank God! John was okay.

'What did he say?'

There was a moment's silence on the other end of the line as I waited for her answer.

'He asked for you, so I told him, "No, sorry, Helen's out at the moment, can you ring later?"'

'And what did he say?'

'He said no ... he said, "It'll be too late."'

The phone box suddenly became hot and claustrophobic and I felt like I couldn't breathe. A sticky panic coated my skin and the palms of my hands sweated with fear. Fear of what John might do.

'Too late? What did he mean by too late?'

My mind galloped as horrible, unspeakable visions of what he might do overwhelmed me.

'I don't know, but he sounded really upset. He says he's put a letter in the post to you.'

'A letter?'

'Yeah …'

I returned to her house and waited for the letter to arrive, fearing its contents. The following day was a Friday and I wasn't that surprised when the letter didn't arrive, but there was nothing on the Saturday either. An agonising weekend followed, as I waited for news of John.

Was he even still alive? I wondered in my darker moments. I travelled again to Regent's Park in the hope that I might bump into him there, but to no avail.

On Monday, John's letter finally dropped through the letter-box – all ten pages of it. He'd started the letter on 27 March but it spanned a whole week. He began with mundanities; work and the weather, then declared he was missing me 'heaps and heaps'. Three days later he said he'd finally picked up the pile of cards and letters from the post office and had gone to a pub at Winkwell, a place we'd visited in the early days of our relationship, to read them and finish his reply 'without getting interrupted or spied on'.

He said I'd been right to express my frustration in the angry letter I'd sent on 12 March. He recognised that he'd kept me hanging on for a long time without resolving anything. He thanked me for writing the letter as it had helped him to make a decision.

His words sounded increasingly desperate as he told me about his life, how he'd never felt loved or that he had a home. 'Yes, I've always wanted to love someone and be loved too but the truth is till I met you, I never was. No, not my father and, no, not my mother either … I've got little (now) scars from being slashed with a chopping knife as a kid when she got into a rage'. He felt guilt when she died. He said he'd barely described his life to me. 'I've been running from beatings, chastisement, abuse, etc., for as long as I can remember ... when I'm on my own I feel free, I feel lonely too – but I'm free'. It was so hard reading those words and being unable to comfort him, but also frustrating hearing him say he wanted to be with me, when he had deliberately put physical distance between us so we couldn't be together.

He railed, 'I've got no hope left in people'. I was heartbroken and worried, he sounded so desperate. He implored me to 'please, please, please believe that I love you'.

The final paragraph was dated Thursday 7.30pm, the exact time I'd phoned Sinead from Tring and she told me he'd just called. Then, finally, he wrote, 'I'm going on a flight to South Africa – then – well then I deal with then – I've loved our every minute together, Hels.'

That was it. He'd gone. To *South Africa*.

I was shocked by that as well – although Nelson Mandela had been released from prison, apartheid was still in force and it seemed a very strange choice of destination for a political activist. It surely reflected what a state he was in.

I was distraught, out of my mind worrying about him but unable to do anything about it. I fell apart and cried uncontrollably. I blamed myself for pushing him away with my impatience at his 'little by little' comment. What had I been thinking? He was so obviously distressed and struggling with trauma from his past and now I had driven him away. I would never see him again and there was a risk he might do something stupid and kill himself in the process, given the state he was in. And I would probably never find out if he had done either.

In the week that followed I tried everything I could think of. I rang the Samaritans, the Citizens Advice Bureau, I checked the flights from London to South Africa for the evening he said he was leaving, rang the airlines and asked if he had been on the flights, but either they refused to answer or they said he wasn't on the passenger list. I rang the South African embassy, backpacker hostels in Johannesburg ... Everything drew a blank.

I felt hopeless. The man I loved – who I wanted to spend the rest of my life with – was alone and in a perilous mental state and I had no way of contacting him.

I visited the address in Derby where John had been born, hoping to find his aunt and discover if she had heard anything from him. Even though he viewed her as a bigot, he still might have been in touch, or if something bad had happened she might have been notified. But despite visiting the house several times during the day, no one ever answered the door. The following morning at 7.30am I rang his Aunt Dorothy in New Zealand and asked if she had heard from him – but no, nothing there either.

Penistone, South Yorkshire, late April 1992

It was freezing cold, living in the caravan on my own. I missed John so deeply that I felt as though I was slowly dying inside. It was a real struggle to get up and face the world every day. The only thing keeping me going was hoping that he would get in touch again.

Living in a rural area, the postbox was at the end of the drive. Realising that letters could remain in there for days without anyone knowing, I began obsessively checking the postbox several times a day. It helped that from the postbox I could see across the road and down into the valley below, so the sense of emptiness I felt every time I checked the box and there was no news from John was at least tempered by the beauty of the valley. But equally, that beauty made me miss his presence beside me all the more.

Three weeks after he left I received a letter telling me I had won £50 on the premium bonds, and on the same day I finally got somewhere with my research. I had written to the home affairs department in South Africa and a woman got back to me and told me that if I could give them John's passport number, they could check whether he was in the country. I rang the passport office and a man told me that he didn't think he could tell me the number, as it was confidential information, but then unexpectedly rang back a few hours later and gave it to me. I thought it must be my lucky day. As I rang the South African home affairs department back and gave her the number I was on a high, thinking I was finally going to find John. She went off to check and a short while later returned.

'There's no record of him in South Africa,' she said. 'He can't be here or he would be on record. I'm sorry, I can't help you further.'

My hopes crashed back down. It wasn't my lucky day after all. I'd tried so many things, but I kept hitting a brick wall.

Penistone, South Yorkshire, 23 April 1992

The following day I made the trek to the postbox again. This time there was a letter. I recognised John's handwriting immediately. On the front was a South African Express delivery sticker and a postmark saying Benmore, a suburb of Johannesburg, and dated 16 April. On the rear was a Johannesburg postmark.

I took a deep breath and let it leave my lungs in a long sigh of relief. *He was still alive.*

My hands trembled as I hooked my index finger underneath the back of the sealed envelope and opened it. Inside the envelope were three letters, written on different dates, another ten pages of script. The first said he was on the plane, it was 2.30am and he couldn't sleep and he was sure I couldn't either. He said I was right to have made demands and he was very angry with himself for sodding me around. He reiterated several times that he loved me and how the problems we'd been having were all down to him. He felt bad for lying to Pete and other friends that he'd visit in a few weeks, he couldn't bring himself to tell the truth that he was leaving the country. He tried to explain why he hadn't phoned me, adding 'you must believe Helen that I was being sincere when I talked about kids, a home, travelling with you and making a pond. But it'll only ever be a dream now. I must start to realise that'. He said he hoped he hadn't put me off men.

The second letter described arriving in South Africa. It felt like a crushing blow that he began it with 'Well, I've escaped.' Was that how he felt about our relationship? He talked about his travel plans and said he was waiting for the banks to open. He described 'lots of military/police, big fat bastards' at the airport, who'd harassed him, and suggested there was an air of tension at the airport.

In the third, he sounded confused and empty. He reflected that he'd been wasting my time for too long, and said he wanted me to know he was alive and well and that he would be in the future. He ended by saying, 'I had intended to write on – why I don't know any more, so I'll just say goodbye, Helen – all my love. J.'

I felt ripped apart reading those final words. There was no hope left; he definitely wasn't coming back.

It had finally happened. John had gone – this time for good. I retreated to the caravan and hid myself away, feeling like I was going out of my mind with grief and worry.

A couple of days later I decided, despite John's warnings, to phone Dorothy again. I needed to know if John was alive and okay, but she said she hadn't heard from him, so I continued to worry, struggling to take any interest in anything else in life. There just seemed no point to any of it now.

Needing an outlet for my emotions, I began writing a letter to John that I assumed I would never get the chance to send.

23 April
The last three weeks have been exhausting, I've thought about you non-stop all day every day. The only time I've had any respite is when I've been reading newspapers to try & shut you out of my mind. But even that doesn't work. I'll read something about NZ or Africa or someplace we've been or something that's happened that reminds me of something we did together. I've had nightmares about you some nights.

29 April
Last time I saw you I remember walking through Lordship Park and telling you I would wait as long as it takes to sort yourself out (and that still holds true) but that was if you were going to try &

do it, which you said you were. You said you'd give yourself three
months & if you hadn't got anywhere by then you'd go & see a coun-
sellor & that I'd have an answer by September. I said as long as you
were trying I wasn't putting a deadline on September. I suppose
it's like if I see that I matter to you then I don't mind waiting, but
if it seems like I don't matter enough then what's the point in me
hanging on anyway?

Penistone, South Yorkshire, 29 April 1992

Unexpectedly, a week later, another letter from John arrived in the
postbox, postmarked Benmore, 23 April. I expected the worst as I
pulled it from the envelope. But in contrast with his previous words,
now there was a glimmer of hope.

The letter was twelve pages long. John said he had found it
'impossible' not to write again and talked about his feelings for me
and the 'words of love and affection' we used to have for each other.
He apologised for any anger in his letters and said it was directed at
him, not me. My words had made him realise he had achieved nothing in the last six to nine months, and that I had been 'strung along
hoping, hoping, hoping. The situation perhaps only endured so long
because of the depth of your feelings for me'. He said he wrestled
and argued with himself for days and days on end.

He said he had in fact read the intros to all the books on the
night I gave them to him, 'some of it was really sound. There was
something real good on what happens if you resist or ignore reality,
if you don't grieve and more. Well, I recognise that in me'. My heart
lurched as he talked again about childhood traumas, 'the fact that I
can now at least admit there was a lot of cruelty, bordering on wick-
edness is perhaps a step forward, I don't know. I do know that no kid
should be beaten senseless for years on end'.

He apologised for telling me a 'mega lie' at the start of our relationship – inventing a series of prior sexual encounters that hadn't
happened – he thought most people had them and that was what he
needed to say. 'I can only say I'm really sorry for telling you these

stories Hels. I hope you can forgive me for it … I don't want to seem blasé about having misled you. I've felt sorry about it for a long, long time'. I was surprised by how guilty he sounded. I thought he was daft to invent stories about previous sexual encounters, but it wasn't the worst crime in the world.

He said there was no particular reason why he'd chosen to go to South Africa. He 'only had one thought and that was to put a lot of distance between us'. He had to stop himself getting in touch with me and let me get on with life. 'I don't want to leave you alone but I must. I have to stop hurting you any longer'. To me this felt the wrong way round, the overwhelming hurt I felt now was from his disappearance out of my life and at the end of our relationship. This still wasn't making any sense.

He talked more about his feelings for me and reiterated that right from the start of our relationship he'd been in love with me, saying that 'even before we got together I thought you were some-one special. I was right too. I can honestly say you are the closest "friend" I've ever had. You're far and away the person I've loved most and been closest to'. He said that he loved me so much it hurt – 'so bloody much it makes me cry'. He thought I was the best thing that ever happened to his life. No one had ever expressed this inten-sity of feeling for me. I felt the same and it was really heartbreaking to read those words knowing he was the other side of the world and wouldn't be coming back to me.

He said there'd never be another person in his life after letting me down so much. He knew he had to confront his past and future, but he didn't know when. 'I do know I'll never forget you and all the precious times we've had together, I wish I could still have a home and kids with you and tell them the things I was never told and give them the love I never had and wrap you all around me'. My eyes filled with tears again as I thought about the disappearance of our whole planned future together.

Then, just as I reached the point of utter despair and acknowl-edgement that our dreams were over, John said that if he ever stopped running, he'd write and tell me. The final page ended, 'I hope I can stop running away from you and my problems some day – if I can, I'll come running back to you. I'm not assuming, presuming or asking you for anything more, love, I just had to say it.' He signed off 'cheerio, love. Take care of a great person. All my love, J x'

It seemed John did really want us to get back together.

Inside, my emotions were scrambled; just when I'd begun to grieve, John had offered an unexpected lifeline I could cling to, some hope for the future. He was alive and well, and dealing with some really difficult emotions. He had been abused as a child and he wanted to work through those things. Now there was the chance that one day we might be able to make this work. I clung onto that with both hands.

Unsent letter to John, 13 May 1992

Staying in my old room in Tottenham. I woke at 5.30 & couldn't get back to sleep. It was light outside & the dawn chorus had started. I thought back to two years ago, when we used to wake up about that time & sneak glances at each other, till we worked out we were both awake. Then looking at you. You always looked so beautiful.

We went to Winkwell & walked along canal banks for the first time. I remember you saying you thought our relationship would be a two-day wonder. You thought I wouldn't want to see you again.

Letter from Republic of South Africa's Department of Home Affairs, 11 May 1992

A couple of weeks later, another letter arrived with a South African postmark, referring to John by his first name, Philip (which he never used). But this time it wasn't good news.

Madam,
Whereabouts: PHILIP JOHN BARKER
I acknowledge receipt of your letter dated 9 April 1992, and have to inform you that no record can be traced for the above named person.

They must have missed recording John's entry to South Africa. After all, he'd sent me two letters from Johannesburg, so he must have been there. But while his last letter had filled me with hope that there might be a letter to follow, none came. I picked up my pen and continued my letter to him.

Unsent letters to John, May–June 1992

29 May

Two years back Camber Sands ... remember you walking to the sea & when you were halfway down the beach, me putting shorts on & being worried you'd see my legs & not want to know me anymore – daft really.

Then the following day your car being nicked (& my first letter to you) – bastards. I remember wanting to comfort you, to put my arms round you & protect you, but you telling me it didn't matter, mostly I didn't believe that, but I felt I had to accept your word. It wasn't till a long time later that you admitted it had hurt.

11 June

Today's the day two years ago that we arrived in Oban. Real nice sunny day today, same as it was then. Remember going for a walk near the shore, beautiful views across the sea. Buying drinks at that sailing club then laying in the grass relaxing. Feeling really happy. Then that dog peeing on your feet. Staying at a B&B for the first time ever.

Getting the ferry to Barra the next day. I've got a really clear picture in my mind, I've never forgotten it The boat was passing an island, we were both looking out to sea, towards the island, you were facing the back of the ship, I was facing the front, we were right up close & you had your arms around me. It was beautiful.

Hertfordshire, July 1992

A month later, and despite John's warnings, I decided to try Dorothy again. I was desperate to know whether John was still alive. I called early on a Monday morning, and this time she told me she had heard from him, and he was back in the UK, working at his old workplace. I felt gutted that he hadn't got back in touch with me too, but thought perhaps he felt too guilty about what he had put me through. I decided to try to find him. John had previously written to me on headed notepaper from the company he worked for – Construction and Technical Services in Ware, Hertfordshire – so I looked up the address and then rang British Rail to find out train times. The next day I caught the first train and travelled down there on a massive buzz of adrenalin, convinced I would find him and at least be able to see him and talk to him again.

I walked into the office and approached a woman at the reception desk.

'Hi, I'm looking for John Barker, I've been told he's working here at the moment.'

She stood up and went into a back office to ask someone. Moments later, she reappeared.

'He left on Friday.'

I was absolutely gutted. It was like riding an emotional roller coaster. I had been so full of hope, but now everything had come crashing down around me again.

Unsent letter to John, July 1992

14 July

Woke up this morning & felt down. Cried for a while then persuaded myself to cheer up, as there might be a letter from you in the post. 8.45 & I went to check. No letter from you. It hurts, it really hurts. It's hurt ever since you went away except for about two weeks after I got your second letter, when I felt hopeful that you'd be in touch again. Then after those two weeks, although it hurt I told myself to be patient, that eventually you'd come back from Africa, there was no point in me tormenting myself over what might have happened to you. It was difficult, but it worked. Until last Monday when I rang Dorothy and she told me you'd been back in England six weeks, then it hurt again, why hadn't you been in touch?

That's the hardest part, just not knowing. If you don't love me any more, well I know I can survive that & get over it with time. But right now I'm just hanging on & it's tearing me apart. All I really want just now is another chance to talk to you, not to try & persuade you of anything, but so I at least know what the situation is.

London/Derby, July 1992

I also tried to follow a lead through details of John's parents in New Zealand. I knew when they had died and I had details of the sale of the family home. I figured if I could find the estate agent whose name Dorothy had told us or if I could get hold of a death certificate for either of them, then I'd hopefully get an address where I could contact John. I took a train to London and visited the New Zealand High Commission. I was told to fill in a form, pay a fee and wait a couple of weeks. A few weeks later I received a reply saying that there was no trace of either of them. Alarm bells were going off in my head, but I told myself it was possible that they had different surnames to John, so I shouldn't assume the worst.

Then I thought of the house in Derby where John said he'd been born. He'd told me that his family had long since moved out but I decided to visit all the same. With no other options it had to be worth a shot. I borrowed a friend's car and drove down. However, when I knocked there was no answer. Undeterred, I returned a few hours later and knocked again. This time, a woman answered but she'd never heard of him. I'd just hit another brick wall.

Unsent letter to John, my birthday, August 1992

Dear John, I'm gutted, I'm really hurting. So many times in the last four months since you've gone I've set dates, hoping to hear from you. Today has always been the last one. And nothing. Not even a card with just your name. Why? I can't understand. In your last letter you said you still loved me. If that's so I can't understand why you haven't been in touch, especially since Dorothy told you I wanted to hear from you. And especially why you couldn't manage a card to me on my birthday if you still love me? If you don't, then why can't you at least write and tell me that so I can stop being tormented by wondering.

Penistone, South Yorkshire, August 1992

The mystery of John's disappearance was bugging me. I had come across a book called *Tracing Missing Persons* and read it from cover to cover. The book said that the Salvation Army ran a tracing service, forwarding letters via the National Insurance system to put people back in contact with loved ones. Two days after my birthday I wrote to them to ask if they could find John. I described him as my common-law husband in the hope that they might take me more seriously. After all, we had lived together for over a year and had been planning to start a family at some point.

The Salvation Army sent a reply on 21 August acknowledging receipt of my letter and saying they would look into it, although 'enquiries could take some weeks and we cannot of course guarantee success'. Still, it gave me hope to think someone was helping me search for him.

The book also suggested using a private detective to find a missing person. I was nervous about doing this as I knew that many private detectives were former police officers, but equally, maybe they had channels I didn't have access to, so they might be successful. I phoned a few companies and eventually met up with a man at Sheffield Station to pay him and give him John's details. A couple of months later he got in contact to say he could find no trace of John. Another door slammed in my face. I had no luck with the Salvation Army either. They confirmed in writing that they had been able to forward two letters to John, but that so far they had not received any response.

Tottenham, London, early 1993

Towards the end of 1992, I felt both physically and mentally spent. John's disappearance still consumed my thoughts every day and I missed being able to talk freely to my long-term friends in London.

Although Pete and Sue had been supportive, I felt my ongoing gloom in their household was an unfair burden for them and was worried they might start to resent my presence. The McLibel case had been hotting up and was increasingly taking up my time and energy, with more pre-trial hearings and deadlines for providing details about our case. It felt too much to try to fight the action from Yorkshire, so I decided to move back to London, to focus on the case and to be close to my old friends again. I rented a flat in Tottenham – where I had lived for so long and where John and I had once been so happy. It felt like a lifetime ago, and John had become a ghost.

All too soon, the McLibel trial took over my life. In some ways, it was good to have a distraction – anything to stop me from thinking about John, what had happened to him and what might have been.

It was a huge effort to assemble pleadings, documents and witness statements for the McLibel trial and to attempt to rebuff McDonald's efforts to have our case struck out and to deny us a jury trial.

Royal Courts of Justice, London, 27 June 1994

Finally, we made it to the start of the McLibel trial. We had publicised a protest outside the court on the first day and I hoped John might see the publicity and turn up, but I knew it was unlikely. The start of the trial also made the news and I wondered if he might see it somewhere and get back in touch, at least to wish me well if nothing else.

The case began with opening speeches from McDonald's lawyers followed by speeches from Dave and me. McDonald's were asked to come up with a timetable for the trial, and to list the huge number of witnesses to be called on subjects ranging from nutrition and advertising to employment rights and animal welfare. At pre-trial hearings, McDonald's had estimated that the trial would last a few weeks. Now, they had set out a timetable lasting three to four months. It felt daunting even then, but within a couple of months it had become clear the trial would last much longer.

As part of my daily routine, I took the Tube to Holborn, then walked to the Royal Courts of Justice. On the way I passed St Catherine's House, which at the time held the register for all the births, deaths and marriages in England.

I'd first visited it years before with my younger sister to research a school project on family history, and later I had been back there to look up John's family records to help in his search for his father. One day in December 1994, on my way home from court, and purely on instinct, I suddenly decided to go into St Catherine's House and look through the death records for Barker, starting from 1960, the year of John's birth. In the 1968 volume I found a record of a death that matched John's name and place of birth. I felt a chill down my spine, but knew that I had to see the certificate itself before I could be sure it was the same person. I filled out the application form, paid the fee, then went home to wait.

A couple of weeks later I returned to collect the certificate. I found a quiet corner of the building and sat down to look at it.

CERTIFIED COPY OF AN ENTRY OF DEATH
In the County of Derby
PHILIP JOHN BARKER: Male, age 8 years.
CAUSE OF DEATH: Acute lymphatic leukaemia

This was John – my John. The name, the address and the details of the father all matched; it was definitely him.

John had been using the identity of a dead child.

John Barker – the man I'd loved, the man I'd planned to spend the rest of my life with – didn't exist. He never had.

I'd spent two years with him; I'd shared my bed and my deepest hopes and fears, but now I didn't even know his name. *Who was he?*

And if the person I had lived with, had been in a relationship with and thought I had known best didn't really exist, what did that mean for all my other relationships? If I missed that John wasn't real, how could I know whether anyone else was who they said they were?

I wanted to talk to friends about what I'd discovered, but how could I know who to trust?

I decided if John had been an infiltrator in our circle of friends and activists, that meant there could be others, so I'd better not talk about it in case word got back to the police about what I'd found out. Or maybe John had been on the run from the police or someone else and had used a false name to avoid detection, then equally I needed to protect him from potential danger. So many possibilities raced around my head, driving me frantic with worry.

Who was he?

Nausea rose inside me as I remembered all the things I'd shared – all the things we'd discussed.

I knew from the court case that McDonald's had, at one point, hired private detectives to spy on our group, so that was another possibility.

Had John been working for them?

It didn't seem plausible but then, nothing did – not any more.

Had John been a private detective sent to spy on us by the multinational? Or had John Barker been a detective working for the state?

Solid ground – my whole world – had been pulled from beneath my feet and I didn't know who I could and couldn't trust. Through the fog of uncertainty, there was one person I knew was real: Dave Morris – the other half of the McLibel Two. I sat down and told him what I'd discovered. He could see how upset I was and tried to reassure me.

'Helen, even if he had been a police officer then he could have genuinely loved you.'

I shrugged.

'I don't know, there are just too many unanswered questions.'

It was comforting to think at least something of the relationship might be real, but I knew I'd never rest until I got to the bottom of it all.

Alison

(Officer: Mark Cassidy)

My mum first introduced me to politics. She didn't agree with Dad about most current affairs but her socialist perspective of why the world was so unfair had a strong influence on me and my older brother, Ben. My university years were spent with Mick – my long-term boyfriend, who I'd been seeing since sixth form – as well as reading literature and closely following politics but taking part in zero political activism. Mick always warned against getting too involved.

'They had files on everyone who was a member of the National Council for Civil Liberties,' he told me. 'As soon as you join a party – especially a left-wing one – they start watching you.'

Our years together spanned the Miners' Strike, which ended in 1985, but I did little more to support the miners than attend the occasional march, throw money into a bucket outside the university bookshop and read about their struggle.

I left Mick in 1992.

Colin Roach Centre, Clarence Road, Hackney, London, early 1995

I'd joined an independent, politically non-aligned group two years previously, based at the Colin Roach Centre – named after a young black man who died from a gunshot wound at Stoke Newington police station in London. The eclectic group included anarchists, Marxists and members of the Labour Party, and had already successfully exposed corruption in the Met Police, raising awareness of systemic racism in the force with a particular focus on the disproportionate number of black people killed in police custody. The centre had also compiled a database of corrupt police officers. I liked the people in the group who were unpretentious, bright and serious about what they were doing. I was particularly interested in police monitoring, anti-racism and trade unionism.

I was working as an English and media studies teacher at that time, so I had a video camera and was interested in recording and editing film. My relationship with Mick had ended three years before and I was ready to start seeing someone new when I met Mark Cassidy.

I'd grown up and lived all my life in London and was drawn to him first by his accent: a Liverpudlian lilt. He had a bashful charm, and an authentic presence. He wasn't the typical middle-class campaigner who often turned up in left-wing groups. Mark was a working-class joiner from Birkenhead and he fitted in well with some of the men at the centre. He was a breath of fresh air; down to earth, practical and, above all, warm and friendly. He'd first turned up on the day of the annual 'We Remember' justice march that the Colin Roach Centre (CRC) had been co-organising. The march was followed by a meeting at the Halkevi community centre in Dalston where the human rights lawyer Gareth Peirce was the keynote speaker. I hadn't gone along but Mark had got talking to Mark Metcalf – a key organiser in the CRC – and soon began to attend our regular meetings. It was at one of these meetings that I first noticed him. We chatted, and I liked him. Mark had a van so when he offered to give us all a lift home at the end of the night, I readily agreed. I was the last one he dropped off and, by the time we said goodnight, I'd hoped something might happen between us.

London, a few weeks later, spring 1995

One evening after a CRC meeting, instead of letting him drive off into the night, I invited Mark to join me in my flat for a beer and a smoke.

'Do you smoke cannabis, Mr Cassidy?' I asked, hoping my jokey tone would cover the embarrassment if he never touched the stuff.

He laughed into his hands.

'Cannabis?' he repeated, still chuckling. 'Oh aye, I have been known to have the occasional spliff.'

We drank, smoked and talked for hours, and one thing predictably led to another. The following morning, we were lying in bed when the alarm sounded loudly at the side of my head.

'Fucking hell, that's a racket! What's the time?' Mark asked, half-smiling, half-grimacing.

It was 6.30am, and our clothes were still strewn across my bedroom floor – reminders of the night before. Empty bottles lay beside an ashtray of crushed-out joints.

Mark stretched and yawned.

'Right,' he said unexpectedly. 'I better get going.'

His Liverpudlian burr made me smile.

'Me too,' I said, exhausted from our sleepless night. I leaned forward and kissed him gently on the forehead.

I felt self-conscious as I climbed out of bed. My hands searched around, trying to find a towel I could wrap round myself before hitting the shower. By the time I'd emerged, my hair still dripping wet, Mark was already out of bed, dressed, and sat lacing up his workman's boots. I felt a pang of uncertainty.

'Don't you want a shower?'

He looked up at me as he clambered to his feet.

'Nah, I'll have one at home. I need to get my tools and I haven't got a change of clothes.'

'Cup of tea?' I offered.

He shook his head.

'Nah, I'd better head off … you know, or I'll be late. I'll just pop to the loo before I go,' he said, gesturing over towards the door.

I smiled as he left the room. As I did, I caught sight of my own reflection in the bedroom mirror. My eye make-up had smudged around my eyes, leaving dark, unsightly rings; my naturally curly hair was matted, and my face bright red, partly from rubbing against the stubble of his chin, and partly through embarrassment.

With him in the loo, I quickly grabbed some clean underwear, my jeans, which I found crumpled in a fabric puddle on the floor, and a fresh T-shirt. The jeans stank of stale smoke from the night before.

'Right then,' he called from the hallway.

I left the bedroom and walked him to the door to say goodbye.

I wonder how he feels about monogamy and casual sex?

'Erm,' I mumbled, trying to find the right words. 'Do you want to do this again?'

Mark grinned.

'Do I have to make an appointment?' he laughed.

And then he'd gone. I watched as he bobbed down the steps to the path outside, and then into his van.

Make an appointment? What did he think? That I have a different man here every night?

Later that evening, I pulled the curtain closed and stared down at the telephone on the side. I wondered if I should call. I was more than aware of the rules governing 'how to keep a man keen'. The ones repeated in countless useless magazine articles about who should call first after sex. I shook my head.

I don't have to wait for him to ring. It's 1995; I'm an independent woman in charge of my own destiny.

I stretched out a hand and picked up the phone. Dialling his number, it rang a few times before he answered.

'Hi, it's Alison. I had a good time last night.'

The previous evening flashed through my mind as I blushed at the intimacy we'd shared. I twiddled my necklace. Holding my breath, I waited for his response.

'Yeah, me too.'

'So, how was your day?' I asked, wondering what being a joiner actually involved.

'Apart from the fact I'm knackered, it was sound.'

I laughed and understood exactly what he meant.

'I could hardly keep my eyes open during lessons,' I admitted. 'I spent most of the afternoon with the kids, watching cartoon versions of *Macbeth*.'

He laughed and the awkwardness dissolved a little down the phone.

'To be, or not to be,' he said in a posh accent that wasn't his own.

Now it was my turn to laugh.

'That's *Hamlet*!' I pretended to scold. 'Out damned spot! It's the Scottish play …'

'Oh yeah, damn spot – that bloody dog gets everywhere …'

There was another silence – a slice of dead air between us – until Mark spoke.

'So, fancy going out for something to eat at the weekend, then?'

A grin spread across my face as I imagined Mark brushing a nervous hand across the top of his head, waiting for my answer. I let his question hang for a moment in mid-air.

'Definitely.'

'Right, it's a date then; pick you up Saturday?'

I nodded eagerly even though he couldn't see me.

'Yes, see you then.'

Putting down the receiver, I squealed with delight and allowed myself to flop down on the bed. Staring up at the ceiling, I continued to smile.

Was that it? Was Mark my new boyfriend?

Mark's bedsit, North London, June 1995

After our first date – a meal in an Indian restaurant – our relationship moved quickly and almost immediately, he was spending most of his time at my place. It was a mutual decision. On my first visit to his bedsit, half a mile away from my flat, I hadn't been impressed. The corridor leading to it was lined with faded 1970s paisley wallpaper that was peeling away in places. The building was dingy and had the aroma of overcooked cabbage. Mark's bedsit consisted of a single bed with a narrow sleeping bag laid on top of a mattress and a sad greyish-white pillow for his head. There was a battered old chest of drawers that looked as though it had been picked up in a house clearance. On top was a plastic kettle and a couple of chipped, tannin-stained mugs that had been lined up alongside a pile of anarchist and Class War pamphlets. A cheap woven rug covered most of the brown linoleum flooring and there were two Class War posters that he'd Blu-tacked to the walls along with a newspaper cutting on Tranmere Rovers' promotion. The whole place had the feel of a boy's student digs.

He'd told me his father had been killed by a drunken driver when he was eight. He'd fallen out with his mum when she remarried her new partner, John, who he didn't get on with. His grandma had brought him up during his teenage years, but she had died in 1993. He'd said his grandpa was still alive but they weren't particularly close.

'You all right with instant?' he asked, spooning some into one of the mugs.

'Yeah, course!' I lied.

'Fancy coming with me to a footie match some time?'

I sat up.

'I'd love to.'

I smiled and went over to him as he stirred the coffee. Lifting my hand, my fingers stroked the synthetic material of his blue and white Tranmere Rovers top.

'I even like the feel of your shirt which, by rights, I should find repulsive.'

Mark snorted with laughter and shook his head as I continued to tease.

'It's all part of your authentic charm, I suppose.'

My eyes scanned the bare room that I had no desire to ever wake up in. I spotted a twelve-string acoustic guitar leaning up against the bed.

'Do you play that?'

He turned his head away from the cups and the kettle.

'I'm learning.'

I beamed.

A van and a guitar!

'Bring it over to mine. You can practise.'

Mark grinned; he wandered over to the guitar, picked it up and rested it against his knee. I watched as he began to clumsily pluck at a few chords.

'I'm pretty shite at it.'

I laughed.

'But why a twelve-string? Surely it must be much harder to learn?'

He lifted his face and looked directly at me.

'Probably, but I like a challenge.'

Fundraising benefit, Molly Malones, Hackney, London, summer 1995

Mark and I went with a few others from the CRC to support a fundraising benefit gig at a venue called Molly Malones. It was noisy and overcrowded, with people packed in tightly next to each other; there was a grey curtain of smoke hanging in the air and the place stank of spilt beer. Mark spent much of the evening talking politics with various people at the bar while I danced and chatted with friends. We didn't want to be joined at the hip and I liked that we trusted each other to socialise separately without fear of betrayal. We found each other at the end of the evening to go home. He seemed really upbeat.

'You'll never guess what,' he grinned.

'What?'

'Some bird only made a pass at me – she said I should come back to hers.'

I asked who she was and, when he said her name, I nodded in recognition. I'd never met the woman but she was a well-known figure in the Revolutionary Communist Party. I felt a thread of jealousy twist inside.

'And what did you say?'

Mark pulled shut the van door, dusted the palms of his hands against his jeans, and looked at me.

'I told her I was here with my girlfriend.'

My girlfriend. I repeated the words inside my head, trying the title on like a new overcoat. I liked that. He'd not only turned the woman down but, by calling me his girlfriend, he'd cemented our relationship both for us and to the world outside.

'And what did she say … to that, I mean?'

He grinned and shook his head.

'She told me to fuck you off and go back with her.'

'Fucking cheek! I'll kill her!' I said, only half joking.

'The London left's a fucking knocking shop,' he chortled to himself as he started up the engine.

I could see why he thought that but was relieved it didn't include us. It had been our first test and he'd passed with flying colours.

He had turned her down because he was loyal and trustworthy.

One morning soon after, he left me in bed to go to buy ingredients for a cooked breakfast. As he stood by the bedroom doorway, I was struck by how lucky I was. It was almost too good to be true. Members of the Colin Roach Centre were acutely aware of the possibility of being infiltrated, and the thought suddenly crossed my mind. He'd turned up not knowing anyone. He fitted in quickly. He was interested in getting to know the radical, London left. I didn't *really* believe it but asked anyway.

'It's like you've just dropped out of the sky. From nowhere. You're not a cop, are you?'

Mark's smile broadened as he broke into a chuckle.

'Yeah! Gotta report back to Hendon later!'

I laughed at the ridiculousness of the idea along with him, forgot all about it and was grateful for the tasty breakfast that appeared soon after.

My flat, North London, July 1995

By now, Mark had pretty much moved in, claiming one half of my bed as his own.

As we lay there propped up on our pillows, I was complaining about my dad and the dysfunctional side of my family. I'd been thirteen years old when I discovered he'd been cheating on Mum for years and, as a result, I explained, I'd decided that most men lie.

'I hope you're not one of them.'

Mark laughed and pulled me towards him. I snuggled in, inhaling the scent of his skin, now so familiar. I rested my head against his chest; I felt contained, safe and protected by this big bear of a man.

'He left my mum and I don't really get on with my stepmother,' I continued. 'Birthdays, Christmases and the odd occasional phone call was about the sum total of our emotional commitment.'

I paused and contemplated my next question. I didn't like to pry, but I was dying to know more about his family.

'What about your background? You don't talk about your dad much. What was he like?'

I felt Mark shift uneasily next to me.

'I can't remember that much. It's hard to know if I really remember it or if it's just from old photos.'

Pushing myself up onto one elbow, I faced him.

'I'd love to see those photos. Do you have them back at your flat?'

He shook his head quickly.

'Nah, they're all up at Mum's. But you'll see them someday.'

Mark shifted again and readjusted the pillows beneath his head.

'Anyway, I've been thinking. How about we take the van up to Scotland for our first New Year together?'

So, he was thinking long term. I hoped it would be the first New Year of many.

'I've been a couple of times before,' Mark continued, interrupting my thoughts, 'and there are some great places to stay; stunning views. You should see them, Ali. We can go cross-country skiing. It's brilliant!'

I'd never heard of cross-country skiing before and the closest I got to an outdoor adventure in my family was a roast chicken picnic on Hampstead Heath.

'Sounds great but camping in January? Won't it be freezing?'

Mark laughed.

'That's half the fun; we'll be cosy inside the van and as long as you wrap up during the day, you'll be fine.'

He grabbed the edge of the duvet and pulled it up over my naked shoulders. Suddenly the excitement vanished from his face and his brow furrowed.

'Listen, I've got to spend Christmas with my grandpa in Birkenhead, but I could pick you up at Liverpool train station.'

'Deal!' I replied, delighted we were already making plans together.

West Belfast, August 1995

The Colin Roach Centre had organised a delegation to the West Belfast *fleadh* (a community festival of entertainment and events). I'd never been to Northern Ireland, and neither had Mark, but he agreed to drive everyone over in his van. With his working-class, Irish background, he seemed far more comfortable than I was. Even when he accidently drove us down the Shankill Road, unlike everyone else, he didn't seem bothered and brushed it off with a joke.

At one point we were walking in a group by a parade of shops. My eyes darted around, hyper-aware of the unfamiliar surroundings. Somehow, Mark had drifted behind us when out of nowhere there was a loud bang. I jumped and screamed, my mind going straight to a gunshot. I turned around to find him doubled over, laughing. He'd stamped on a crisp packet.

'You bastard!' I screamed, but he couldn't stop chuckling.

I laughed along but felt embarrassed. He knew I was tense and took the piss.

Derry Walls, August 1995

Part of our reason for being in Belfast was to learn from the local community how they organised to resist police brutality. We'd been invited to support the local Catholic community in Derry, which was protesting the Apprentice Boys' annual march through the centre of town. We had to climb the Derry walls, which defined the old town quarter at the heart of the city. My ascent was clumsy but finally we joined the crowd. I was pressed between young Catholic men and women, listening to Republican leader Martin McGuinness as he addressed everyone. I could see Mark from where I was sitting. It wasn't long before the Royal Ulster Constabulary (RUC) had arrived in their stiff-as-cardboard green uniforms to pull us all off the bridge, and Mark and I were separated. The throng of the crowd swept me away and I was steered in a sea of unfamiliar faces. I scanned each one, looking for him, but he was nowhere to be seen. My heart pounded and my mouth was dry.

Where is he?

The police navigated us away, and I felt stranded and alone in a strange town. As the crowd moved, I spotted a familiar YHA sign up ahead, peeping over the top of a brick building, and I headed towards it. I had no plan – nothing – but I knew I had to try to find Mark and the others. I walked inside the hostel, feigning the confidence of a guest, and headed up some stairs, slipping through a door with a 'no entry' sign on it. It led me through to a corridor that had windows overlooking the square – a perfect vantage point to try to spot Mark and the others. I pressed my face against the cool glass to search; all I could see were green lines of police and clusters of protestors but Mark wasn't among them. The sound of the drums grew louder, echoing back from the buildings as the Protestant marching band approached. My stomach knotted.

Suddenly, I became aware of a man standing near me, a little further along the corridor. He was wearing a smart Barbour jacket and I felt his gaze boring into me. I made a determined effort to look calm, and to not return his stare.

Where the hell are you, Mark?

Then, the man started whistling along to the band's marching tune, tapping his fingers in time with the drums. We were entirely alone in the corridor, and there was something about him, he was obviously undercover, placed there to keep an eye on me having wandered off from the crowd. There to spook me.

I had to escape. I knew about undercover cops, especially in Northern Ireland, and I wanted to get away. Retracing my steps, I fled the building and ran over to the main square; I turned and turned again, my eyes scouring every inch of pavement, every shaded doorway, every break in the crowd, looking for Mark. I felt a heady mix of nerves and adrenalin.

Has he been arrested?

Is he safe?

I carried on walking, trying to hold my nerve.

What should I do?

I was beginning to wonder if I should pretend to go shopping but was worried the others would never find me. I was calculating how long it would take the CCTV cameras to spot me if I continued to pace up and down the same streets, when I heard a familiar Liverpudlian voice behind me.

'There you are!' Mark called, taking me in his arms.

I finally felt safe – the coursing adrenalin began to subside.

'Mark, thank God!'

'It's fine, I'm here now.'

His voice oozed relief.

It was my thirtieth birthday during our trip, and Derry City were playing Lokomotiv Sofia at Brandywell Stadium in Derry. Mark and I went with others from the CRC. It wouldn't be every woman's ideal birthday night out, but the atmosphere was electric and I was so happy with Mark that little else seemed to matter.

Liverpool Lime Street, 27 December 1995

Pulling into the railway station, I disembarked onto a freezing cold platform as a vicious wind whipped against my face. I followed the signs for the taxi rank, where Mark told me he'd be waiting. Beyond the line of taxis, there, parked in a loading bay, was his trademark ex-postie van and him waving at me from behind the wheel. I ran over and clambered into the seat next to him. With my rucksack perched on my lap, I leaned in to kiss him.

'It's so good to see you,' I said, unable to hide my excitement.

'You too.'

I pulled down the sun visor to check my frizzy hair.

Maybe I should tie it back, make it look neater?

'So, what time's your grandpa expecting us?'

Mark looked at me with a look of exasperation.

'He's only gone and signed up for some church outing, hasn't he?'

My heart sank and I felt bitterly disappointed; I'd been looking forward to finally meeting him.

'Oh no, what a shame!'

Mark slapped his hand on the top of the steering wheel in annoyance.

'I know, typical, eh? I told him weeks ago we were coming, but the silly bastard forgot.'

He leaned forward and twisted the key in the ignition. The van spluttered and then fired into life as the engine chugged.

'Come on, we'll see the old man another time.'

Pushing the gearstick into first, the van lurched forward and we set off on our holiday. But I couldn't shake the feeling of regret. His grandpa would have been the first member of Mark's family I would have met.

Suddenly, there was a reassuring hand on top of my knee, as Mark gave it a squeeze.

'Anyway, tell me about your Christmas.'

I rolled my eyes dramatically.

'Our Jewish Christmas was fine. The usual, really; overeating, family tension and crap telly!'

He threw back his head and began to laugh.

'Sounds great!'

'Yeah,' I smirked.

I dug out a pack of tobacco and began to roll a cigarette as we hit the road to spend the New Year and our first holiday together in the Cairngorms.

New Year, Cairngorms, Scotland, 1995/6

I'd expected Scotland to be cold, but not this freezing. We camped in the back of the van. We'd brought everything we needed to create a cosy nest against the icy air outside. Our breath formed condensation that seemed to cling against the cold air as we tried to maintain our body temperature against the –22°C frost. Outside, the snow was knee-deep, but we had love, alcohol and cannabis to keep us warm and comfortable. We finally toasted in the New Year with a nip or two of whisky.

'Happy New Year!' I smiled.

My face had become numbed by the alcohol and temperature. I leaned forward and kissed him passionately; then I raised my mug to chink his.

'Here's to 1996!'

My flat, North London, February 1996

Mark gave notice on his bedsit. We'd been spending all our time together and since I'd never wanted to stay at his shabby place, we agreed he'd move in with me permanently.

My flat, North London, summer 1996

We'd soon settled down into a life of domesticity, and I hadn't felt this happy for years. Mark would leave for work at 6.30am as a joiner at the Manor Works, in Clapham. I also worked full-time, teaching, and when we weren't at political meetings or events, we enjoyed our evenings watching TV or hanging out with friends. Weekends were spent walking, riding our bikes and travelling the country to watch Tranmere Rovers away games. He loved football and I was entranced by the crowd.

In mid-June, Mark told me he'd landed some work in Spain because Terry, his boss, had a mate who owned a villa over there.

'It's a painting job, but it's very intricate work that Terry specialises in. I'll be gone about a week.'

I missed him and was greedy for him when he came back. His skin glowed from the Spanish sunshine. He was as keen as I was to make love, and seemed flattered by my urgency.

In August, we went on holiday for two weeks in Crete. We trekked the Samariá Gorge and I had my first experience riding pillion on the back of a hired motorbike. We had a wonderful time and were becoming closer every day.

Mum's wedding, London, September 1996

My mother married her long-term partner Sid at a registry office in North London, and celebrated with a big party back at their home. Mark already knew my immediate family well but at the wedding he met everyone, engaging them all with his down-to-earth manner and friendly personality.

We'd often go for Friday night dinner at Mum's home. Mark would wear a koppel and stand respectfully as Mum and Sid recited the Friday night prayers and lit the Shabbat candles.

One Friday night, Sid, who'd returned to university study in his senior years, started talking to Mark about his recently completed MA dissertation.

'If that appeaser Lord Halifax had been PM, God knows what would've happened,' said Sid.

Mark nodded briefly. I was ready to step in, worried that he didn't know how to respond. But, before I had the chance, he spoke up.

'I know, Churchill has his critics, Sid. But, like you say, it would have been a very different history if he'd not been in charge.'

I was proud that my self-educated, working-class boyfriend from Birkenhead could hold his own.

He was able to fit in anywhere.

Helen

(Officer: John Barker)

The High Court, London, 17 July 1996

Our evidence to the High Court in the McLibel trial finally drew to an end. Somehow, we had to condense the evidence that had been presented in court – 40,000 documents and 20,000 pages of testimony – into a compelling closing speech to convince the judge, Mr Justice Rodger Bell, to rule in our favour. The closing speech alone was expected to last six more weeks. Dave and I were exhausted, but we couldn't stop. We'd come too far to fall at the final hurdle.

The High Court, London, 1st November 1996

The McLibel trial had hit 292 days in court and had officially become the longest trial in English history. It certainly felt like it!

The case continued for a few more weeks after that with closing speeches and legal arguments, then the Judge said he was reserving his judgement and didn't know how long it would take to write.

Now all we could do was await the verdict.

Alison

(Officer: Mark Cassidy)

My flat, North London, 8 December 1996

I'd been thinking about my ex-partner, Mick. Although we'd split over three years ago, we still met up as friends a couple of times a year and always in the build-up to Christmas.

It was freezing outside, and I pulled the curtains tight to keep out the draught whistling through the window.

'I'm going to give Mick a ring,' I told Mark. 'I haven't seen him in a while. We usually meet up for a Christmas drink.'

I looked over at Mark; he glanced up from a TV programme he was watching.

'You don't mind, do you?'

He shook his head, before his eyes returned to the screen.

'Course not.'

I leaned in and kissed him gently on his cheek, grateful for his trusting attitude.

Picking up the phone, I stretched the cable and carried it through into my bedroom for privacy. Mick had moved back into his mother's house after we'd separated so I found her number and began to dial.

'Hello,' a woman answered on the other end of the line.

I was taken aback. I'd expected Mick to answer – or even his mum – but it wasn't either of them. The woman's voice sounded oddly familiar but I couldn't place it.

'Hi, it's Alison; is Mick there?'

Without warning, the woman's tone changed.

'Mick isn't here. I'll get someone to call you back,' she snapped before hanging up.

I looked at the receiver as if it had bitten me before replacing it in its cradle. Resting my back against the headboard, I tried to place the familiar voice.

Who was the woman and, more importantly, where was Mick?

I rewound her voice over and over until suddenly it clicked.

Of course! It was Joan, Mick's sister.

She'd never really liked me, but this was unusually curt, even for her.

But why was Joan at Mick's mum's house, answering the phone?

I picked it up again, but decided against calling back in case Joan answered a second time. Instead, I began folding green and red paper in preparation for the following day's Christmas-themed writing lesson at school. I was creasing the last few pieces when the phone rang behind me.

'Alison, it's Karen.'

It was Mick's cousin, but she didn't sound herself; her voice was sombre, deep and slow.

Why was she there? Something was very wrong.

'Karen! What is it? What's going on?'

She tried to speak but, as she did, her voice cracked with emotion.

God, what is it, and where's Mick?

'I'm sorry no one has told you, Alison, but Mick died last Sunday. It's been his funeral today.'

A darkness washed over me; I opened my mouth to speak – to say how sorry I was – but no words would come, only tears.

'What do you mean? Karen, I don't … I don't understand,' I spluttered. The news, my words, this awful feeling that had swamped me – nothing made sense.

'There's no easy way to explain it. It's not your fault, Alison.'

Not my fault? What was she talking about? I hadn't seen Mick since spring, when we had that row … oh God!

A hand flew up to my mouth as I tried to stifle the high-pitched cry emitting from it.

'My fault?' I repeated, sucker-punched by the two words. 'What do you mean, it's not my fault?'

I heard Karen take a deep breath on the other end of the line.

'He loved you so much … he just never got over you two splitting up.'

I'd killed Mick; I'd killed him by breaking his heart.

It didn't feel real. Nothing felt real. A crashing roar sounded in my ears.

'How did he die?' I asked, holding in the tears.

'It was a burst ulcer – stress-related, we think. He wouldn't get treatment. He was in lots of pain but he refused to see a doctor … you know how stubborn he could be.'

I shook my head in disbelief as my chin trembled. I couldn't believe I'd never see Mick again.

I'll never be able to speak to him or ask his advice; I'll never be able to pick his overfilled analytical brain ever again …

The pain was too much; the reality too hard to comprehend.

'But why … why didn't anyone tell me?'

I felt there was more Karen hadn't said. She paused for a moment, as though trying to find the right words.

'I'm so sorry, Alison, but Joan and his mum – they blame you, for all his stress. They didn't want you at the funeral. I'm really sorry.'

And that's when I let go. Sinking down the wall onto my knees, I began to sob until soon my body was shaking with pain and grief.

'I loved him so much,' was all I could say before hanging up.

My eyes were raw from crying as I stumbled to my feet and made my way back through to Mark. He noticed the state I was in immediately.

'Ali, what's wrong?' he gasped, rising from his seat to hold me in his arms. 'Christ, what's happened?'

His hand brushed damp strands of my hair away. Then he cupped my chin and tilted my face towards his.

'What is it?' he whispered gently. 'What's wrong?'

I couldn't look at him; I couldn't face anyone. Instead, I buried my head against his chest and sobbed.

'Come on, whatever it is we can …'

'It's Mick,' I said, blurting out his name between breaths. 'It's Mick … he's dead.'

Mark's arms stiffened around me as he became rigid, as though he'd been filled with concrete.

'Oh my God!' he said, letting go and backing away from me.

He crashed back onto the sofa. I was taken aback by his shocked reaction, and knelt down beside him.

'They blame me, Mark. The family blame me. It was his funeral today and they hadn't even told me.'

He leaned forward, rested his elbows on his knees and covered his face with his thick fingers.

'Oh my God ... oh my God ...' he said over and over again.

I was surprised and confused. I'd spoken to him about Mick, but the pair had never met so his reaction seemed excessive. After a few moments, he got up and went into the kitchen. I heard the chink of glasses as Mark returned with two shot glasses and a bottle of whisky. He unscrewed the lid and poured two large measures.

'Come on, I think we need this ... I just can't believe it.'

I picked up the glass and threw the alcohol to the back of my throat, scorching it. Then I poured another. Mark's face looked ashen; his neck sunk deep between his shoulders

'I know why I'm so upset, but why are you taking it so hard?'

There was shock in his eyes as he twisted towards me. He wrung his hands and I waited for an answer.

'It's just that I knew how much you'd loved each other and, I know it sounds strange, but I always thought if we split up, you'd get back with him.'

I wiped the back of my hand against my eyes to rid them of tears.

'Oh, Mark, we're not going to split up.'

Helen
(Officer: John Barker)

Judgement day in the McLibel trial, the High Court, London, 19 June 1997

It was pouring down in London as Dave and I sheltered under my umbrella on our way to the High Court. The grey pavement was wet and reflected London's skyline like a mirror. We reached the court and found a mounting press scrum awaiting us. We stood there awkwardly, posing for photographs, knowing that the next few hours would be crucial. As the camera flashguns exploded, I again wondered if John might see me on the news and think about getting in touch to explain everything.

I hope you regret what you did, I thought as the barrage of lights blinded me.

It felt like such a momentous occasion. Dave and I had spent 314 days in court and, finally, Mr Justice Rodger Bell would give his judgement and the case would be over.

Although the judge made many findings in our favour, he ruled against us on some points and then ruled we would be liable to pay McDonald's damages of £60,000. We weren't that surprised – we'd been warned it could happen.

As we emerged from court, the rain had stopped and the sun had appeared. A large crowd had formed outside and, as we stepped out, a huge cheer rose and we punched the air in triumph. Despite the damages order, it felt like a victory because through the court case we had exposed the reality of McDonald's and opened them up to public scrutiny – and there were now some damning rulings against their core business practices. In short, the trial had been a public relations disaster for McDonald's.

Afterwards, at an organised press conference, we were asked how we felt about losing the case and paying damages to McDonald's.

I explained that what would have been a loss was if we hadn't fought the case and had instead allowed McDonald's to intimidate us into backing down. Then I told the reporters: 'We're not going to pay the damages. McDonald's don't deserve a penny and, in any event, we haven't got any money!'

Mass defiance day across the UK, 21 June 1997

Two days later, in an act of defiance and celebration, protests took place outside over 500 McDonald's restaurants in the UK and further stores throughout the rest of the world. McDonald's hadn't seen the last of the leaflets – far from it – because people handed them out in their thousands. McDonald's had applied for an injunction and had threatened that if we continued to distribute leaflets, they would have us jailed. I didn't want to go to jail, but I would have been ready to do so because the alternative would have been to give into McDonald's tactics, which I wasn't prepared to do. The mass defiance day was intended to show them that if they tried to suppress their critics, more people would step up to publicise the issues. In the end, McDonald's never collected a penny in damages. I think they knew that if they did try, the resulting publicity would have been catastrophic for their already bruised company image.

Alison

(Officer: Mark Cassidy)

My flat, North London, July 1997

Since the end of my relationship with Mick, I'd spent years with a raft of unsuitable men until Mark had appeared on the scene. I watched as he cooked dinner in my kitchen.

It had been seven months since Mick had died. The grief had shifted something in me and I needed permanence. I wanted a future with Mark and one that included children. It felt too early to broach the subject. I didn't want to scare him off. For now, I decided to keep the idea locked in my head.

After dinner, we snuggled on the sofa and watched a rented DVD, which were fast beginning to replace videos. It was his favourite film, he said: *The Day of the Jackal*. Set in the 1960s, it told the story of a professional assassin who was called The Jackal. A master of disguise and false identity, he had been hired to assassinate the French president, Charles de Gaulle.

'This bit's great,' Mark said as he gestured over at the TV. I had a more interesting plan, however, and soon we'd missed a large chunk of the film, making love on the floor.

'I love that film,' he remarked as the credits came on and I sat and rolled a post-coital joint.

'Here,' I said, passing it over to him.

'Cheers.' He inhaled deeply. 'The Jackal's disguise at the end is brilliant.'

We'd smoked most of the joint when Mark suggested a game.

'Have you got any wigs?'

I looked at him oddly.

'You know,' he said, 'from a fancy-dress party, or something?'

'Why?' I asked, blowing smoke out of the corner of my mouth.

'How about we put on disguises, blast some classic tunes on the CD player, mime along to the words with my guitar, and film it on your video camera?'

I burst out laughing.

'Are you serious?'

He nodded with a cheeky grin.

'Come on, it'll be a laugh.'

I leaned over, grabbed his head in both my hands, and landed a huge smacking kiss on his lips.

'Fantastic idea. I do love you!'

I'd blurted the words out impulsively and, as soon as they hit the air, I felt my face flush.

'Yer not so bad yerself!' he responded, slapping me on my backside.

I got up and wandered through to the bedroom to dig out my camera while Mark searched his jacket pocket for a pair of dark shades. He pulled on a khaki green German army shirt and made himself comfortable in the chair. Lifting up his twelve-string guitar, he perched it on his knee and opened with his favourite Johnny Cash song. It was 'Wanted Man'.

I pressed record and watched, impressed, as he mouthed along to every line. He was word perfect.

'How do you know all the words?' I asked, as he brought the song to a close.

'A combination of a "sticky" brain and my dad playing loads of Johnny Cash when I was little,' he replied, before leaning forward in his chair to give my knee a squeeze.

'How about a duet of "Bohemian Rhapsody"?'

I threw my head back and laughed.

'You don't know all the words to that too, do you?'

I'd never been able to master the words to any song all the way through.

Mark looked bashful.

'You do! No one knows all the words to that.'

He nodded.

'I think I do, anyway. Let's give it a go.'

As he mimed the lyrics that questioned whether this was 'real life' or 'just fantasy', it became apparent he knew every single word to Queen's 'Bohemian Rhapsody'.

Israel, 3 August 1997

We'd booked to go on a three-week trip to Israel, where I was looking forward to introducing Mark to old family friends who lived there. We were both excited to go; Mark explained how he'd been fascinated by Israel and its history, and joked about the grilling he was prepared for from El Al security, who scrutinised travellers at the airport in London before they got on the plane.

I knew it would take ages to get on board. The Israeli airline's security was well known for examining everyone, especially those who weren't Jewish. I waited in a queue while the female security officer glanced up from my passport to my face and back again several times. She was petite and humourless.

'Are you Jewish?' she asked, dressed in her regulation blue shirt, her tanned arms bent at the elbow as she gripped my British passport between her fingers.

I nodded.

'Have you been to Israel before?' she demanded.

I gave my answer as she looked down at my passport again; my stomach clenched. Even though I had nothing to hide, I felt guilty.

'Do you speak Hebrew?'

'A little,' I replied.

'What is the purpose of your trip?'

The answer to that was easy.

'I'm with my boyfriend,' I replied nodding back at him, waiting behind me. Mark had his eyes cast downwards as he leaned his weight forward against the luggage trolley. 'We're touring the country and visiting old Israeli friends.'

She asked more questions and, after what seemed like an age, finally waved me through. I stood on the other side of the barrier, waiting for Mark, wondering how long she'd take with him.

'Okay, thank you.' She smiled, indicating he should go through with a flick of her petite wrist.

I couldn't believe it – she hadn't asked him a single thing.

'How did you do that?' I said, open-mouthed.

'It must be my natural charm and good looks,' he teased, and soon we'd boarded the plane and left the grey tarmac of London's Heathrow airport behind, bound for Tel Aviv.

That evening, we stayed with friends who lived just outside Tel Aviv, before travelling north the following day to the city of Kiryat Shmona. The day after, we visited a nature reserve and the next day we climbed Mount Hermon and stayed on a campsite at the Sea of Galilee. Enjoying lunch at a fish restaurant at the Ein Gev kibbutz, I reflected on how lucky I was. If I'd fallen in love with a more stereotypical activist, he'd never have come with me to Israel. He'd be too restricted by anti-Zionist dogma to countenance it. Mark wasn't like that.

We visited a spa and then Nazareth and the town of Caesarea on the Mediterranean coast, before heading back to my friends in Tel Aviv for drinks on the eve of my birthday.

The following day, I celebrated my thirty-second birthday. We'd just reached the beach when Mark said he wasn't feeling very well.

'What is it?'

'I don't know, I just feel hot; like I've got a fever or something.'

It was over 90°F so everyone was hot but I was concerned for his welfare. I tried to push away the disappointment of my birthday celebrations being cut short.

'Come on,' I said. 'Let's get back.'

The following day, Mark said he felt as though he was burning up, so my friends called a doctor, who told us to take him to casualty. We rushed in their car to Tel Hashomer Hospital where doctors X-rayed Mark's chest and hooked him up to IV antibiotics. I paced the air-conditioned room as the doctor explained they'd diagnosed him with pneumonia. I glanced down at Mark's face; it was pale despite our first week spent in the sunshine. The hospital wanted to keep him in for two nights. He was released on 14 August but just three days later, he said he felt dreadful again, so we drove him back to the hospital, where he was given another chest X-ray.

The medics held the black and white negative against the light. They seemed to see it all.

'The pneumonia is still there. He's got more pleural fluid on his lungs; he needs to fly home,' the doctor advised.

I couldn't fathom why the advice would be to fly home when he was already in hospital, being cared for, but I just wanted Mark to get better. With his mind made up, the doctor wrote a letter to give to our insurance company, so we could catch an earlier flight. We'd only been in Israel two weeks when we boarded a plane back home to London, cutting our holiday short by a week. I was gutted. I'd looked forward to it all year but the priority was to get Mark back and on the mend.

Strangely, once we'd got home – despite my protestations that he needed to rest – he returned to work almost immediately. When I suggested it was too soon, he told me not to fuss. We'd been told to expect a three-month recuperation period, but Mark made a miraculous recovery.

The funeral of Princess Diana, 6 September 1997

Along with the rest of the country, Mark and I sat on the sofa side by side, watching the funeral of Princess Diana on TV. She'd been killed in a car crash along with Dodi Fayed – son of Harrods department store owner, Mohamed Al-Fayed. The country was still in a state of shock and national mourning. As we watched the pomp and circumstance of the day's proceedings, I became dismissive of the outpourings of grief; I was scornful of the privilege. I rolled my eyes as I got up and made us a cup of tea, bringing through a plateful of digestive biscuits.

'Parasites!' I mumbled under my breath but loud enough for Mark to hear.

His head turned round to meet mine – a look of surprise, almost disgust, on his face.

'They're still children, you know!'

Mark seemed cross but I didn't fully understand why. We were anti-monarchy. I thought back to his grotty bedsit and the Class War posters he'd pinned up. One had been a photograph of the royal family, waving from the palace balcony with the word 'WANKERS' emblazoned across the bottom of it. But, right now, he seemed defensive, almost protective of them. I was struggling to comprehend the disconnect.

'Whoever they are, those boys have lost their mother,' he said, by way of explanation for his sudden outburst. 'They'll never get over that.'

Reprimanded into silence and knowing he was right, I sulkily dunked my digestive in my tea until it became soggy.

Dover, 15 November 1997

Mark travelled with a group of anti-fascists to stop a BNP march in Dover. They blocked the fascists' way with the strength of their physical presence. I followed the news coverage of the protest during the day and captured on the video recorder a sighting of Mark on the news. Wearing a black woollen hat and a dark bomber jacket, he'd been standing on some raised ground with others, shouting down at the racist thugs below. They'd been surrounded by police trying to move them. His eyebrows formed a deep V as he invited the sea of white men to take him on.

Mark faced them and began to bellow.

'Come on, then!' he shouted, a look of menace on his face.

It wasn't pretty to watch, but I was proud of his role.

My flat, North London, November 1997

I don't know what I was looking for in his jacket pockets that morning. It was the weekend and he'd gone out to the shops to buy a paper. As the front door closed, I had an impulse to search. I felt he was hiding something from me. I expected to find a leaflet, I think. Or evidence of some meeting he'd attended without telling me. I thought he was possibly dipping into more radical political stuff he'd know I'd try to talk him out of.

Instead, I found a NatWest bank card in the name of M. Jenner. The signature on the back was in his handwriting. I didn't understand.

What was he doing with this and whose was it?

As soon as he returned, I confronted him.

'Who is M. Jenner, and what are you doing with their bank card signed in your handwriting?'

He turned to grey stone – frozen in time with his hands on his head, a posture of submission.

'Oh, my God! I'm so stupid.'

'What's going on, Mark?'

His arms dropped to his sides and his face took on the expression of a small child confessing a misdemeanour. He explained he'd bought it off a bloke in a pub. He knew it was really stupid and said he'd only used it to buy some petrol.

'Please, Ali, please don't ever tell anyone. I can't believe I've been so stupid. Please, promise me, you won't tell anyone. I'm so embarrassed.'

Taking a sharp pair of scissors, I cut up the card into the bin. I was furious with him for being so reckless but agreed I wouldn't tell a soul.

Helen
(Officer: John Barker)

New Zealand, December 1997

By coincidence, a few years after John disappeared, my sister met and married a guy from New Zealand, then later emigrated. With the McLibel trial and all the work in lodging our appeal finally over, I felt like I desperately needed a long holiday, so I booked a flight to New Zealand for a few months. As it turned out, my sister lived about an hour's drive from Tauranga – the town John had said his parents had lived in. My sister offered me the use of her car to explore on days when she didn't need it for work. One day, I decided to visit the town to see what it was like and on the off-chance I might find John or someone who knew him.

I pulled up near the beach on a glorious sunny day and went for a walk around the base of Mount Maunganui, an extinct volcano, and then up to the summit. Tauranga was a stunning place, so beautiful, which made me grieve for John again because I wanted someone to share the experience with. The pressure and intensity of the McLibel trial had forced me to put my feelings and investigations on hold, but the mystery of his existence and disappearance bugged me and I decided that while I was here, I should try to find out more.

John's aunt Dorothy had an unusual surname, which stuck in my memory – Wabernoth – and John had said she lived in Auckland but had previously lived in Tauranga, so I thought it would be worth a shot trying to find a trace of her. I called at the library and searched through the electoral register. There were only three people with that surname listed in the town, and one was called Dorothy. I made a note of the address and drove over there.

A woman in her seventies answered the door.

She seemed welcoming until I told her I was looking for John. Her smile instantly faded and she put her arm across the doorway defensively.

'I haven't seen him. I don't know where he is,' she replied curtly.

I explained that I was worried about him and wanted to make sure he was okay. But she insisted she knew nothing.

As a last shot, I told her that as part of my search I'd applied for the death certificates for his parents, but both had come back with no trace. I suggested I may have had the wrong surname.

'What was his mother's surname?'

She seemed vague.

'I'm sorry, I don't remember now.'

As she closed the door and I walked away, I knew something was wrong. I wasn't sure if Dorothy was supposed to be his mum's sister or just a close family friend he called an aunt but, either way, she would have known his mum's surname. Her response had been distinctly odd.

A couple of weeks later, I went back over what I knew about John's New Zealand connection: he'd moved there with his parents as a teenager and his dad's death had been in December 1988, his mum's in February 1990. Although the registry office had come back with no trace, I knew now it was likely they had a different surname. It hadn't occurred to me that he might have made up their deaths. I decided to look through the death notices in the archives of the local newspaper. I wasn't sure about anything any more, but I had to start somewhere. I searched through the paper for the months of their deaths and for any names that might fit. Nothing. I widened the search to a few months either side. Nothing. Then I wondered if I had the wrong year for his dad. As I continued my search, Dorothy's surname caught my eye.

I read the notice:

Wabernoth – Ken. Dearly loved husband of Dorothy, loved father and father-in-law of Debbie and John (London).

This had to be Dorothy, John's aunt. And John had talked of a significant ex who'd broken his heart who'd been called Debbie.

This couple were also said to live in London so it felt like there were so many similarities, it had to be a piece of the jigsaw, even if it didn't seem to fit or make sense. The thought that Dorothy might actually be John's mother-in-law, and Debbie his wife, seemed too far-fetched. I told myself it was probably a coincidence. I needed to do more research.

Now I had a potential surname to search and, thankfully, it was unusual enough to find likely matches. John had been born in 1960 so, I reasoned, the earliest he would have got married would have been 1978. I began my search between 1978 and 1989 under the name Wabernoth. Nothing. Then I checked for births too, in case they'd married in England but had kids in New Zealand. Nothing.

Back in London a few months later, I repeated the searches without any success. But I had the McLibel appeal to work on so I gave up for the time being.

Alison

(Officer: Mark Cassidy)

London, end of 1997/beginning of 1998

Mark and I spent Christmas Day at my mum's with my family then we brought in the New Year up in Scotland. It had been the anniversary of Mick's death, and my urge to have children with Mark felt even stronger.

In February, we went on a walking holiday with friends to the Peak District in Derbyshire.

In May, Mum celebrated her sixtieth birthday. With Mark by my side, we beamed as my brother pointed the camera towards us and clicked the button. The camera flashed, and we stood there, frozen in time, surrounded by my family in full celebration; I was as happy and settled as I could remember.

May–June 1998

We had a busy few weeks planned – bank holiday in Lyme Regis, Glastonbury Festival and then my stepbrother's wedding at the Savoy Hotel. Mark bought a new suit for the occasion where we drank champagne, danced to the live band and indulged ourselves in five-star luxury that neither of us were used to.

On 30 June, England were due to play arch-rivals Argentina in the World Cup; Mark was excited about the game even though his support for England seemed a contradiction. Everyone we knew on the left shared the generally accepted position in all international sports events to actively support A.B.E: Anyone But England. It was an anti-imperialist position, not without irony and humour. But Mark, it seemed, didn't subscribe.

So when he arrived home from work on the night of the match – the quarter finals of the World Cup – I was surprised to see he'd bought and was wearing an England commemorative sweatshirt.

The cross of St George was planted on one side of his chest with patriotic pride.

'What the hell are you wearing?' I asked, astonished that he expected me to go to the pub with him and our friends dressed like that.

He brushed off my concerns.

'It's the World Cup! Who do you think I'm going to support?'

Any team but that one.

I shook my head but, at the same time, I quite liked his refusal to follow the crowd when he didn't agree.

'I am English, y'know.'

I couldn't believe it.

'But look at it; it's got the flag of St George on it. You look like ...'

'What? What, Ali? What do I look like?'

I hated myself for saying it, but I couldn't hold it in.

'You ... you look like you're in the BNP!'

Mark snorted with laughter, trying to defuse the situation.

'Agh, don't be daft! My politics isn't defined by which football team I support.'

I didn't know anyone in our political circles who would choose to wear that top. But there was something about Mark that meant he got away with it.

Perhaps it was his honesty.

My flat, North London, summer 1998

I was late starting my period and, although we'd never really talked in any detail about having kids, I thought that Mark might secretly like the idea. He had a lovely way with my nephew and niece – Ben's children – and I knew he'd make a great dad.

He was busy washing up when I decided to broach the subject.

'Mark?'

'Hmm,' he replied, half-distracted, his hands soaked in washing-up suds.

'My period's late.'

I kept my eyes on his face the whole time; I'd expected him to laugh or maybe just smile, as he usually did whenever I mentioned anything serious or tricky. Instead, the blood drained from his face as it turned the same colour as his grey sweatshirt.

Well, say something.

'Are you serious?'

'Er, I'm sure it's just late … but it wouldn't be the end of the world, would it?'

He turned back to the dishes and pans in the sink and scrubbed them furiously.

'I'm not ready for kids, Ali.' He kept his gaze fixed on the washing up. 'Maybe one day.'

Counselling, Relate, London, September 1998

After the false alarm of my late period, whenever I tried to discuss the idea of starting a family, it always ended badly. It became increasingly obvious to me that the only way we'd resolve it was with couples' counselling. Mark wasn't keen, but eventually agreed. We went for weekly sessions for eighteen long months, and while I talked openly and honestly, Mark never seemed to have that much to say. Our counsellor, Max, tried her best to draw information, feelings, anything from him, but he would sit, ensconced in the peach-coloured tub chair next to me, answering direct questions but offering very little to explain his reluctance to start a family. It wasn't that he didn't love me, he explained. He just wasn't ready. As I listened to week after week of excuses – including a fear of passing on epilepsy that his father had apparently suffered from – I wondered how deeply damaged from childhood he really was and whether any amount of counselling would ever break through his emotional guard.

London, January 1999

In spite of Mark's block about having children, we were still happy. Apart from union meetings at work, I'd remained in the background of political activities since my ex Mick had died, doing little more than accompany Mark to the occasional benefit gig or helping with a leafleting campaign; our comfortable, domestic life continued.

Then it was my step-aunt's golden wedding anniversary party and, as we mixed with my relatives and drank in celebration, I wondered if we'd be together that long and how we'd look in our old age.

Helen

(Officer: John Barker)

McLibel appeal, 31 March 1999

The appeal we lodged at the end of the McLibel trial was finally heard in January. In March, three appeal court judges ruled that it was fair comment to say that McDonald's employees worldwide 'do badly in terms of pay and conditions' and to say that 'if one eats enough McDonald's food, one's diet may well become high in fat, with the very real risk of heart disease'. As a result, they cut the damages awarded to McDonald's from £60,000 to £40,000. However, they also upheld some finding against us, so we lodged an appeal with the House of Lords, which was turned down later that year. Then we applied for permission to appeal to the European Court of Human Rights.

McLibel appeal, 5 July 2000

Following a lawsuit Dave Morris and I had initiated in 1998, the Metropolitan Police agreed to pay damages to us after they admitted they had been passing personal information about us to McDonald's spies before the McLibel case started. To us, this collusion between the police and McDonald's showed the political role of the police in undermining protest activity.

As part of the settlement the police issued an apology to us and agreed 'to bring this settlement to the attention of the three Area Commanders of the Metropolitan Police Force and ask them to remind their officers of their responsibility not to disclose information on the Police National Computer to a third party.'

Alison

(Officer: Mark Cassidy)

London, December 1999

On 14 December, my dad was admitted to intensive care at a Surrey hospital; my brother Ben and I were told it was a suspected heart attack. The following day, Mark and I went to visit Dad in hospital where the doctors told us they now believed he was suffering a bad chest infection. My dad looked terrible and the next day he was so unwell that he had to be sedated and pumped full of adrenalin to try to boost his blood pressure.

When I was fifteen, Dad had married an Irish woman called Mary and had converted to Catholicism for her sake. Mary told Ben that the priest had been called to give Dad the last rites.

I'd always had a complicated relationship with Dad but I loved him and I wanted to be there. For the next week Mark and I took it in turns with Ben to visit.

A few days later, on 23 December, Mark received a call on his pager. He'd always worn one for work and his boss had used it to contact him with an urgent message to phone the family priest back in Birkenhead.

'It's my grandpa, Ali; he's had a stroke. I've got to go back and see him. I'll go up there tomorrow.'

'I'll come with you,' I insisted. 'Christmas doesn't mean anything to my family. No one will be bothered if I'm there or not.'

Mark turned away from the TV; he took my hands in his with a seriousness and sensitivity I hadn't seen before.

'I know, but I've got to go on my own. You need to stay here for your dad. And for Ben.'

I shook my head.

'But I want to spend the holidays with you.'

'I know, but I'll be back,' he said, pulling me against his chest. 'I know I've treated you like shit, Ali. But when I get back I promise

I'll make it up to you. I'll introduce you to my mum – she'll be so proud to see I've ended up with someone like you. But this … well, I have to do this alone.'

We'd already arranged to see Dad in hospital and to go for lunch afterwards with Ben. On the way there, despite being a superb driver, Mark pranged the van, hitting the bumper of the vehicle in front.

'Shit!' he cursed, unclipping his seatbelt to get out and inspect the damage.

I was about to say something but thought better of it. I knew he'd been shaken by the news of his grandpa.

This was turning into one hell of a Christmas.

Dad had been in a coma but was now showing some signs of improvement; he'd opened half an eye but wasn't obeying commands.

The next day was Christmas Eve, and Mark readied himself to go back to Birkenhead to see his grandpa. I was still trying to persuade him to let me go with him. I buried myself into his warm body, trying to make sense of why he seemed so adamant to go alone. Before my half-finished thoughts formed into speech, the telephone rang. It was my brother Ben. He sounded bewildered.

'Ali, they're moving Dad to Torquay. The hospital has just called. Apparently, the hospital is trying to empty as many beds as it can. They think they're going to need them because of all the Millennium stuff going on – London overspill or something … I don't know. All I do know is, they're going first thing tomorrow with a police escort. They wanted to fly him over in an air ambulance but they reckon it's going to be too windy.'

I was stunned.

'But it's Christmas Eve – a *police escort*?'

'I know, that's what I thought, but I suppose a motorbike will clear the traffic. He's back in a coma. They need to move him quickly.'

'But a police escort? Is that normal?'

'I really don't know. I'm just telling you what I've been told.'

I was as confused as he was. Suddenly, a thought occurred to me.

'We don't have to go down to Torquay, do we?'

I scratched my scalp anxiously and, before my brother could answer, I continued. 'It's just that Mark's grandpa had a stroke yesterday and he's going to Birkenhead tomorrow to see him. I want to go with him.'

'Well …' Ben's tone sounded disapproving. 'I'm really sorry to hear about Mark's grandpa, but I'm going to see Dad. I'll let them settle him in tomorrow then I'm going to go – for Boxing Day. I think we have to.'

'For fuck's sake!' I spluttered. I was irritated by my brother's sense of duty and his self-righteous tone. 'Okay, I suppose I have no choice, do I? I'll come with you.'

Mark was still lying stretched out on the sofa, listening in to the conversation. As I put the phone down, he held out his hand and drew me over towards him.

'It's for the best, you know,' he said, kissing me softly on my forehead.

Torbay Hospital, Torquay, 26 December 1999

Ben and I arrived at the hospital early on Boxing Day morning to be greeted at the desk by a perky male nurse.

'Good morning and Merry Christmas!' he chirped, popping his head over the top of the counter.

We told him Dad's name.

'Ah, you're here for Joseph?'

We both nodded.

'Well,' he said, smiling warmly, 'I am delighted to tell you that your father's come out of his coma!'

Ben and I looked at each other and then down at the nurse as he sifted through a pile of papers on his already-cluttered desk. There was a silver mini-Christmas tree, a selection of reindeer cards and a bumper-size tin of Quality Street all jostling for position in between patient notes. He drew his finger along a long list of names to check for Dad's room number. Snapping his hands together, he looked up at us both and gestured to the direction of his bed.

'He's the Christmas miracle!' he said, smiling. 'I'll take you to see him right now!'

As we followed him down the hospital corridor, I stole a glance at Ben to acknowledge the weirdness of the whole situation. Before we'd reached my father's room, the nurse glanced down at some notes on his clipboard.

'Now, I have to warn you that Joseph is still a little confused at the moment but he's making fantastic progress and early signs are showing he should make a full recovery!'

Relief flooded Ben's face.

'That's great news!'

He turned to share the moment but, I couldn't help myself – I couldn't stop thinking one thing.

He didn't die. He's still alive. I could have gone with Mark.

However, now wasn't the time to try and explain to Ben or the nurse why I felt so disconnected from Dad. Instead, I forced a smile.

'Yes, fantastic!'

I didn't want to be there, especially not now it was turning into one flamboyant false alarm.

The nurse pushed against the door and sashayed through into our father's room.

'Joseph!' he called out a little too loudly. 'Your lovely children are here to see you.'

I watched from a distance while the nurse gently stroked my father's veiny hands, as though trying to bring him back into the world. Dad's skin looked yellow against the starched, white hospital pillows. His eyelids fluttered and then opened to reveal bloodshot eyes. He struggled to focus and then a flicker of recognition passed over his face.

'They've kept me in an internment camp the last few days: Alcatraz – in New York. I'm not giving them information about you,' he said, looking directly at me. 'I wouldn't give it them. The hospital is on an RAF base. I've been in the Sahara, but I was helicoptered out of New York.'

Ben and I looked at each other with raised eyebrows and tried to suppress our giggles. I went over to Dad's bedside and held his hand in mine.

'You're hallucinating.'

Laid out in his hospital bed in a semi-delirious state, my father seemed unable to answer our bland and repetitive questions.

'How are you feeling? Have you been eating? Have the doctors said when you might be going home?'

We stayed for as long as the four-hour drive on Boxing Day justified and I felt relieved that he was feeling stronger, even if he didn't make much sense. Once home, I spent the next few days shuffling around in my slippers, watching mindless, festive television, waiting for Mark to return.

My flat, North London, 28 December 1999

I heard the diesel engine chug before it cut out, then the sound of the van door as it slammed. I pulled on a jumper and ran outside to welcome Mark. My excitement, however, was met by emptiness as he trudged up the path with his head bowed low. I noticed his eyes were hollow, his face unshaven, and his lips pursed. He was still wearing the same clothes he'd left London in. He gave me a cursory peck on my cheek as he strode past me and the posters in the hall-way, through into the bedroom.

'Are you okay?' I asked, following him as he threw his small rucksack on the floor. 'What's happened?'

'Are you making a cup of tea?'

Even his voice sounded different as he wandered through into the kitchen. Lifeless. He sucked in his cheeks and, with elbows propped onto the kitchen table, hung his head in cupped hands. All I could see was his short, cropped brown crown.

I put the kettle on in silence as I waited for him to speak. Finally, he did.

'I had a fight with John.'

John was Mark's stepdad. I knew the two hadn't always seen eye to eye, but a fight?

'A fight? A physical fight?'

There was another pause.

'I hit him.'

My mouth gaped open as I pictured Mark landing a heavy punch to his stepfather's jaw.

'What happened? Why?'

He still had his head in his hands, as though trying to avoid eye contact.

'He wound me up.'

I wanted to ask more but thought better of it. Mark seemed so upset and I didn't want to make him worse. Instead, I busied myself brewing the tea. I noticed him picking at the skin on his fingers as I put the tea on the table between us and sat down next to him. I remained quiet, hoping he'd volunteer more.

'He started on at me,' Mark said. 'Like he always did. Normal shit. How I didn't do enough for my mum. How I'd let her down. What a disappointment I am to her. Same bollocks I'd put up with for years. I wasn't having it, so I lumped him one.'

He seemed so upset that I thought it best not to press further.

'How's your dad?' he asked, looking at me for the very first time.

'He's out of the coma. Still a bit confused, but amazingly seems to be on the mend. He's still in hospital. They're monitoring him for another few days and then, all being well, he'll go home.'

Mark didn't seem in the least bit surprised; I assumed it was because he was still so angry and absorbed by his own family drama. *Maybe he hadn't taken it in properly.*

We sat in silence, drank tea, ate dinner, and watched compilation TV programmes that attempted to summarise the top ten everything of the twentieth century in just thirty minutes. He didn't seem to have much else to say; instead, I allowed the fight to fester inside him.

The following morning, he was still so quiet that I worried there may be more to it.

'You haven't killed John, have you?' I asked, cracking a pair of eggs into a pan of sizzling butter.

'Don't be daft,' he said to the table rather than me.

'Well, it's just you're behaving as if it's something that bad!'

'It feels that bad,' Mark mumbled as he continued to chew at his finger.

I pushed the eggs around the pan, burning hot fat spitting out, scorching the skin of my hand. I glanced over at Mark; he was hunched over the table, shutting me out. I knew he was thinking about something painful, and not just John. There was more to it, there had to be. I wasn't sure what it was but I was determined, as soon as his mood had settled, to try to find out more.

My brother's house, Millennium Eve, December 1999

With my niece and nephew safely tucked up in bed, I sipped more red wine in Ben's lounge. We'd eaten enormous amounts of perfectly cooked beef, Yorkshire pudding and roast potatoes, and Mark and I were now sitting on the chocolate-brown sofa. His arms were folded, his legs crossed – his body language padlocked. As the evening drew closer to midnight, we watched the fireworks on TV. Despite the anticipation of a special New Year's Eve to remember, Mark's mood was dark and not long after midnight, we retired to my brother's guest room to sleep off the wine.

My flat, North London, 15 March 2000

I gathered together our dirty laundry from the bedroom floor, as Mark watched from under the duvet. I dropped the worn clothes into the wicker basket and sprayed deodorant under my arms, filling the air with scent.

'What's wrong now?' I asked, feeling irritated.

He'd been working crazy hours on a job in Luton since the New Year, leaving before 6am and arriving home after 9.30pm. He'd been withdrawn and low all year but this was the worst I'd seen him since the depression had set in.

'Nothing,' Mark grunted as he tugged the duvet up around him. 'I'm just not needed in until later.'

I pulled on a top, kissed him on the cheek, and stroked my hand through his bristly hair. He didn't respond to my touch and instead lay there motionless.

'I'll see you when I get back then,' I said, blowing him a kiss from the bedroom door.

I knew he'd seen it, but nothing came back.

When I'd got in from school later that day, I walked into the kitchen to find a letter from Mark waiting for me on the table.

He'd left me.

The edges of my vision blurred and panic took over. I was devastated. I picked up my phone and dialled his mobile.

'Mark, what have you done? Please ...' I begged. 'Mark, please come back. We can sort this out, whatever it is that's wrong. We can sort it.'

He replied by saying things to try to calm me down; he finally agreed to meet me that weekend to talk about it.

My flat, North London, 18 March 2000

When he came in through the door, I wrapped my arms around him, so relieved was I to have him back. I knew he'd been battling with depression, but I was committed to helping him get through it. We talked things through and Mark agreed to come home. He said he had stuff to sort out at work but that he'd be back on Thursday. We kissed passionately and one thing led to another until soon we were making love on the sofa. Afterwards, as we lay there, Mark seemed embarrassed. He propped himself up against some cushions.

'What? What is it?' I asked.

I just wanted things to return back to normal between us. But Mark seemed sombre.

'It doesn't feel right doing this ...'

I looked at him oddly. He was speaking as though we were strangers on a one-night stand.

'I don't understand.'

He said he didn't either.

My flat, North London, April 2000

Mark was feeling edgy so to help calm his nerves we decided to walk into town. On the way back through Islington, I noticed a silver saloon car pass us twice, slowly. Inside were two men with short, crewcut hair. I thought I saw them point and laugh at us.

'That car has just driven past twice. Did you see?' I said, pointing at it.

Mark looked blank.

'Well, it definitely did and I think the blokes inside were looking at us. They were laughing,' I explained, feeling a little unnerved.

'Take no notice,' Mark replied, keeping his eyes fixed downwards.

I wanted to ask, but I could see he wasn't in any mood for being pushed. I stayed silent, wondering who those men were.

My flat, North London, 11 April 2000

It happened again, the exact same way as before: another letter waiting for me on the table. In it, Mark explained that he had to get away.

He'd written that we wanted different things and that he couldn't love me like I needed.

This time I knew it was over. And I knew he wouldn't be coming back.

But I still loved him, and was worried sick. *Where had he gone and why did he need to run away like this?* I tried to call but his phone went straight to answerphone. I knew he wouldn't answer so I emailed instead.

I can't believe you've done it again. It seems that you want to make me hate you but I can't do that. I love you and want to be with you. I suppose it wasn't that hard to leave this time: less stuff, more practised. Apart from anything else, you owe me and my mum money. I break up this week for two weeks and I was desperately looking forward to having some time away with you – we talked about it, for Christ's sake. How do you expect me to be strong like this? I can't think straight and don't know how I'm going to cope. I need a break, too, and wanted it with you. What are you trying to do? How can you say you love me (I notice you didn't say it in this note) and then treat me like this? What have I done to deserve it? This time you don't even keep the phone on so we can't speak. You've taken complete control and left me quivering ...

I've slept a little and am now going to work. You could phone during the day and I won't be here. I really don't know what to say. I'm very worried about you. I'm unclear about what does matter to you right now since I've tried reading between the lines of your behaviour and your note and I think I keep getting it wrong. I thought you cared about me. I thought we'd been making things get better. I thought you had a nice weekend. I notice you've left your slippers and the bike again and so, reading between the lines, I hope that you'll be coming back some time. But when, and how do I know? I think I deserve some kind of explanation. I know you'll be checking your email – I hope you've had the courtesy to read all this. I'm angry, hurt and missing you terribly. I want you to come home quickly and I want you to communicate with me.

I was devastated and straightaway tried to trace someone who might have known him from home. I found my address book. In it, he'd crossed out hard in a furious scribble the name of his grandpa's address in Birkenhead. He'd even scored through his own mobile phone number but, of course, I'd memorised that. It was immediately clear that he didn't want me to find him, which made me all the more determined to try. I contacted his bank, the DVLA and tracked down his boss Terry, at the Manor Works in Clapham, to ask if he had any contact details for him. Everything resulted in a dead end.

Email from Alison to Mark, 19 April 2000

Dear Mark,
Where are you? Why haven't you contacted me?
Alison

In late April, I received a phone message for Mark. It was an activist from another group he'd been involved with. Mark had said he'd explained to anyone who needed to know that he was dropping out of politics for a while so I didn't understand why this activist hadn't heard. I arranged to meet him in a London pub.

'It would be good to just cross-reference a couple of things about Mark,' he told me as I sipped at my drink. 'Rule out he's not a spook.'

A spy? Mark?

My brain whirled with the possibility. I'd been with this man for five years.

A spook? Surely not.

But I processed the idea quickly. It started to make sense. Mark's interest in radical politics, his sudden change of personality, his depression, his recent vanishing act and his wish to be untraceable.

We went through more details about his background, how he paid for stuff and why we thought he might have left. The more we talked, the more convinced I became that the bizarre idea that he was a state agent was true. But the activist thought otherwise.

'I don't think he was a spook,' he said, draining his pint glass, trying to reassure me. 'You said you wanted kids. Sounds to me like he felt trapped and took off. He won't be the first or the last to do that.'

He was confident he was right. I wasn't so sure.

My flat, North London, 11 May 2000

As my theory developed, I replayed in my mind every memory of Mark I could conjure. I wanted to test each moment to see how it fitted with the proposition that he had been fundamentally lying about who he was and why he was in my life. Then I remembered the name on the bank card.

Could Jenner be his real name?

I became convinced I was in possession of classified information and was being watched. If I was right about Mark being a state agent – MI5 or Special Branch – then those who employed him would be monitoring me. I started seeing cars and vans following me everywhere. I began to take notes of number plates, descriptions and what the driver did or didn't do. I stored them all in a book, wondering if my observations really were to do with state secrets or simply paranoia.

There were workmen at the property next door. By now, I suspected anyone and everyone of spying on me, including them.

Or maybe they'd been keeping an eye on Mark.

I couldn't be sure.

The workmen's van had disappeared from its regular pitch when I returned home one day. I sighed with relief. I decided to go over to my computer and check my emails to see if there was any more news from Mark. The connection seemed to take forever.

But then my arms prickled with goosebumps. Two new emails appeared in my inbox – both from him. I opened the first without breathing, but was immediately disappointed by its brevity. It was barely one line long. Mark wrote that he was all right and 'travelling on' and asked me not to worry. In the second, which was similarly short, he implored me not to wait for him as he was not 'worth it'.

I read them again and again. Hunched over the screen and blurry-eyed, I stared at the words, hoping they would transform into something infused with love, truth and hope if I looked at them for long enough. Large tears fell onto my wrists as I smeared them against my face and walked into the kitchen.

Later that afternoon, I saw a message flashing on my answer-phone. I dialled 1471 but it said the number wasn't available. The call had lasted a minute or so and, from the background noise, it sounded as though it had been made from a public place such as an airport or railway station.

Had it been Mark? Was he in trouble?

My flat, North London, 15 May 2000

Arriving home from work, I pushed open the front door and there, sitting on the doormat, was an airmail letter with a German stamp and a postcard of the east side of the graffitied Berlin Wall. I tore open the thin blue envelope, unfolded the paper inside, and turned it over quickly to find he'd covered four sides of A4.

Wanting to savour the moment of having a piece of him in my hands, I read each word slowly, trying to make them last. He wrote that he was now in Berlin, that he was sorry, that he had felt 'desperate, alone and frightened' and that he couldn't love me the way I wanted.

I looked at the letter again and blinked through the tears, wondering how much – if any of it – was true. Then I glanced down at what he'd written on the back of the postcard; it was a line from a Sex Pistols song. Remembering his sticky brain for lyrics, I carried the card to my computer. I typed in the phrase and started to roll a joint as the page slowly loaded. I clicked through to the band's official site, where the homepage appeared in a bright pink with bold yellow typeface taken from the band's famous album cover: *Never Mind the Bollocks, Here's the Sex Pistols*. I knew Mark's superb memory for lyrics, but the song 'Holidays in the Sun' about communism, futility and paranoia were more resonant than I could have anticipated. The final line of the song was blunt and to the point: it instructed me not to wait for him.

My flat, North London, May 2000

A friend of mine, Jude, came round for supper. I had become obsessed with my theory that Mark was a state spy. I didn't know if it was MI5 or Special Branch but I explained my thinking, in micro-detail, to anyone who was kind enough to listen. It was the only explanation that made sense to me and, to know I wasn't going mad, I needed others to see it that way too.

'I'll start with his driving skills. He drove like a professional. He could get that van in and out of *tiny* spaces; he drove in blizzards without a problem – do you remember what I said the weather was like that New Year we went up to Scotland? It was fucking awful and it was like he enjoyed it. He got in the car in Crete and drove in the middle of the night in the middle of nowhere as if he'd been there all his life. I know lots of people can do that, but he was like it in Israel too and it's harder there with the different alphabet. He just read the road like a professional. And he had endurance; drove for eighteen hours in one stint and didn't complain, and drove that time to Sunderland and back in one go for that football match we went to. Do you remember?' I paused for breath. 'And what about those parking tickets he used to throw away? He'd said they never chased them up and they never did ...'

Jude remembered it all and nodded, her features drawing closer. I ploughed on.

'He said his favourite poet was Rudyard Kipling. Rudyard-fucking-Kipling! I took the piss out of him at the time saying he was the archetypal poet of the Empire and he just said he liked it, bought a little hardback of his works once when we were out in a bookshop and read "If" aloud to me, saying it was his favourite poem. He took that little Kipling book with him. Do you know the poem?'

Jude shook her head.

'It's all about surviving the trials of being a boy and a man and, if you're thinking in the way I am, there's bits in it which are so appropriate it makes my stomach lurch.'

I recalled the lines: 'If you can wait and not be tired by waiting, / Or being lied about, don't deal in lies ... If you can bear to hear the truth you've spoken / Twisted by knaves to make a trap for fools ...'

'And there's something else,' I told Jude.

She looked up, worry in her eyes.

'Go on.'

I swallowed hard and decided it was time to break my promise to Mark not to tell anyone about the stolen bank card in the name of Jenner. Jude was the first person I told.

Later that afternoon, I called Elaine – one of my oldest friends from school. I'd exhausted Jude and I needed someone else to listen to me. If I was right about my theory, I was sure my calls would be tapped and maybe even my home bugged. But I wanted 'them' to know that I knew.

'He was military, police, I'm sure of it,' I explained to Elaine. 'I'm not sure what exactly: MI5 or Special Branch, but something like that. I think maybe he had been in the army at some point. There's loads I don't know, but I'm pretty sure that's what he is.'

Elaine was speechless. Most people were.

Relate, London, May 2000

I made one final visit alone to Max, our counsellor at Relate. I didn't need the Kleenex on the table because I was too numb to cry. It was the first meeting since Mark had disappeared and I was telling Max that I thought he was a state agent.

'The thing is, I'm not entirely surprised by what you're telling me,' she replied.

I looked up at her, startled. Most people I told looked at me like I was mad.

'You see, I wouldn't normally do this. It would be considered unprofessional. But under the circumstances I think it's appropriate.'

I watched as she reached over to retrieve a manila folder containing pieces of paper. She searched for a document. The piece of paper had a line down the middle. On one side was Mark's name, on the other was mine. My side was filled with writing but Mark's was virtually empty. Max looked over at me.

'This is the assessment I made of you both when we first met. To be honest, I wouldn't have been surprised if you'd told me he was a hitman.'

I pondered her response and knew I needed some answers. I needed to know what, if anything, he'd told me was true. My starting place was the Family Records Centre. It had moved from St Catherine's House to near Exmouth Market in Islington. In oversized folios, I searched for the registration of his father's death and that of his grandma. There was no record for either. I cried into my coffee in a nearby café and tried to process the fact that my theory was stacking up. I had no hard proof that he was a spy but everything I did have pointed that way and I needed to find out more.

My flat, North London, June 2000

Spy or no spy, I was still worried sick for Mark's wellbeing and began to theorise that he'd run away from everything. That he'd fallen in love with me and was trapped. He'd had to get away – from me and from his employers – whoever they were. I emailed him asking that one question.

Had he run from it all?

Soon after, I received a ton of emails from an organisation called University Diplomas and some strange phone calls from unknown numbers. I began to exist in a world of paranoia – apart from people I'd known all my life, I didn't know who I could trust.

By the end of June, after dozens of unsolicited emails, I noticed that my washing line had been cut. I was sure I was being watched and they wanted me to know it. The internet and emails in general were still fairly new at the time and I wasn't clued up about spamming and junk mail. I'd become convinced the phrase 'University Diplomas' and the contents of the email were some sort of coded message, so I typed the words into an online anagram generator. It churned out lots of meaningless anagrams, but one chilled me as I sat back and read it:

I'm a spy. Lost ID. I've run.

I was convinced I was right: the emails were a coded message from Mark.

My flat, North London, 12 August 2000

I called my friend Jude's number only to be connected to my own answerphone. Two weeks later, Jude called another mutual friend and it triggered my answerphone, which then taped their entire conversation.

Something weird was happening.

Somewhere in the UK, December 2000

A friend of a friend worked in a UK passport office. They agreed to do a search on Mark's passport details for me. I didn't know what I thought it could show but it seemed worth a try. All they needed was his full name, place and date of birth.

Mark Steven Cassidy – Dublin – 7 March 1967

I had little hope of learning anything new but when the call came through a couple of days later, I was surprised by what I heard.

'It's a bit weird, to be honest,' my friend began.

'Go on.'

'Well, my mate's been working at the passport office for donkey's years. Never seen anything like this before.'

'What was it?' I asked, my mind racing with possibilities.

'They put in his details and it said "File stored in CE". It usually just gives a number, which refers to a paper requisition file. This CE thing was something different. They'd never seen the code before and just shut down the search. Sorry they couldn't do more but they freaked out a bit.'

'CE? What does it mean? Did they have any idea?'

'Not a clue. But they said it was weird.'

CE? Classified Entry? Covert Evidence? Confidential?

I didn't understand its meaning but I knew I'd discovered something significant. Another piece of the jigsaw. Another slice of the truth.

London, January 2001

I was meeting former activists from the Colin Roach Centre to discuss Mark. It was a freezing cold night. My friend Jude's breath mixed with my cigarette smoke as it billowed up into the icy air.

'It'll be okay,' she said, trying to make me feel better.

I looked at her.

'I don't know what I'm going to say. I know we've been through it, but I'm not sure I can.'

I stuffed my freezing hands deep inside my coat pockets. I needed to be there, to hear what Mark Metcalf from the Colin Roach Centre would say. He was the first person to get to know Mark Cassidy when he'd approached the CRC stall at the meeting after the 'We Remember' march. He'd reached the same conclusion as me about Mark Cassidy: he was a spy.

Mark Metcalf had suspicions before he'd disappeared, apparently, but nothing he'd ever shared with me at the time. I needed to witness other activists' responses. I just didn't know how to play it.

'Say whatever you want to say,' Jude insisted.

A clutter of thoughts collected in my head but before I was able to give them voice, I spotted a small group of people congregating on the opposite side of the road.

'Oh, they're there,' I said, indicating over with my chin.

Standing outside the old building was Mark Metcalf with a couple of others. I looked down at my feet as Jude and I walked the remaining five yards to the zebra crossing and approached the huddled group.

'Hello,' I said quietly, noticing how embarrassed everyone seemed.

'Why are we out here?' Jude asked, shivering.

'There's some confusion about which room we've booked,' Mark Metcalf told her.

Jude suggested we go in for a drink to get out of the cold.

We sat with our drinks at a small table in the corner of a nearby pub; soon we were followed by some of the others.

'How've you been then?' I asked one of the other women.

She fiddled with the strap of her handbag, nervously pushing it higher onto her shoulder.

'Yes, not bad. You?'

'Not too bad,' I lied.

There was an uncomfortable silence.

We slowly sipped at our drinks through the awkwardness. Despite being as embarrassed as everyone else huddled around the table, one of the other male activists turned and addressed me with a directness I appreciated.

'How long since Mark has been gone, Alison?'

'Er, about nine months or so.'

'I see,' he replied.

The first woman took the opportunity to express her concern, her eyebrows furrowed together.

'And how are you feeling?'

I replied with my perfected, cast-iron defence.

'As little as possible.'

I placed my palms together and shoved them between my legs; my eyes cast downwards.

'Okay, shall I begin?' Mark Metcalf said, addressing the group.

I nodded along with everyone.

He opened a notebook and began to read aloud:

'I have called this meeting because I believe Mark Cassidy was working for the British state. Not only do I believe it is important for you to have an opportunity to hear my reasons for this, but I think you should be aware of the fact that the security services will hold a file on each and every one of us ...'

'Okay. Alison, perhaps you could start us off then?'

I scanned the eight people around the table.

'I don't really know what to say,' I said as my face flushed. My throat felt hot and dry as though it might close in on itself. 'Um. I ... er ...'

'Look,' Jude butted in kindly. 'You have to all realise that Ali has emotional difficulties around this issue. We need to treat it with sensitivity.'

I breathed deeply, nodded over to her and launched into a heavily amended version of my story. I told the group about the bank card and the fictitious dates of the deaths of his father and grandmother. I told them I'd never met any of his family, and the sob story he'd recounted had prevented me from probing further. I told them about a few strange things he'd done while we were in Ireland, like checking under the van before we boarded the ferry, and disappearing for an early morning walk down Shankhill Road while we were in Belfast. I discussed the surveillance I thought I'd been under.

'There are hundreds of details but I don't want to go through every minor thing here. It's not that I don't want you to know, I just haven't got the energy. The point is, Mark here and I have reached the same conclusion. We're convinced Mark Cassidy was working for the state. I don't know doing what exactly, but I don't believe his passport would have got him through El Al security if it wasn't a pretty convincing copy, and things like that don't come cheap. I can't prove it, but that's what I believe.'

I gulped down my nerves and watched the others as their thoughts and suspicions scurried across their foreheads like spiders. A web of paranoia, scepticism and pity.

'I want to say what a dreadful experience it sounds,' said one of the male activists. 'I know how it feels to be monitored and watched. You start to think you're going mad. It's unbelievable the lengths the state will go to.'

I looked down into my drink and crossed my arms tightly.

'I think it's *awful*, Alison. I feel so sorry for you,' said Celia Stubbs kindly. Celia had been fighting for justice since 1979 after the killing of her partner Blair Peach by the police at an anti-Nazi demonstration in Southall.

'I don't know what he was spying on anyway,' she said. 'We were hardly the Baader-Meinhof gang.'

'Oh, I don't know,' one of the men teased. 'We've tabled some pretty radical motions at my local Labour Party meetings recently.'

A ripple of laughter floated across the table, momentarily lifting the tension.

'Alison and I have spoken about doing other things in terms of warning other groups and so on,' added Mark Metcalf, 'but nothing has been acted on.'

'You think we should be letting other groups know?' one of the male activists asked, clearly interested in the prospect of a wider campaign.

'I don't think so,' I said. The last thing I needed plastered all over the internet was a campaign illustrated with my holiday snaps. 'We can't prove it. I don't think we should be doing anything more public than this. It's not the sort of thing you go shouting about.'

'But maybe someone might recognise him from other groups,' he suggested.

I felt my blood rise with a mixture of panic and annoyance.

'I just don't think we're at that stage. It's a double-edged thing. On one hand, I am totally convinced he was a spy; I don't need it proved any further than it has been for me – I believe it. On the other hand, to warn others requires proof, not belief. I have proof he lied to me, that's all. The rest is circumstantial. It's enough for me but I'm not sure it's enough to go on record with. It's a serious allegation. It's not something you go spreading without hard evidence. Apart from friends and family, I've told no one in a public, political setting like this before. I'm really not ready for it to be any bigger.'

'I *will* write about it at some point in the future,' Mark Metcalf remarked. 'I think it's important to expose how the state operates. That's why we were all involved in the CRC, isn't it? To understand and challenge state abuses, especially those perpetrated by the police.'

I looked down at my hands. I knew he was right, but it was easy for him. He hadn't been in love with a state operative.

London, June 2001

I needed more evidence. If I was ever to be able to expose what Mark Cassidy had done, I needed harder facts.

I arranged to pay £175 to a private investigation firm based in Oxford. It searched for a Mark Steven Cassidy, born in Dublin on 7 March 1967, formerly of my address in London. But the searches drew a blank. It traced Mark's former boss as I had done, but he told them nothing I didn't already know – that he'd stopped working for him in early 2000, and that he'd let Mark keep the work van.

Mark didn't seem to be registered for tax and there was no trace of his National Insurance number. In fact, his name had only been listed on a medical record at my address. The investigations revealed that Mark had once applied for a duplicate driving licence. The private investigator wrote:

This is an old dodge, when persons take on someone else's identity, which looks highly likely in this case. They even sometimes research the persons who have recently died and take on their persona. We

had several instances of this nature, and they are normally done by
persons on the run from the Child Support Agency, Tax Authorities
or are wanted by the police, and many other fraudulent reasons …

The investigator hadn't found Mark but he'd proved that he'd been living under a false identity. I was one step further towards proving my theory and showing the doubters I wasn't going mad.

He had been woven through the fabric of my life for five years. My brother, mother, father, step-family, all my friends, everyone in my life had known and liked him. As I slowly explained to them what I thought he was, I observed a common response. It was like a syndrome. No one wanted to admit that they'd been so duped, so manipulated.

'I really thought he was my friend,' they all said, refusing to believe that he could have used them; that the friendships could have been pretence. Most perceived me as delusional. He'd left me because he'd had enough; not because he was a spy. But for those who allowed themselves to run with my theory, they needed to believe he'd come over to 'our side'. That we'd turned him into one of us – someone with a social conscience. They even made excuses for his behaviour. That maybe it really *was* the nervous break-down scenario. Or maybe he had to get away but couldn't say why. Everyone tried to explain away Mark's lies to survive the pain and confusion he'd left behind. There must be a psychological term for it, like Stockholm syndrome, where hostages build an allegiance with their captors. Maybe seeing some humanity in the cruelty of others made it easier to cope with.

London, November 2002

I knew I'd never get any answers. I'd proved to myself what Mark Cassidy was and if others didn't believe me that was their problem. It was clear he was never coming back and, if I had any prospect of a normal life, I had to put him behind me. I had to start meeting new people but I knew trusting someone again was going to be difficult.

Through the smallness of the London Jewish community, I was reconnected with David, who I'd known since primary school. When I was thirteen, his name was inscribed in a heart on my school books. We'd had a clinch and a kiss when I was sixteen and then had gone our separate ways until now. In a local Turkish restaurant, we exchanged stories from our missing years. He had some explosive tales but I trumped them all with the story of my five-year relationship with a spy.

'You don't deserve that happening to you, Alison,' he said, looking shocked. 'The thing is, if some people told me a story like that, I'd think they were mad. But not you. You're not mad. You're completely credible. It's a nutty story, but I totally believe you.'

It was a crucial moment. Not only did he believe me – when so many didn't – but I could trust he was who he said he was. I'd known him for decades. He was kind and generous, and I knew I must not let this opportunity die.

Helen

(Officer: John Barker)

New Zealand, late 2002/early 2003

I returned to New Zealand. Shortly before I left, the BBC broadcast a three-part documentary – *True Spies* – about a secret squad of undercover police who had infiltrated trade unions and campaign groups, including animal rights and environmental campaigns such as those I'd been involved with. They were called the Special Demonstration Squad, and it was the first time I'd heard of them. Watching it brought home that the police did send long-term agents into campaign groups. One of the officers even referred to having sex with people he was spying on. I felt sick. I knew I needed to investigate more.

I packed a video of the series into my rucksack to show to friends who had been involved with politics and had known John, but who now lived in New Zealand.

With Christmas over, I decided it was time to restart the investigations. I discovered 'Aunt' Dorothy had died in 1998, six months after I'd visited, so I obviously couldn't ask her again. Then I found the address of her son, who also lived in Tauranga, so I went to see him. Knocking on the door, I waited for him to open it before showing him a photo of John. I asked if he recognised him.

'No, he could be anyone,' he replied, which I thought was a strange answer.

I explained I was worried about John because he'd been in a bad way before he'd disappeared.

Dorothy's son said he didn't know him and suddenly changed the subject. He spoke of guns and how he'd previously been in the Marines. I sensed he was trying to freak me out and, although I didn't entirely believe what he was saying, I decided that as I was alone in a remote place it was probably better to leave.

Back at my sister's house, I studied the notes and photos I'd brought to help with my search. I looked through a list of New Zealand resources for those researching family history and discovered it was possible to order wills. I visited Auckland to order wills for Debbie's – John's ex – parents. However, both documents only named the son, so I drew a blank.

I went to visit friends in Wellington and, while I was there, visited the archive centre in town. I discovered the will of Debbie's grandmother. Debbie was named in the will and when I saw her surname, I realised it was exactly the same as the surname of the man John claimed was his biological father. Debbie *had* to be married to John, despite me being unable to find the certificate. I went through the marriage records in New Zealand all over again, searching under Dines as well as Wabernoth this time. But still nothing. A total blank.

London, March 2003

Back in England, I repeated my searches for John without any success. One dead end followed another but, just as I'd begun to lose heart, I decided to expand the search years. *Maybe I'd calculated them wrong?*

Then I hit the jackpot – I found a match for Debbie Wabernoth and John Dines, so I ordered the marriage certificate. A week later I picked it up. As my eyes scanned it, I recognised John's handwriting on the signature immediately even though it was a different surname to the one he'd used with me. At last, I had an answer. It was definitely him and I felt sick knowing that he'd kept his marriage secret.

My eyes scanned along and that's when I spotted something else. His occupation.

Police officer.

I felt my blood run cold from my head down to my feet.

I thought I was going to collapse so I slumped into a nearby chair. My head felt as though it was about to explode; I wanted to scream and throw up all at once, but I was in the middle of a silent research room and the last thing I wanted was for people to stare at me.

I knew I was going to burst into unstoppable tears and I was still struggling to breathe as I made my way to the doors to escape. There was a payphone on the wall so, in a panic, I picked up the receiver and called a friend. As soon as she answered, I struggled to get the words out.

'I'm at the Family Records Centre. I need to meet urgently. I need to talk to you,' I sobbed down the line.

I walked around in a daze until I met her.

'What is it, Helen? What's wrong?' she asked.

'It's John,' I said, beginning to break down. 'He lied to me. He wasn't an activist after all, he was a police officer.'

It was so hard to say those words out loud for the first time but over the next few weeks it was something I had to face again and again. The discovery of the extent to which John had been deceiving me for years had shaken me to the core and destroyed the foundations of everything I'd ever trusted and believed in. I still felt I couldn't be sure who anyone was but, with my head exploding, I spoke to a few long-term close friends – some of whom questioned my interpretation of events.

The grief and doubt were like a form of torture.

On a visit to my parents, I talked to my dad about what I had discovered.

'He was spying on me, Dad. John lied to me. He lied to me about his age, his name and what he did. He was a police officer spying on me and my friends – he was in the group spying on us for years.'

But my dad didn't seem convinced. He had met John and knew we had been living together and planning our future together.

'I think you're being paranoid. That wouldn't happen in this country. There's probably a far simpler explanation.'

I looked over at him.

'Okay, then why would he lie to me?'

Dad thought for a moment.

'Do you know what I think, Helen?'

'What?'

'I think he was embarrassed.'

'Embarrassed?' I said, almost laughing out loud.

My father nodded.

'Embarrassed, but why?'

'I think he was a former police officer and he was embarrassed by it. That's why he didn't tell you …'

Could that be it? Had John just been ashamed?

If Dad was right, then that could mean maybe John really did love me, that he hadn't been spying on me. I wanted to believe it so much because it was far less painful than all I had right now. Really, was I just paranoid?

Alison

(Officer: Mark Cassidy)

Meeting with Helen Steel, London, August 2003

My boyfriend David and I had just started living together when I was contacted by Helen Steel. She'd been put in touch by a mutual friend who'd heard us both speak separately about our ex-boyfriend spy theories.

The Colin Roach Centre had supported the McLibel campaign, so I knew quite a bit about Helen and we had lots of friends and acquaintances in common. We'd been at many of the same events before but had never really talked. I invited her round to the flat so that we could share our stories about our ex-partners.

'A similar thing happened to me,' she said.

I felt a chill run through me.

We told each other the details of our relationships and the similar searches and discoveries we'd made to expose Mark's and John's true identities. Their vans, their elusive families, their troubled pasts, their nervous breakdowns ...

Helen said there were probably others out there. I'd thought the same but I was doubtful we'd ever find them. A few weeks later, Helen sent me a couple of photocopied pages of a chapter from a book about Scotland Yard. The pages included details about a number of Special Branch squads and their roles. Following on from what I'd told her about the strange 'CE' passport search results, she'd highlighted a paragraph entitled 'CE Squad' about a unit of undercover police infiltrating left-wing and anarchist groups.

I knew it was still an interpretation of the facts. I knew it wouldn't hold up in a court of law as incontrovertible proof. But, for me, it was the final piece of evidence I needed. There was no longer any doubt that Mark was in Special Branch. An unaccountable, secret police force that had sent my head spinning for years.

It was time for me to stop dwelling on a dead relationship and a puzzle I'd already solved. I had a loving new partner who I didn't want to lose to a ghost.

Helen and I would never get any more answers than those we'd unearthed ourselves. It was time to move on.

Helen
(Officer: John Barker)

London, August 2003

I had still told very few friends what I had discovered about John. I didn't want it to get back to the police and I didn't know who I could trust. But one of those I did share it with told me a short while later that he knew another woman with a similar story – Alison. I arranged to meet with her and we shared our respective stories. It was chilling to hear the similarities, but a part of me wondered if this was a ruse, to find out what I had discovered about John. I had felt unnerved at discovering that John had been a police officer. If John had been spying on me, the police would obviously want that kept secret, so what might the state do to stop me exposing it? I knew it needed to be exposed for what it was and brought out in the open to public scrutiny, but I had to bide my time until there was a safe way to do it.

I went to see solicitors who specialised in actions against the police, to see if it might be possible to bring a case against the force, as a way to bring the abuse out into the open, but I broke down while explaining what I had discovered. Then, somehow, their responses gave me the impression that they thought I was going mad and I began to doubt myself further.

Had I somehow lost touch with reality?

I turned away from bringing a case until I had sufficient proof that no one could doubt the story.

In the meantime, I embarked on more research to see what I could find out about John. I managed to trace him to an address inside some police accommodation, which took me up to where he'd been living in 1980. However, in the middle of this, something happened that turned my world upside down all over again – my father was diagnosed with terminal cancer. I was devastated and stopped my research. Instead, I focused on my father. He died within just six months.

Lisa
(Officer: Mark Stone)

London, September 2003

You didn't often see environmentalists wearing designer gear and expensive mirrored wraparound shades, so Mark Stone stood out.

The day I first became aware of him I was at an anti-arms fair demo in London. I thought his shades made him look a bit dodgy, and might spoil our chances of springing up unexpectedly at the arms company offices. But my friends seemed to trust him, so I did too. Mark also had a white pick-up truck, so he'd drive himself everywhere and transport people around. Lots of campaigners were very anti-SUV and his white pick-up had that same gas-guzzling vibe, which was completely at odds with our environmentalist beliefs. Although he caught some flak for his truck, he didn't seem to care. He was, in many ways, an unlikely environmental activist.

I lived in Cornerstone, a housing co-op, in Chapeltown, Leeds. It consisted of two large Victorian houses that provided a community and a home for around fourteen people, and also a base for green activists to work from, in the office downstairs. I moved in during my mid-twenties, when I was an idealistic young activist, campaigning on all kinds of things – anti-GM crops, CND, climate change, anti-roads protests and the Iraq war. I thought we had a chance to make a big difference in the world, and I was passionate. We really walked the walk in those days, living communally, wearing our ethical, sustainable ideals on our sleeves, so you'd think Mark Stone was an unlikely fit in my world, but we also had a lot of fun and his irreverent humour went down well in our group. We campaigned, partied hard and spent time in the outdoors climbing and walking, and Mark joined in with everything.

The Sumac Centre in Nottingham – which Mark was just starting to get involved with – had a similar scene around it, and we worked closely together. The people there were environmental, animal rights and peace activists. There was a lot of crossover between Leeds and Nottingham, and Mark used to come up regularly from Nottingham to visit an activist friend who lived on our street. I'd seen him on a few protests and at parties and hanging around our house. I knew his face, and had already noticed the friendly and open way he spoke to me.

Leeds, Autumn 2003

Mark was starting a relationship with a friend of mine called Kate. They'd got together at a big party at my housing co-op in November.

He came to Leeds that autumn to do a rope access technician course, because he wanted to work in industrial and commercial climbing to supplement his other work as a delivery driver. As an avid climber myself, I knew people who already did that line of work, so it was familiar to me. Mark would later joke how well paid it was and that he earned 'Hollywood money'. I remember him greeting me like an old friend on the stairs at Cornerstone one afternoon, even though I feel like I'd only met him a couple of times. It was what made me take notice of him properly for the first time.

He started going climbing with friends of mine. We all had a real love of climbing, mountaineering and the outdoors, and so he fitted right in. He became part of our extended social scene over the months to come.

Kinlochleven, Scotland, January–February 2004

Mark had organised a winter mountaineering trip to Scotland for me and my friends. There were around ten of us staying in a hostel; we had a great time. It was my first introduction into climbing snowy mountains in crampons, and I was instantly hooked.

As a group, we used to go on regular social climbing trips. It was on one of those trips in 2004 that Mark first turned up with all of his shiny new climbing kit. It was unusual for anyone to be able to afford so much gear at once – most of us would collect it piece by piece.

'I had all my climbing gear nicked, so I had to replace it all at once,' he said by way of explanation.

We jokingly called him 'Flash' because of his flash new gear and the pick-up truck he drove, and it stuck as his nickname.

I began to get to know Mark a little. He had a special kind of charm because he was always so open and friendly. He was also instantly flirty with me and I was flattered.

Lake District, September 2004

We were going on a group climbing trip to the Lakes, and Mark turned up with Kate, who joined us for a couple of days. As usual, he was wearing his regulation mirrored shades.

'You look like a drug dealer,' one of the others teased over his sunglasses and pick-up truck.

Mark nodded and smiled.

'That's not too far off the truth.'

It added to his mystique, this hint that he'd had a bit of a chequered past.

Kate had previously spoken to me about Mark. Like me and my boyfriend at the time, Merrick, I knew theirs was also an open relationship.

To an outsider it must have seemed casual, but it wasn't. All our relationships were about mutual respect, honesty and trust. We believed in living by our ideals and that extended to every aspect of our lives. But, in some ways, Mark was quite different from all that; he claimed to have a more traditional view of relationships, but he was willing to learn.

On the last night of the trip, after Kate had already left, Mark seduced me. We'd been staying in a camping barn and we were all playing silly games and having a few drinks. He'd been larking around and flirting with me. Again, I felt special in his company and we got together in the back of his pick-up truck. I remember him saying my name in a particularly intense way, like he was paying me special close attention.

Although I really liked the way Mark made me feel about myself, I didn't expect it to go the way it did. It was just a bit of fun at the beginning. He shared my passion for the mountains and for activism. Slowly but surely, he got under my skin.

Naomi

(Officer: Mark Stone)

Leeds, autumn 2003

I first met Mark Stone in late 2003, coming and going from my old home at the Cornerstone housing co-op, on the same street where I still lived. Assuming we had friends in common, I stopped to talk most times and was always struck by his warmth, how approachable he was, his easy sense of humour.

I'd moved into Cornerstone in 1999, to be involved in environmental and social justice campaigns and for the sense of community. I'd been involved in campaigning since I was a teenager, galvanised by the anti-apartheid movement and the Campaign for Nuclear Disarmament. As a bisexual woman I had also gradually begun campaigning for LGBTQ rights, overcoming the silences and homophobic prejudices that had stifled my sense of self growing up. My move to Leeds in my late twenties was part of a larger shift in my life, away from a career in academia that I found isolating, into a new career in horticulture.

I started seeing a new girlfriend, set up a gardening business with friends and, after a couple of years, moved into another housing co-op on the same street, this time with my own flat. Mark became part of my friendship network from that time.

Leeds, autumn 2004

A year after first meeting Mark, he started seeing my close friend Lisa. I was pleased for her and interested in where it was going to go. I knew that Mark was in a relationship with another woman, Kate, for about a year when he started seeing Lisa and that relationship hadn't finished. I also knew Lisa had been with Merrick for several years at this point. I knew and respected them all and the polyamory they believed in. I respected the openness, honesty and integrity that they were looking for in their lives.

This was another of the ideas that had been introduced to me through being part of Cornerstone: the idea of open relationships, of being deeply honest about desire, about the possibilities of being true to different relationships with different people. It was a challenging thing to take on, much discussed in my friendship circle with strong views on all sides. For me, in a society that labelled my own desires unacceptable, that had told me from childhood that 'normal' did not include my bisexuality, I felt open to exploring what other truths there might be.

Lisa

(Officer: Mark Stone)

Leeds, October 2004

Mark invited me to go down to Nottingham to stay with him for the
weekend. There was a climate change gathering at the Sumac Centre
that he was helping organise. Kate was away and he asked me to stay
with him in his room in the shared house he lived in with her and
other friends of mine.

'I'm so lucky you want to come and stay with me,' he remarked
back in his room.

'Why?'

'Because you are beautiful.'

I laughed it off because it sounded so cheesy, but he was serious.

'Come on, let's open a bottle of whisky,' he suggested, pulling an
expensive bottle of single malt out of a cupboard.

I asked him to tell me more about himself as we settled down
with our drinks.

He paused.

'I've taken risks,' he explained, sipping his whisky.

I didn't want to pry, but he went on to tell me that he'd had very
little love during his upbringing.

'My parents split up when I was younger. I don't see my dad, and
I have a very strained relationship with my mum. Then I got in with
some dodgy people ...'

However, he brightened as he spoke of his brother, Ian, who lived
out in Ohio in the States and was two years younger than Mark.

'He's the only person in the world who means anything to me;
I go over there to visit him. He owns his own landscaping business.'

Mark was a bit rough and ready, a bit more working class and
laddish than some of the others in our social circle; it made him

feel down to earth somehow. In many ways he was like a breath of fresh air because he was different. He didn't always want to chat about politics even at a political gathering. He was definitely not an earnest academic type of activist.

He wore his hair long and tied it back in a ponytail. Beneath his mirrored shades, Mark had a noticeable squint in his left eye. He explained he'd had an accident as a toddler, playing in a cardboard box when he'd caught his eye on a staple. Mark told me he'd had operations to try and correct it but they hadn't worked so, growing up, he'd had to sit at the front of the class and wear an eyepatch. As a result, he'd been badly bullied and had developed a nervous stammer. He explained he'd had years of speech therapy but whenever he was stressed or tired, he would trip over his words, especially the letter 'g'. I found it all so endearing and it gave him a vulnerability that I found disarming.

'You seem to like all the bits about me that I've never liked about myself,' he laughed.

In spite of this, Mark had a worldly air about him. He confessed that, at one point in his life, he'd been involved with drug-running and had met some nasty people along the way.

'I've done things in the past, things that made me feel very scared ... so I decided to break away and make a change. I wanted a new life. That's why I like you lot, because you are doing good in the world rather than trying to fuck people over, and that's what I want to do. I went too far the other way before, that's why I've made such a big change now.'

The story made sense; it explained the fact he was quite cagey about his past, and why he always had plenty of money.

Helen
(Officer: John Barker)

European Court of Human Rights, 5 September 2004

Dave Morris and I travelled by Eurostar to Strasbourg for the ECHR hearing. Although we had won many of the issues in McLibel, we still had the order for damages hanging over our heads, and anyway, the draconian nature of English libel laws was acting as a barrier to freedom of speech for many. Our appeal called for greater protection of freedom of speech about issues of public interest and challenged the lack of legal aid to defend libel cases, which had led to the serious inequality of arms between us and McDonald's. We had our day in court, this time represented by Keir Starmer. Then we had to sit tight and wait to see what the court's ruling would be.

Lisa

(Officer: Mark Stone)

Leeds, Christmas 2004

Mark was flying out to Thailand to take part in a Thai boxing camp.

'I'll see you when I get back. You won't be able to get hold of me out there.'

I nodded.

'It's okay, I'll see you after New Year.'

On Boxing Day, I was sitting at home when I heard the news – a massive tsunami had hit the south-west coastline of Thailand, with waves reaching up to sixty-four feet in places. Thousands were feared dead and thousands more were missing.

I was thrown into a panic. Although he said he'd be uncontactable, I tried his number anyway and left messages, but I didn't hear back. I was unsure what to do, so the next day I messaged Kate, to see if she'd heard anything. 'Kate, it's Lisa. Have you heard from Mark? Have you seen the news? I've tried his number but there's no answer.' I waited anxiously for her reply.

I couldn't believe Mark was over there, caught in the middle of one of the worst natural disasters the world had ever seen.

'He's fine,' Kate replied. 'He's just messaged, saying he's okay.'

I felt a huge sense of relief.

Yorkshire Dales, January 2005

The news of the tsunami had been a bit of a wake-up call; it made me realise that I cared for Mark more than I had thought.

On his return, we went walking in the Yorkshire Dales, and he seemed haunted by what he said he'd witnessed.

'We weren't affected by it, but we travelled from the boxing camp to the bit that had been really badly hit. We wanted to help with the rescue effort, but it was so intense,' he recalled, rubbing his hands against his forehead. 'Everything had gone.'

'Gone?'

'Yeah,' he said, sweeping out his hand, '… totally destroyed – washed away.'

Mark paused for a moment as though he were still trying to come to terms with it, and then he continued.

'We were digging bodies out of the sand …' he explained, his voice fading with the trauma.

I allowed him to talk – to open up – and I didn't want to press him for details. Still, he was desperately upset.

'I slept in a doorway because there wasn't anywhere to stay but I didn't care. I just wanted to help those people, especially the ones searching for their relatives.'

He paused, his hands still trembling, as he tried to compose himself.

'There was a mother, she was searching for her dead child. We all helped her dig in the sand and rubble, helped her find her dead child.'

'Mark, I don't know what to say.'

We stayed in a room above a pub. Mark supposedly had much more mountaineering experience than me but, in truth, while his rope work and his safety were good, he didn't seem as capable at being in the mountains as I'd expected.

That day we were walking up Ingleborough – the second highest of the three Yorkshire peaks. We'd just reached the top when a heavy mist came down. Mark dug the compass out to study it. I had some compass skills but he was the one with more experience.

'I hope we're going to be able to get down off this mountain,' I remarked, watching him trying to work it out with the map and compass.

As I waited, I realised he was struggling.

'Shall I have a go?' I offered.

He shook his head.

'No, no, I can do it; I want to do it. I'm just trying to work it out …' he mumbled.

It took a while, but eventually we worked together and managed to find our way safely down off the mountain.

'Oh brilliant, we did it!' he whooped.

His reaction confused me. He seemed genuinely relieved he'd managed it.

I thought you were supposed to be really good at this sort of thing.

There was also a certain confidence to rock climbing that Mark didn't seem to possess. I suppose I'd expected more given what he'd told me about his experience.

He talks a better climb than he actually does.

But then, so many men do.

I reasoned it was all part of male bravado, and Mark could sometimes be a macho type of guy. But I felt even closer to him when I got to see his softer, more vulnerable side.

After this, we slowly started to see each other more often, we'd meet up every couple of weeks and I'd go and stay with Mark or he'd travel up to be with me. We'd meet up when he wasn't working away on a contract; even then, he always kept in touch.

Naomi
(Officer: Mark Stone)

Yorkshire, January 2005

Mark and I were at the same weekend-long tree-planting event, as part of a campaign to stop flooding in the Calder Valley and combat climate change. He and I ended up getting together that weekend. At the time it felt very mutual, one of those nice things that sometimes happens. Although Mark was still with Lisa, we had lots of conversations about it and we were both aware of what the other one was doing. We all lived on the same street and often when Mark came to visit her, or me, we'd all be part of the same group hanging out.

Helen
(Officer: John Barker)

European Courts of Human Rights ruling, 15 February 2005
We held our breath for the email from the court to arrive with its
ruling. The clock ticked. We had to keep dialling into the internet
to see if it had landed or not. Finally, it dropped in our inbox, and
Dave watched over my shoulder as I opened up the message. My eyes
scanned it, trying to read as quickly as my brain would allow.

'Yes!' I cried.

I punched the air as Dave cheered behind me.

The European Court of Human Rights ruled that the original
McDonald's libel case had breached our rights to a fair trial and to
freedom of expression. As a result, it ordered the UK government
to pay us a total of £24,000 in compensation, towards the time and
money we had spent fighting the case. The ECHR ruled the trial
had been unfair because of the lack of resources we'd had available
to us, and the complex and oppressive nature of UK libel laws. It
was a landmark legal victory for the little people, like us. And, as
a result of all the publicity surrounding the trial, McDonald's had
spent an estimated £10 million on the case – about three hundred
times as much as us – and despite that, it had been dubbed the worst
corporate PR disaster in history. It had been a victory in more ways
than one.

Lisa

(Officer: Mark Stone)

Leeds, 2005

By now, Mark and I were seeing each other regularly, even though our relationship wasn't exclusive and we both had other relationships. Kate split up with Mark around this time, as she had moved away to live in Spain in early February. We were starting to be with each other every couple of weeks and he would take turns to stay with me in Leeds. In the basement of the Cornerstone house where I lived was the main office for various different campaign groups. It was where we kept all the computers to help organise and plan future campaigns. It was a busy, bustling activist hub as well as the house where I lived. We socialised and ate dinner with my housemates – who weren't all activists – and we also spent a lot of time in my room watching films on his laptop and listening to music.

I was thirty-one years old and really into drum and bass music. I did a bit of DJing at house and squat parties. Mark got into drum and bass too. He was also into different types of music – country and guitar rock – and later we would go to lots of gigs together.

We weren't a very mobile phone-loving group of people in those days. I had a really basic mobile phone – a Nokia – but I didn't use it much. We didn't like the idea of carrying tracking devices around and you weren't allowed into any activist meetings if you had a phone on you. Instead, you'd have to take the battery out and leave it in a box. But Mark had a BlackBerry he said he needed for work. I didn't know anyone else with such a sophisticated phone, and he seemed to always be on it. He began sending me nice messages each day, so I wanted to keep my phone with me in case he texted. He was the first person to ever shower me with messages like this.

Festival of Dissent, Lanarkshire, Scotland, 6–10 April 2005

There was going to be a preparation meeting to campaign against the G8, which was to be held in Scotland. We headed to the festival and, although it had snowed, we planned to camp. The event was to inform others about the issues behind G8 and what it represented, and to try to plan actions around the summit. People were due to travel from all over the country.

'It's going to be brilliant,' Mark insisted.

We'd already done winter mountaineering, so I knew he'd be fully equipped.

'Come on, Lisa. I'm way more prepared than the rest of these activists. I've got a base-camp tent, down sleeping bags – a warm bed! We'll be fine,' Mark said, trying to persuade me to go.

And we were. Other people struggled with the cold, as it snowed that weekend, but we were snug with our whisky and treats and spent a lot of time avoiding meetings and staying in bed getting to know each other.

Naomi
(Officer: Mark Stone)

Scotland, April 2005

In the spring, I travelled to Scotland with Lisa, Merrick and a group of friends, but Mark couldn't come. We climbed a mountain called the Merrick for Merrick's birthday. Mark had given me a framed photo he'd taken of Merrick, wearing an amazing costume at a fundraiser in Nottingham earlier that year, to present to his friend at the top of the hill. Merrick loved it. The photo and the thought behind it. That was how close we all were.

Holiday in Northumberland, May 2005

One of the things that struck me about Mark was what an attentive person he was; he seemed interested in who I was. He was so complimentary: about me, about my friends, about the whole community.

'You're a very beautiful person, you're a special person, you're so kind,' he told me.

He also presented a level of vulnerability that surprised me. He opened up pretty early on about the impact on his self-esteem of his father abandoning the family when he was young, the feeling of loss and confusion this left him with. He spoke of his self-consciousness about his wandering eye, caused by the accident as a very young child. He liked that I looked him in the eye, despite this. Somehow this took me off guard.

'When I was growing up, I was a real geeky child,' he said.

I could relate.

'I went to see Bros at Wembley. You should have seen me,' he said, laughing to himself at the thought. 'I wore this long peach-coloured cardigan. No wonder I never really fitted in at school.'

I laughed too, because I understood. Like me, Mark said he had found his community and people who accepted him. He said he had a lot he wanted to learn from us, about relationships and how to live life.

We went on holiday together in early May, cycling up the Northumberland coast. It was so beautiful. I loved cycling and Mark seemed really keen on the idea when I suggested it, putting a lot of effort into organising the five-day trip and buying a bike rack for the back of his truck. To keep costs down, we did a mixture of camping and a few B&Bs along the way. A highlight was the day we spent on Lindisfarne island, reachable only when the tide was out. We timed our trip just right, following the tide times and arriving as the island became cut off by the tide; it was quiet and otherworldly. Later, we cycled back to the mainland, through the sand dunes in the dusk: with Lindisfarne in the twilight behind us, time seemed to stop still and that moment felt magical. We returned to the mainland just as the tide crept back in and covered the island road.

Leeds, summer 2005

Mark was hugely committed to activism; in fact, he was so dedicated that it almost felt above and beyond. He made himself useful and put himself at the centre of things. He was always prepared to go the extra mile. He had a van and would offer to drive the length and breadth of the country just to collect stuff – tents or equipment.

One time he called from a demo, all fired up with enthusiasm.

'You should have seen me, Naomi. I hung a banner off this bridge … and I'm really excited! Are you impressed?' he asked.

I was taken aback and not sure what response was expected.

'Yes, that's great, Mark; well done.'

His enthusiasm sometimes overwhelmed him and he could go a little overboard, bordering on immaturity – there was always a sense of him wanting to impress people.

I was a big fan of country music and Mark said he was too. I decided to learn to play the mandolin. I'd played the guitar when I was younger, but I'd never quite got the hang of it. However, I loved the sound of the mandolin, so I thought I'd give it a go.

I bought a mandolin and a CD to try and learn. Talking to Mark about it one day, he mentioned he'd always wanted to play the banjo. It seemed slightly odd but then I knew he used to go and see opera with Kate and later got into drum and bass DJing with Lisa. In many ways he just seemed to fit the person and blend into their world.

Lisa
(Officer: Mark Stone)

Peak District, early June 2005

We went wild camping above Burbage Edge in the Peak District before meeting friends to go climbing the next day. It was a bright evening and we headed up onto the moors laden with whisky, luxury chocolate and comfy bedding, stuffed into our rucksacks. It was both romantic and hilarious that we were carrying so much. I laughed at Mark's top-heavy bag towering above him as he walked along the stony track, pretending not to struggle under the weight.

That night it was clear and starry and our tent was nestled cosily in the heather.

'I love you, Lisa,' he said, pouring me a dram of the peaty, smoky liquid in one of the glass tumblers he'd carried all the way up.

'I love you, too.'

He looked at me with such deep sincerity and I felt a shift in the dynamic between us. He explained he'd never felt like this about anyone before.

Naomi

(Officer: Mark Stone)

My brother's wedding, Leeds, June 2005

Mark came to my brother's wedding with me. He met my whole family that day. They welcomed him and he was his usual friendly self: it felt like a good day. But in among the ceremony, the food and the dancing, the moment jarred when Mark asked not to be in the official wedding photo. He told me he was finding things difficult and was going to take some time to himself.

He'd already told me that his father had abandoned him when he'd been young; it seemed to have had a huge impact on him. Not only did it have an impact on his self-worth, it had also dented his confidence and, in turn, had affected his whole life. He always explained that this was why he loved his brother so much.

Mark often received calls from his Uncle Phil, who he was very close to and who he said was like a father to him. I felt for Mark and his situation, and I was impressed at how honest and open he was about his feelings and his family. So, on the day of my brother's wedding, when he told me he had found it tough, I tried to be understanding.

'I just find it all so very difficult and emotional to see such a strong family, Naomi.'

I tried to reassure him.

'You know you're welcome here. You're part of this day. I'll be right beside you.'

But he shook his head, wouldn't let me change his mind and vanished until all the photos were finished.

Lisa
(Officer: Mark Stone)

G8 protest, Gleneagles, Scotland, 6–8 July 2005

Mark had played a crucial role in the demonstration at the G8 summit. He hired and organised a fleet of minibuses; he was logistics manager for the protesters and had earned himself a new nickname – 'Transport Mark'. He was also the 'Logistics Man'. I was there, but we had our different roles and he was busy. I went on some of the protests and volunteered with the medics and then helped in the kitchen; I basically helped out where I was needed, while Mark was right in the thick of things. While we were there, we also celebrated his birthday on 7 July. The day had been significant because it was the same day as the 7/7 bombings in London, and the news of the attack had shaken us all. In particular, Mark had seemed very affected by it because he was a Londoner.

Iceland, July 2005

We'd heard about a demonstration being held in Iceland during the summer. Some Icelandic activists had been at the Festival of Dissent in Scotland, and had spoken about a protest to protect the wilderness. There were plans to try and industrialise Iceland in a way that hadn't been done before. There was talk of the construction of lots of hydroelectric dam schemes to flood the landscape, and the building of over half a dozen aluminium smelters. The protest was to stop the build of the first one – the Kárahnjúkar Dam.

Although there had been protests about dams in the past, there had never been a protest camp like this one in Iceland before, so they needed activists with experience and I was very excited to go. I asked Mark.

'What do you think?'

He seemed unusually cagey.

'Well, I don't really know, I might have to go and work then.'

He seemed to dodge the subject for a couple of weeks then, one day, he announced he was going to come.

'Let's go together,' he said, suddenly excited by the idea.

We travelled to the eastern highlands in Iceland for three weeks. It was the longest time we'd ever spent together. We caught the ferry – a trip that lasted three days – from Aberdeen to the Shetland Islands and then over to Iceland. The whole trip was so romantic from start to finish, drinking whisky on the ferry and eating amazing seafood in the restaurant. I loved a little taste of luxury because it always felt a bit illicit, as other activists were less likely to eat in restaurants. We also sat outside on the deck to watch the stars – it was magical. We arrived in Iceland and pitched up our tent at the protest camp.

There were around thirty activists staying in the camp, who had travelled from all over the world. When the protests began, I locked myself onto a dumper truck; the wheel of it was the same height as me. Another activist and I D-locked ourselves to the wheel to stop it from moving; we'd fastened the locks around our necks. It was the kind of thing I was used to doing on blockades like this – it was a common tactic, and we knew that we were quite lucky as Western activists, in that we could do this kind of thing knowing we wouldn't be killed or injured, and work would have to stop. This time, though, the driver started up the engine and half a dozen people jumped on to disable it, including Mark, who pulled a hydraulic hose to stop it dead. Afterwards, he turned to me.

'The thought of something happening to you – I just saw red.'

He'd caused the most damage so a security guard pointed him out to the police. They came towards us so we legged it and changed our clothes. Others were arrested, but Mark hid the overalls he'd been wearing so we were never caught.

Life was exciting. That summer it felt as if we were living years in just one day; our relationship was played out in these intense, exhilarating times. We spent twilight nights together in Mark's tent. It never got fully dark at that time of the year in Iceland, so we'd spend a lot of time having sex. One night the condom slipped off by accident and I needed to get the morning-after pill from a chemist in a nearby town. Mark seemed quite shaken up, but I was much calmer.

Forest Fields, Nottingham, summer 2005

Mark moved out of the house he'd been sharing into his own rented, two-bedroom terraced place in Bradgate Road, Forest Fields. I travelled down to help and realised how few possessions he really had.

He did, however, have lots of photographs, mainly of him and his brother. He also had pictures of us in Iceland and, in pride of place in the middle of his bedroom, there was a four-poster bed built from scaffolding. The bed hung from chains, and everyone teased him that it was his sadomasochism bed, which I found funny because he wasn't that sexually adventurous. In reality, he was much more tender and gentle – a big softie. Whenever he emailed, he'd sign off with 'BSI' – Big Soft Idiot.

He bought himself some decks so he could do some drum and bass DJing with me. He had books and more photographs of me dotted around, which I somehow found a bit weird. I put it down to the fact that, beside his brother, he didn't have much family.

Mark would often buy me presents – climbing gear, underwear, a bottle of whisky. I felt a bit strange about it, not being into material things.

'I'm not that kind of girl, I don't need that,' I insisted.

His gift-giving sometimes left me feeling awkward. At the same time, it made me feel cared about, and it was nice that he thought about me when he was away.

Leeds, 2005/6

Something had shifted. After Iceland, things became more serious between us; we were much more publicly a couple.

In summer 2006, I left the Cornerstone housing co-op and started renting my own flat in Leeds. Having my own space for us to spend more relaxed time together was great for our relationship.

Naomi

(Officer: Mark Stone)

Poland, July–August 2005

I couldn't explain it, but I felt Mark slowly drifting away from me. He was really involved in the campaign against the G8, in Stirling, Scotland. He'd been busy with it so I put it down to the fact it was because he was so preoccupied. It took all his time and got to the point where he seemed to be working around the clock on it, 24/7.

That summer Mark was also seeing another woman, Sarah, as well as me and Lisa, which I accepted. In August, Mark travelled to Iceland with Lisa and I was travelling with an old friend in Poland, when he sent me an email talking with vulnerability about the difficulties he was having in managing open relationships and stressing the importance of honesty. He was loving and affectionate and talked about how important it was to him that things were good between us 'cos I hate hurting people'.

Leeds, September 2005

Mark and Lisa returned from Iceland. I knew he'd been trying to negotiate his relationship with this other woman and I'd already felt him move away from me. So when Lisa and Mark arrived home from the Icelandic protest, I spoke to her directly. I could see she had fallen in love with Mark so deeply and significantly, and that's what I'd felt from him too. All his messages pointed to it. Something within me told me I needed to back away and leave their relationship to grow. It dawned on me that my main priority had become my friendship with Lisa and Mark – I loved them both dearly. I knew he'd fallen for Lisa and I didn't want to be the person on the edge. Instead, at the end of September, when Mark called in to visit me, I told him how I felt.

'Let's stop having this relationship,' I began. 'Let's be friends, and let's be honest – I think that's where we're at now. I think when you were in Iceland things really shifted for you and Lisa; I really care about you, but I think it's time for this relationship to change and become a friendship instead.'

To me, it was all part of having an open relationship – that, when you ended things, there didn't have to be anger or rejection.

We were both standing in the kitchen inside my flat; Mark had his back to me when I realised from the shudder of his shoulders that he was crying. I was shocked because I thought he would be relieved, not upset. In fact, I'd almost expected him to say something like: *Thanks, Naomi, it's not you, it's me*.

Only he didn't; instead, he sobbed.

'I feel I've let you down,' he wept.

I shook my head.

'No, no, you haven't.'

'I really wanted to be there and I couldn't be. I tried to do it – to do open relationships – but I can't.'

Eventually, Mark composed himself and we parted on good terms. But I still couldn't quite reconcile his reaction.

A week after our split, Mark sent me a heartfelt and emotional email. In it he reflected on the positive impact I'd had on his life and his disappointment in himself. I was genuinely moved by the affirming way he'd described me. He expressed regret that our relationship had not gone the way we'd hoped since he'd become closer with Lisa. I valued the way he also considered the importance of my friendship with her. He promised that I'd always have a best friend in him. I was touched by his message and proud of the way we were going to be able to remain good friends.

It wasn't until years later that I realised the irony of him thanking me for my honesty, as well as his parting comment that while he had tried to explain himself, some things could never be fully explained.

Lisa
(Officer: Mark Stone)

'Reclaim Power' and 'Camp for Climate Action' environmental protest, Drax Power Station, North Yorkshire, 31 August 2006

Activists decided the organisation of the protest at the G8 summit in Stirling had been so successful that they wanted to replicate that way of organising against climate change, which was our main focus. We would organise a series of national 'Climate Camps'. In 2006, the first one was held at Drax and around 600 protesters attended, including us. Mark was part of the main logistics organising team, alongside a woman called Lynn Watson. Everyone was working together from different groups to collectively squat a piece of land to occupy as a camp. We'd turned up with marquees and things were erected quickly so by the time anyone knew what was happening, we had a whole camp set up with infrastructure and security. The police knew it was coming but they didn't know exactly where it was going to spring up.

On the day of the big demo, there was a huge group of protestors who planned to march to the main gates to try to shut down the power station; we were aware they would shut the gates and divert people, containing the protest, in order to keep the power station open. I was part of a group that had planned to break off from the main demo to try and get in through the fence around the side, to lock ourselves onto something and get the power station shut down. Lynn and I approached the fence around the back of Drax. I knew Lynn from the activist scene in Leeds; surprisingly, she'd suggested we 'buddy up' that day even though we weren't that close. She was friends with a lot of people I trusted and I'd been round her house. She'd even chatted to me about my relationship with Mark, but it was the first time we'd done anything like this together.

That's odd, I thought. But it was good to have a buddy for safety, so I agreed.

Someone started making holes in the fence with a pair of bolt cutters. The police arrived and tried to get us to stop. But there were only two of them and more of us so we carried on. There were a couple of holes in the fence, and the police were distracted arguing with the others, when Lynn turned to me.

'Let's make a break for it, through this hole,' she suggested.

So we did. We made a run for it but almost immediately we were nicked because the police were waiting on the other side. Lynn and I were handcuffed together, and then something bizarre happened to her. She was mouthing off with the cops, then whispering to me that we should make a run for it despite having been formally arrested already. It was as though her adrenalin had shot up. She was behaving really out of character.

She obviously hasn't been nicked before.

We were taken to a local police station and held for hours. We'd been arrested in the afternoon, but we weren't released until the early hours of the morning so I had absolutely no idea what had happened back at the power plant. One of the protesters from the 'arrest support group' came to meet me.

'Just so you know, Mark's back at the camp and he's okay,' she said.

'Why wouldn't he be okay? What's wrong with him? What's happened?'

The woman became flustered.

'Didn't you know?'

I stared at her.

'Sorry, I thought you knew. Yeah, he's been beaten up. But I don't know any more than that.'

We walked over to a minibus then called at all the different police stations to pick up other demonstrators who, like me, had just been released. I asked if someone could call the camp and find out what had happened. I was frantic as we slowly made our way back there. Information filtered through in dribs and drabs how Mark had been beaten up by the police and then arrested. But, for some reason, he'd been released much sooner than I had. As soon as I reached camp, I asked someone where he was.

'He's in the medics' tent.'

I ran over and found him; he was fast asleep. He'd been patched up, given stitches and bandaged up in hospital, and was now being looked after by our medics. He was sleeping in their tent so they could keep an eye on him.

'He's okay,' one of them said, trying to reassure me. But I was really worried.

Mark had stitches in his eyebrow and bruises on his face, hands and body. As I waited for him to wake up, I crept into the bed where he was sleeping and snuggled up. He woke, turned to me and we had a whispered conversation about what had happened. He told me they'd stamped on his back. Six officers had piled on and beaten him up. He already had back issues, but the attack made it much worse. His bravado stories followed the next day.

'I told the copper that my mum punches harder than that,' he laughed.

It seemed like his way of coping.

'I refused medical attention in the cells because I wanted someone to photograph my injuries.'

The following day, he wanted to go. He drove a van he'd borrowed from Uncle Phil but, as we tried to leave, the police insisted on searching it. They found his climbing gear and confiscated it. Mark was furious but there was nothing we could do. He was so angry, I feared for his mental health.

Once home, his strange behaviour continued and he insisted he had to return straight to work.

'What do you mean? You've just been beaten up; you can barely walk – let me look after you.'

But he refused and we had an argument. I was really worried about him.

'Look, I can't just sit here dwelling on it. I've got to go and be busy, otherwise I'm going to get too angry.'

Wales, November 2006

My father had been ill for quite a while, having suffered a stroke three years previously. Over the years that followed, his health had deteriorated.

Mark had met him once, and Dad really took to him.

'I'm glad you're with someone nice,' he told me.

He lived on his own, and had a woman in to help clean; one day she found him stumbling and incoherent and called an ambulance. This time, he'd suffered a much bigger stroke.

Mark was very supportive and drove me down to Wales to see him. He had already met my mum and sister. They liked him, and he got on really well with my brother. He also had a strange connection to Bristol and Uncle Phil, who gave him work, so he said he'd take a detour to South Wales to drop me off to see Dad.

'Uncle Phil's not really my uncle, he's just really good friends with my family,' Mark explained.

Uncle Phil would lend him equipment; he'd borrow a projector for a meeting or a van for a demo. He told me Uncle Phil was a delivery driver, who took marine engine parts all over the country. He talked about him a lot and would go down to Bristol to have Sunday lunch with Phil's family. However, he never invited me. One day I decided to ask why.

'I'd really like to meet Uncle Phil. Who are you embarrassed by, me or him?'

Mark shook his head.

'Oh, him. He's racist and he says the most awful things about people. I think you'd get really offended; I think you'd hate him. I don't want you to meet him because he'll say something embarrassing and I won't know what to do.'

He does sound like the sort of person I wouldn't like, but he's still important to Mark.

Also, Uncle Phil was the only person who lived in the UK who was part of Mark's past. His brother lived in America, and his mum lived in Ireland.

When my father died at the end of that November, my friends helped me through, and Merrick came, although Mark wasn't able to come straight away.

Why can't he get compassionate leave?

He attended Dad's funeral in early December, when he met the rest of my extended family and travelled in the mourners' car. He'd been there for some of my most vulnerable moments and had held me as I cried through the night.

Later that year when the family met up to scatter my dad's ashes, I invited Mark to join us, but he said that he couldn't get the time away from work.

Winter mountaineering trip, February 2007

Losing my dad in my early thirties had felt quite young; I was in a bit of a mess. Most of my friends hadn't lost parents. My response was to cling on tightly to the relationships that mattered. I was still in a relationship with Merrick, who had been incredibly supportive of me in my grief. Although we had a very strong connection, we both had other relationships that took our attention. I was feeling a strong need for someone to make me feel special, and to make me feel like I was the most important person in their world. Mark was very good at that. Despite not always being around he made me feel like I was everything to him. He would message me and call me all the time, as if I was always on his mind.

Early on after my father's death, I felt a renewed need to be part of a close family, and I was worried that without Dad, ours might drift apart. I wondered whether I should create my own family and mentioned it to Mark.

'Maybe I do want kids, maybe I do want to start a family one day.'

But, at the same time, I was frightened I'd scare him off because he'd always been so adamant that he didn't want children. I was also frightening myself with these unfamiliar desires.

'I'm not responsible enough for that, Lisa. I'd make a terrible dad. I don't want to restrict my freedom that way, and I don't think you do either.'

Maybe he was right, maybe it was a terrible idea, but I was more confused about it all now.

USA, early 2007

I was still trying to come to terms with my father's death but, just when I needed him most, Mark left for Ohio, America. He told me he'd be gone for a couple of months and had planned to stay with his brother so he could undergo a private operation on his back. He'd suffered with it ever since he'd been beaten up by the police at Drax. He stayed in touch with me all the time with emails and romantic text messages and frequent calls, but I couldn't help missing him terribly. When he returned a few months later, there was a surgical scar and some improvement, but his back was never right after that.

G8 Summit, Heiligendamm, Germany, 6–8 June 2007

Following my father's death, I began to withdraw a little bit from my previous activism. The grief and loss I felt seemed to diminish my passion for wanting to change things, but Mark had kept me involved in that world. He was heavily into protest stuff connected to the G8 in Germany, so he included me in his plans by saying it would be a nice chance for us to spend more time together.

'We could even turn it into a bit of a holiday,' he suggested, trying to persuade me to go to Germany with him. 'We could cycle there together.'

We'd already been on a cycling trip in Pembrokeshire, so it didn't seem a daunting task, although Mark usually took his pick-up truck when he went to Europe. Instead, we caught the ferry from Harwich to Denmark, and then cycled a couple of hundred kilometres with our camping stuff strapped to panniers. It took us three days to cycle in the intense heat. By the end of it, Mark was mildly delirious and spent the first day in Germany throwing up with sunstroke. Afterwards, he introduced me to some other activist friends he knew from his frequent travels to Germany. He had always been interested in travelling and meeting people. He was one of the links between UK and German activists.

At one point, we went in a small group to try to blockade the road to stop delegates reaching the G8, and we were arrested. There was a makeshift holding centre for all the arrests so that we could be processed. Everyone else in our group was female, so we went to one and Mark was taken to a different holding cell. Later, he was full of bravado stories; he told me he'd refused to be searched and hadn't co-operated over the six hours. But he was the only male in our small group so no one could back up his story. He always seemed to have stories of bravado when dealing with the cops.

If that's what you need to make you feel as though they've not taken your power away from you, then good for you.

In the end, we were all released without charge. Afterwards, we travelled to Berlin for more demonstrations, and got very drunk at a squat party. For the first time in ages, Mark seemed to let off steam. I asked why he had so much energy to release.

'I've been really stressed; I've had such a lot of work on before getting here.'

Glastonbury, 20–24 June 2007

Mark didn't usually take drugs, but he took ecstasy twice with me. Even though he was a big drinker, drugs were out of character.

'I've seen so much bad stuff,' he insisted. 'I don't get the same kind of high other people do; I'm not sure they work on me.'

Mark was delivering supplies to a vegan café at Glastonbury so we got a vehicle pass and he was able to drive into the 'Green Fields' part of the site. We later took ecstasy while watching bands and I'd never seen anyone have so much fun.

Big Green Gathering, Cheddar, Somerset, summer 2007

The second time Mark took ecstasy was when we were part of a collective, helping run a bar at a festival, the Big Green Gathering.

However, that year it was shut down by the police as we were setting up. There were all kinds of theories why the police might have intervened. Some people thought it was because of all the money our bar had raised for direct action against climate change at the Climate Camps. Once we knew it wouldn't go ahead, we had a big party for the crew, as we had a fully stocked bar with no prospect of opening. Mark took ecstasy, and after a while he started to slag people off, which was totally out of character. He said mean things about people as they danced.

'Look at the way he's dancing, he thinks he's great. They all think they're so cool, but they're just a bunch of scruffy wasters.'

I was baffled.

Mark looked over at me and changed his tune.

'This is why I don't take ecstasy; I don't like what it does to me.'

'Yeah,' I agreed. 'You should just stick to the booze, it's more fun.'

Rossport, County Mayo, Ireland, summer 2007

I drove my campervan over to Ireland for a holiday and I'd planned to attend a protest while I was over there. I'd been involved in a campaign to help stop Shell running a pipeline under a stretch of land to bring in gas to a nearby refinery. Some years previously some local farmers had been arrested for stopping Shell from entering their land, and since then a protest camp had been set up. A bunch of us went over to support the local community. I'd wanted Mark to join me on my trip, and maybe come to the camp, but he refused.

'I can't, I'm working.'

But he also told me he needed to see his mum, who lived in Ireland. I ended up doing the road trip on my own. I didn't understand how he could take weeks off at a time to travel to protests in Iceland or Germany or attend Climate Camps, but couldn't get a short amount of time off to be with me in Ireland. I must've seemed really pissed off because, in the end, he did meet me in Ireland but he didn't come to the camp. Instead, he met me closer to the ferry terminal. I'd offered to meet him at his mum's house.

'No,' he replied. 'She's not been well and things are difficult between us.'

We met in a random campsite on the coast near Waterford. Mark didn't want to go out that night. Instead, we went swimming in the sea and spent the evening together inside the campervan before I left for the ferry in the morning.

Naomi

(Officer: Mark Stone)

Berlin, autumn 2007

In November, I met up briefly with Mark again in Berlin. We both happened to be in the city at the same time. He said he was there visiting friends so we arranged to meet and spent the night together in a friend's flat. I only slept with him twice after I'd ended the relationship, and this time was one of them.

It felt good to see him again. Afterwards, he seemed keen to try and sustain our friendship. We promised to keep in touch and, on 10 November, I kept to my word, sat down at my computer and began to type.

> *Date: Sat, 10 Nov 2007 12:07:28*
> *Subject: :)*
> *Hey lovely*
> *Hope everything is good with you. I just wanted to say what a pleasure it was to see you, talk, reconnect and spend time with you in Berlin this week. I am really pleased that happened. It was so good to acknowledge a connection between us. I respect and value the life you lead. I know you are a genuine, loving, respectful person.*
> *Take care of yourself!*
> *Love to you, Naomi xx*

Mark responded the next day with an email sent from his BlackBerry, saying how wonderful it had been to see me. He expressed that it had been hard to split up and promised that there was always a place in his heart for me.

During the year out I'd taken to go travelling, I spent three months in Berlin and then I moved to Spain for another three months.

A chatty email arrived from Mark a few months later. It seemed full of his usual bravado, sharing a crazy story about storming the Japanese embassy in New York City. At the same time, it was a romantic message and he sounded keen to connect, painting a picture of a get-together in an old town bar. I felt that our friendship was standing the test of time.

Lisa
(Officer: Mark Stone)

Leeds and Nottingham, 2008/9

Mark seemed stressed; he was tired and suffering a lot of pain with his back because the operation hadn't worked. Some days he was so bad he struggled to walk. He wasn't registered with a doctor – in fact he didn't seem to be registered anywhere – so I had to take him to an NHS walk-in centre in Leeds, just to get some painkillers. The doctors gave him some Tramadol, but it didn't even touch the sides. He was obviously in a lot of pain. We got him some acupuncture, which seemed to help a bit.

But why was he so stressed?

There was something else that confused me. I knew other people who did the same job as him and they'd progressed or been promoted yet Mark never seemed to. Also, I'd never seen any photographs of him at work as a commercial climber even though others had them.

'Ah well, if I was the manager, I'd be able to take a few pictures,' he explained.

I put his stress down to sciatica and working so hard.

He'd always been so full of energy, but now he seemed strained and had begun to suffer stress-related illnesses.

Did Mark have 'activist burnout'?

Naomi
(Officer: Mark Stone)

Southern Europe, March 2008

I was travelling in southern Europe and had met up with an old activist friend. We were sitting on a rooftop looking out over the brightly lit city; we'd been talking for hours when, out of the blue, they asked me about Mark.

'Do you think we can trust Mark Stone? I think he's spying on us.'

Their words took me by surprise. They explained they thought Mark's behaviour was very erratic.

'He's always going away, and he doesn't explain why he has to go. We've never met his family. Quite a few things just don't add up.'

I couldn't register it properly in my head.

Could this be possible? No, I know Mark. I've had a relationship with him. He's my friend.

My mind couldn't absorb all the questions it brought up; I pushed them back down again. I didn't even talk about it to Lisa, and certainly not Mark.

Nottingham, April 2008

I was back in England for a brief time when I caught up with old friends, including Mark. I stayed with him for a weekend in Nottingham. In many ways, I'd come to see him to put my mind at rest – I had to check it out for myself.

That weekend we both went to a pretty intense self-defence work-shop with a group of friends. We all had to work together closely, to trust each other.

These are my friends, I thought. *I can rely on them. To doubt Mark would be to doubt everyone, even myself.*

Lisa

(Officer: Mark Stone)

Stoke-on-Trent, January 2009

My father had left me some money in his estate so I decided to buy a canal boat to live on. I wanted it to be a joint project between me and Mark, and we had viewed lots of boats together, travelling around marinas to find the most suitable one. Just after the New Year, we found one moored near Stoke-on-Trent. Mark helped me negotiate the price through a broker; he wasn't actually any better at it than me and we didn't get any price reduction, but he gave me the confidence to buy it. The narrowboat – which was fifty-seven feet long – didn't need much work. It was a godsend because while we both knew how to do basic repairs, neither of us was particularly skilled. But Mark was never as available as I'd wanted him to be. I hoped he'd help me move the boat but I had to bring it up to Yorkshire on the canal network alone to move stuff from my flat in Leeds. I wanted him to be part of the adventure but he said he couldn't get the time off.

G20 Summit, London, 1 April 2009

Mark attended protests around the G20 summit in London. It was the day that newspaper vendor Ian Tomlinson died after being struck by a police officer. Mark had spent the day with some anarchist friends and I joined them later, after I'd finished college. The demo had been in the City of London. Mark led me away from the crowd to a bagel shop on Brick Lane. We were both starving.

'Here we are,' he said, holding a hand out as we approached it. 'It stays open all night.'

'How do you know about this place?' I asked.

'When I was a cycle courier, working in London, I always used to come here. It was my favourite bagel shop.'

Nottingham, April 2009

There was a big planning meeting the night before a demo at Ratcliffe-on-Soar Power Station in Nottinghamshire but I didn't attend. In fact, Mark had talked me out of going.

'It'll be chaos – a nightmare. I don't really want to go, and I don't think you should go. It'll be a mess.'

I was so caught up with other stuff that I didn't mind missing this one.

Mark, however, was due to go to the meeting. He was involved with the logistics of the planned action the following day, to try to break into the power station and shut it down. He'd taken up his usual role as Transport Mark and had driven a reconnaissance party to the power station in his van. They'd scouted the area.

Around 120 or so people, including Mark, gathered at a school in Nottingham the evening before the demo – the planning meeting he'd advised me not to go to. Without warning, 400 police officers swooped on the building and arrested the protesters for 'conspiracy to commit aggravated trespass'. It was unheard of for the police to swoop in *before* anything had happened. They must have been pretty confident they knew what would happen, because 114 people were arrested, including Mark. For most people, the briefing that night was the first they'd heard of the plan, but Mark had been involved in the planning and had known for months. Afterwards, his house was raided by police, who trashed it, knocked photos off the wall, and went through his stuff.

Mark felt it was a massive violation and it sent him into a tailspin; as a result, his mental health seemed to plummet. He was usually so bright and chirpy – an early riser and an all-round energetic person – but he became upset and withdrawn. I tried to comfort him but he became very paranoid. He was convinced the police were delving into his background and income. Some people who'd been arrested later had the charges against them dropped, including Mark, which raised a few eyebrows, but it wasn't unheard of for activists to get charges dropped, and it didn't always make sense who got charged and who didn't, so I really thought nothing of it.

Other activists involved in the planning still had charges against them. Everyone presumed the police had messed up and Mark had been lucky. But he didn't seem happy about it. Afterwards, he acted as though he carried the weight of the world on his shoulders.

Yorkshire, June–October 2009

I moved onto my narrowboat in June, and Mark helped me repair a few things, including a leak in the water tank. I'd always expected him to be so much handier than he actually was. We spent a lot of time together on the boat throughout the summer and it was blissful.

'It feels like a respite from life,' he remarked one day. 'I can only fully relax when I'm here.'

I wondered if he'd been taking too much on, planning all the logistics for the recent demos.

Maybe he's just burnt-out.

At times it felt exhausting, trying to hold him together. The only time he was happy was when we'd moored up and there wasn't a phone signal. Instead, we'd drink wine, watch films and stroll down to the local canalside pub. It was idyllic, although I was worried about him.

At this point, I'd become less involved with activism and had decided to return to university to study for a degree. Unlike me, Mark was still heavily involved in protests, although something had shifted. Some days he just wanted to curl up and fade away.

Mark had turned forty along with eight or nine other activists so, towards the end of summer, we planned a huge joint 69ers birthday party – they'd all been born in 1969 – at a farm in Herefordshire. They'd put a band together, and Mark had taken guitar lessons for six months so he could join in. Although he appeared the same to outsiders, beneath his façade I'd been watching him slowly unravel.

On the Friday night of the party, Mark did a DJ set. Everyone was dancing and having a great time, but I could tell he was broken.

We stayed up late but instead of the happy, fun-loving Mark I knew, he seemed like a shell of his old self, and he started to confide in friends that he wasn't doing well.

For the band's Saturday night gig, Mark stood up on stage and performed. They played classic covers and, at one point, Mark took centre stage and sang a Johnny Cash number, as Merrick played drums behind him. I even got up on stage and sang a couple of numbers with them.

But after that evening, he fell apart. We were staying in my campervan but I couldn't get him out of bed; he hid under the duvet. It felt as though the previous months had been leading up to this.

What's happening to him?

On Sunday, we had a day of silly games, but he hid away in the van. Everyone asked where he was and I didn't know what to say. I'd been holding him together for months, but now other people had started to notice. He hung around in the background, and everyone could see he was struggling.

Naomi

(Officer: Mark Stone)

London, 2009

I'd been travelling and had visited Russia, China and Japan, working on community projects. It was during this that I met my partner, who later became my wife.

Mark seemed down and was so much less animated than normal. Lisa told me he'd been struggling and she was really worried about him.

There was a big birthday party. Sitting around the campfire with Mark, he seemed sad, anxious and extremely worried about something. I knew he'd been suffering with his back – he was in a lot of pain – but he also seemed very withdrawn; it wasn't like him because he'd always been so open.

'I feel like I should be stronger, Naomi,' he began.

'There's more than one way to be strong, Mark, and it's okay to talk to people. You've just got to really look after yourself. Look around, you're with friends.'

Mark shook his head.

'I'm going to go away. I'm going to see my brother.'

I nodded; he often visited Ian in Ohio, but then he added: 'I'm not sure if I'm coming back.'

I thought he'd burnt himself out because he'd campaigned for years. Also, it was his fortieth birthday so part of me wondered if this was some sort of midlife crisis. However, I was baffled when he said he might not return.

He will come back because we're all here; Lisa's here, all his friends are here. Of course he'll come back.

But I was also extremely worried.

London, winter 2009

I went out for a meal with a mutual friend of the person I'd spoken to while travelling the previous spring.

They asked me pretty much the same question: 'Do you think Mark is spying on us?'

Even though I'd been asked before, it still wouldn't compute. I argued against the idea but my friend insisted.

How can it be? Where is all this coming from? I thought.

I'd known Mark for years and he'd been with us all this time. All these people had been in relationships with him.

No way.

I couldn't even begin to process the information.

Lisa
(Officer: Mark Stone)

Nottingham, October 2009

By autumn, I was becoming extremely concerned about Mark. I was about to move the boat to Nottingham so we could live closer to each other, as we'd planned. But he was making new plans.

'I need to get away. I'm going to America to stay with my brother for a while.'

'Okay ... how long are you going for?'

Mark seemed cagey about a timescale and it left me unsettled.

I had gone back to university as a mature student and was regularly travelling to London to attend lectures. This new direction for me was one we'd discussed at length, as I always talked to Mark about important decisions, and he was very supportive. I'd bought some tickets for a Pixies gig at Brixton Academy and was really excited because they were one of my favourite bands, so this concert was a big deal to me. I was disappointed when Mark said he was going to the States straightaway, but he agreed to put his trip off until after the gig. In the run-up to it, he did things that seemed so final, they rang alarm bells. He packed up his stuff, sold his truck and said he'd handed in his notice at work and on his rented house.

'You are coming back though, aren't you?'

Mark nodded.

'Yes, of course I'm coming back. I'd never leave you.'

But he didn't seem stable, so I didn't know what to think. The night before he flew, it was the Pixies gig, but Mark started behaving very strangely.

'I think I'm being followed,' he panicked, sounding irrational.

We'd been staying over in a friend's spare room and we were going to meet there and then go to the gig. I'd been in college and realised I'd missed a few calls from him, so I rang back.

'It's me, what's up?'

'It's a bit complicated. I'll tell you when I see you, but I'm going to have to change where we're meeting. I don't want to tell you over the phone, so I'll call you from a call box when I get there. But I'm in Brixton in a pub.'

I travelled over to Brixton, and Mark rang to tell me which pub he was in. But as soon as I walked in, I spotted him looking over his shoulder.

'Right, we're not staying, we're leaving for another pub,' he decided.

I didn't understand.

'Lisa, I can't go into detail, but I'm being followed. We're just going to go to another pub and see if I'm still being followed.'

With that, he got up then we left and walked to another pub.

I tried to ask what was wrong and who was following us.

Mark looked at me.

'I think it's the police. Or maybe it's not the police – maybe it's some dodgy blokes from my past.'

We went from one pub to the next, not staying in any of them very long. We were walking down the street when Mark pulled me behind a phone box.

'We have to hide,' he hissed, dragging me behind a wall.

'Mark,' I gasped. 'I'm really worried about you. I think you're losing your mind.'

He shook his head.

'Maybe I am, maybe I'm not, but I've seen these guys in several different pubs and wherever we go, I see them again.'

I felt exasperated.

'But we can't just keep going around Brixton like this, going in and out of different pubs.'

'They just went past,' he warned. 'That's why I had to pull you behind the wall ... there's two guys.'

I was confused.

'Why would they be following you, why would the police be following you?'

'I know, it doesn't make sense to me, but it's definitely happening,' he insisted, becoming visibly distressed. 'Look, you go to the gig. I'm not coming, I'm going to go to the airport now.'

I was pissed off because I'd been looking forward to it for ages, and I wanted to go with him, not on my own, and what he was saying didn't make any sense.

'But if they are following you now, then they'll follow you to the airport.'

Mark thought for a moment.

'Listen,' I told him. 'If they follow us to the gig then they'll need a ticket to get in. They won't get in without one. Let's have a drink in there and if they come into the gig then something weird is happening. Unless they have a ticket or they're cops then they won't get in.'

Mark agreed.

'Okay, let's go.'

We went into Brixton Academy, bought a pint and sat down at the bar; for the first time that evening, Mark seemed to relax, although he still checked all around.

'Okay, they're definitely not here, so I can stay – I can stay for the evening.'

Although the gig was brilliant, he sat at the bar all night.

Oh my God, he really has lost his mind.

I threw myself into dancing, but I couldn't enjoy it because I couldn't stop thinking about him. I was concerned for his mental health. The only thing that had happened had been his arrest over Ratcliffe and the police raid, but how could that lead to him being followed around Brixton? I didn't believe he was being followed but I knew he believed it. Then I wondered.

Is it really something from his past catching up?

As the gig spilled out onto the street, Mark seemed anxious.

'Let's take different Tubes home,' he insisted. 'Let's split up and reconvene at the house.'

In the end, we caught the same Tube but once we were back near home, Mark insisted on taking a walk to be sure we weren't being watched.

'I'll go up the high street and get us a takeaway; I'll walk around the block a couple of times, then I'll meet you at the house.'

I waited up for him. Our friend who we were staying with sat with me, a little bemused.

'Sorry, Mark's in a bit of a weird mood,' I tried to explain.

He was gone for half an hour before he returned with food. We eventually went to bed, where I held him in my arms and he seemed to relax. The following morning, Mark woke early.

'I know my plane isn't until later, but I'm going now,' he decided, sounding in a rush.

I was stunned; he wouldn't even let me go to the airport with him.

'I'll stay in touch,' he promised, kissing me goodbye. 'I've ditched my mobile in a bin because I'm never going to use it again but I'll be in touch and let you know my new number. I'm not leaving you; I just need to go away and clear my head.'

Part of me felt relieved because I thought he was flipping out and needed to go away to rest and recuperate. However, another part was utterly terrified I'd never see him again.

Nottingham, autumn 2009

A few weeks passed and Mark stayed in touch. At first, he'd ring on Skype and I didn't know where he was calling from. Mark said he'd been paranoid when he'd left but that he felt much better and would email. Even though his communication was more sporadic, it still came, so I never felt as though he'd left me.

'I need to stay here a couple of months. I'll probably stay with Ian until Christmas,' he told me.

Then he said he'd got himself a flat in America.

Was he coming back?

Mark sent me an address but I never wrote to him there because he was always calling, texting or emailing.

'I am coming back; I'm not staying forever,' he promised.

I even suggested he get some counselling, but he refused.

I had moved my boat to Nottingham, just as we'd always planned. Mark had left his house so suddenly that it was in a bit of a state so I spent time clearing and bagging up things I thought he might want when he came home. The autumn was turning into a bitterly cold winter. Mark was still away and I was living alone on my boat. Life was difficult and I felt lower than I'd ever been. Grief for my dad came bubbling up to the surface, but I took solace in my friends and in my studies. I remembered a man called Rod Richardson. He'd been living in a housing co-op with my friends in 2003 when he'd suddenly upped and left, saying he was emigrating to Australia. He'd sent a few postcards but hadn't really kept in touch. Rod left people with a distinct feeling that something was odd. One minute he'd been everyone's best mate, the next he'd gone and hadn't stayed in touch.

One day I said, 'If you disappear then I'll think it's a situation like Rod Richardson – I'll think you're a cop or something.'

Mark was appalled and I felt bad saying it when his mental state was so fragile. I didn't mean it; I was just trying to shock him into coming home.

Nottingham, end of November 2009

Mark rang to tell me he was back in the UK and he'd be in Nottingham for a day and a night.

'But don't tell anyone because I don't want anyone to know I'm around.'

I was absolutely stunned; he was supposed to be in the US. It all sounded so cloak and dagger.

'But you're in America! Why are you in Nottingham for a day? That's really strange.'

It seemed utterly ludicrous, then he explained.

'I can't really talk about it but to make sure I've a job to come back to, I need a medical and an interview, and I've got to do it in person. They don't know I'm in America.'

Mark sounded a bit cagey but I was happy I'd get to see him. He arrived in the morning but didn't want to leave the boat; we caught up and he seemed a little more like his old self, if a bit subdued. We spent the rest of the day and evening together but then his story changed.

'I'm actually around for a few days. I'll pop over to Ireland and see Mum, then I'll go back to America.'

It had all seemed a bit weird and unfeasible but I went along with it because it was a thread of him that I could hold on to.

Nottingham, early January 2010

Mark had returned to the US but said he planned to move back to the UK sometime in January. A few days before my uni exams, he called.

'Guess what, guess where I am?' he asked, his voice brimming with excitement.

'I don't know, where?' I smiled, joining in.

'I'm on a boat; I bought a narrowboat! I'm on *my* boat right now!'

'But I thought you were in America.'

Mark laughed.

'Yeah, I wanted to surprise you. I'm back!'

I sighed.

'Mark, I've got exams. I did tell you.'

'I know I said I wasn't going to mess with your head before your exams, but I'm so excited and I'm desperate to see you. Are you sure I can't see you before?'

'Oh, for fuck's sake! Okay,' I said, relenting. 'Come here, I've pretty much finished my revision, but I'm getting on a train to London in the morning. But come and tell me all about it.'

He explained he'd bought the narrowboat before seeing it.

'It's in Lincoln. After your exams, you can come and see it, but please don't tell anyone where I am.'

He seemed excited to be back and, although he wasn't making a great deal of sense, at least he sounded happier.

Following my exams, I went to visit him on his boat – *Tamarisk* – moored in Lincoln Marina, where Mark told me he had a plan.

'I'm going to bring my boat to Nottingham, then we can do what we'd always planned to do – we can live together.'

He sounded excited; I was so relieved to have him back that I put out of my mind how crazy it all seemed. Part of me was also annoyed.

You can't just bounce straight back into my life, having put me through all that worry, and then pretend nothing's wrong.

I was scarred, but I desperately wanted us to move on together.

'I'll make it up to you, Lisa. I promise.'

Lincoln, January–February 2010

Before we moved his boat from Lincoln, I remembered a pub I'd once been to with an old boyfriend.

'I'll take you there,' I told Mark.

The pub was called The Jolly Brewer, so we nipped in for a drink. We bumped into an activist we knew. However, Mark looked distinctly awkward when he spotted him. The man turned to Mark.

'I wondered if I'd bump into you again after seeing you in November.'

Then he made reference to having met Mark's brother, who'd been with him. I was quite drunk at this point but not enough to know it didn't make sense.

'What?' I said, turning to Mark. 'You didn't tell me about that.'

On our way back to the boat, I began to question him.

'You were in the UK ... with your brother? I've always wanted to meet your brother, but you didn't tell me and you didn't bring him to meet me. You didn't tell me you were looking at boats. You didn't tell me you were coming up to Lincoln to buy a narrowboat and that your brother was with you, and he was helping you buy it. You told me you were back for a medical ...'

Mark sighed.

'I *was* back for a medical. I don't know why I didn't tell you, I'm really sorry ... I've come back for you; I've bought a boat so I can be with you ... Look, I'm just not very good at explaining what's going on ... I'm not in a good place; it's to do with my mental health.'

Things didn't add up. There were inconsistencies – holes in Mark's story.

Is it me?

It was the beginning of the end.

BELINDA AND BOB

Bob and Belinda on a visit to Belinda's parents in north Wales, 1987

Bob and Belinda in a beer garden in Wales, 1988

Two pictures of Bob in the countryside, taken by Belinda, 1988

Bob at the Cambridge Folk Festival, 1988

Bob at Belinda's house, 1988

Tickets from some of the many gigs Belinda and Bob attended together

John (in the blue shirt on the left) sabbing a grouse shoot, 1989

John on a stall at the Anti McDonald's Fayre, 1989

Helen and John on holiday together in Scotland, 1990

John, clean-cut and celebrating his (fake) birthday after his deployment ended, 1992

confront my past and my future. I know I
can keep ~~retracing~~ travelling, but even I don't
think I can keep on running. The thing
is hels I don't know when I'll stop. I do know
I'll never forget you and all the precious times
we've had together. I wish, I still I could have
a home a kids with you + tell them the things
I was never told and give them the love I
never had a wrap you all around me. Those
feelings make me sad. I had intended not to say
these things helen, It's how I feel, but I know
my feelings are no good to you from 5000
miles away.
I want to wish you every single ounce of good
luck, great happiness, peace, fun, safety
a wonderful future - I want all those things
for you hels,
Don't take this as audacious helen, but if
I ever stop running I'll write + tell you. +
hope at least I can keep your friendship. I
can't do that if I still love you though!
I will still try helen, but I'm not asking you
to wait while I do. Helen, my darling,
I love everything about you, I love you,

Extract of a tearstained letter from John to Helen, 1992

John confronted by Helen at Sydney Airport, 2016

Alison and Mark (on the left) on a delegation to the West Belfast Fleadh, 1995

Mark playing Subbuteo 'at home', 1996

Two pictures of Alison and Mark on holiday in Crete, 1996

Mark and Alison on holiday
at Centre Parcs with Alison's
friends, 1996

Mark on a camping trip to
Scotland, photo taken by
Alison, 1997

Mark on holiday in Southeast Asia, photo taken by Alison, 1998

Mark relaxing 'at home', 1998

LISA AND MARK

Lisa and Mark on a trip out from the protest camp against the building of the Kárahnjúkar dam in Iceland, 2005

Lisa and Mark on holiday in the Lake District, 2005

Lisa and Mark in fancy dress in the Environmental Campaigns Tent at Glastonbury, 2008

Lisa and Mark at the big joint 40th birthday party, 2009
(© Sophie Cooke)

Mark on his birthday in
Italy, shortly before Lisa
confronted him about his
passport, 2010

Lisa and Mark on the
Marmolada peak, the highest
point in the Dolomites,
2010. This was their last
trip together before Lisa
discovered Mark's true
identity a few weeks after
returning to the UK

Naomi and Mark on a cycling holiday in Northumberland, 2005

Mark in a 2012 issue of *Rolling Stone* magazine. The photo was taken by Naomi on their holiday in Northumberland in 2005 (not in 2004 as the magazine caption suggests) and was provided by Mark to the magazine. Despite this, he continued to deny his relationship with Naomi at the time

Naomi and Mark at a family wedding, 2005. In the top photo, Mark avoids the official photographer; in the bottom photo, an unofficial snap, he looks more relaxed

Protestors at the Royal Courts of Justice, 2013

Banners outside the High Court, 2015

Lincoln to Nottingham, February 2010

We moved Mark's boat from Lincoln to Nottingham. On our way into the city, it was lunchtime so I suggested mooring up on the canalside, which was close to the magistrates' courts and local police station.

'No!' Mark replied in a fluster and quickly pulled the curtains closed. 'I can't stop here. The police will see me.'

My heart sank.

Oh, no. I thought that paranoia about being followed and spied on was done.

'I'll tell you what,' he said. 'You go out, get some food, and then we'll set off – I don't want anyone to see me.'

Against my better judgement, I went along with it.

In the days and weeks that followed, with his boat moored next to mine, Mark's confidence seemed to return. However, although he spoke of the future, he still seemed set adrift.

'What am I going to do with my life? What am I going to do for a living? I've got no skills, nothing I can build a career on.'

'But you *do* have a career,' I insisted, referring to his rope access work.

He shook his head.

'Oh no, I never really got anywhere with that. I'm done with all that.'

Then I remembered the job – the one he'd had a medical for, but Mark dismissed it as though it wasn't going to happen.

Nothing made sense.

Mark told me an old family friend was setting up a business, delivering motorbikes across the world.

'I need to buy a van I can get a couple of motorbikes in the back of.'

He bought a white Mercedes Sprinter van and started going away for a couple of weeks at a time. Not long afterwards, he seemed to be mulling something over.

'I might change my name. I'm sick of walking around with my dad's name – he was an arsehole and I never really knew him. I could revert to Mum's name; I reckon Ian's going to do the same.'

I didn't think much about it, but he'd just planted the seed of having a different name.

Winter mountaineering trip, Scotland, February 2010

We went away again; I couldn't put my finger on it, but things didn't seem right and I still felt bruised from when he'd left.

One day, on our winter trip with friends, Mark piped up from the corner of the room.

'Do you want to see a picture of my mum?'

I was in the middle of a conversation with a friend when he said it out of the blue, but I'd never seen a photo of his mum so I went over to look.

'Come over here; come, come,' he said, beckoning me over.

I stared at her picture.

'She looks just like me, doesn't she?' He grinned proudly.

And she did. It looked like Mark's face on an older woman.

What was all that about?

It was the first and only time I saw a picture of his mum.

'Why did you do that?' I asked later.

Mark shrugged.

'I feel I haven't been sharing things with you.'

That's when I made a decision.

'Okay, well, we've been together all this time; I think I'd like to meet your family. I know you've said your family is complicated, but it's about time.'

'Yeah, you will. My brother's coming back at the end of this year for a friend's wedding. I'll make sure he comes over and we'll meet up. We'll have a big family gathering.'

For the first time, it felt very necessary to me.

Nottingham, March 2010

Mark began to pursue another woman and they were messaging each other. Although I loved him, we weren't exclusive, and he'd told me about it. However, it soon became clear he was telling us each a different story.

'I'm seeing this other person but I'm only doing it because you've always wanted us to do open relationships,' he insisted. 'Just say the word and I'll stop.'

'No, it'll be okay as long as we're honest with each other.'

Somehow, this relationship felt different because I knew he wasn't being entirely honest with me. I didn't trust him any more. I was no longer as confident in our relationship as I'd been before his break-down. I wondered if he was about to leave and run off with the other woman. It felt as though he was playing us off against each other. I couldn't make sense of his actions – it was as if he was pressing the self-destruct button. One minute he'd push me away and the next he'd bend over backwards to try to make things up to me.

I began to seriously doubt myself.

Naomi

(Officer: Mark Stone)

Bristol, February 2010

In spite of what he'd told me about possibly not returning from the States, Mark did come back to the UK, bought a narrowboat and moored it next to Lisa's on a canal in Nottingham. Then he started seeing another woman. By this time, I was busy with my new life in Bristol, but I was still in touch with them both. I became aware that Lisa was struggling with Mark's seemingly erratic, unreliable and paranoid behaviour. I was worried about her so we met up in Leeds. She didn't seem herself at all and, at one point, almost had a panic attack. I felt angry with Mark.

What the hell is he doing, and what's going on?

I'd never seen Lisa like that before and it unnerved me.

Lisa

(Officer: Mark Stone)

Italy, June 2010

'I've been persuaded to go and help out with the International Animal Rights gathering in July, in Italy,' Mark announced one day.

I laughed. After all, he'd been the one to introduce fish and seafood into my life. I'd been vegan and then vegetarian when I met him; he had led me astray.

'Animal rights, you? You're the least veggie person I know!'

'I know, but they really need someone to come and run a climbing workshop. I can't think of anything more fun than going to Italy with you, doing these workshops, and then we can go off climbing in the mountains.'

I agreed; it sounded amazing. We packed our camping gear into the back of his van. We'd planned to go and do some via ferrata in the Dolomites, which is a style of climbing where you clip onto steel cables attached to the rockface. However, before that, Mark had a job working on a wind farm in Germany and I was going to join him a month later in Italy by train, where he'd pick up and we'd head into the mountains. First, he travelled to Berlin to meet up with friends, where he was joined by the other woman. They spent a week together, which made me quite jealous; I was more relaxed when he started his new job. Then he told me he was going to Italy early for climbing with some other friends of ours and asked if I could come, but I couldn't because I had exams. I was confused, because he knew that, and it wasn't what we'd planned to do. Then he said he was going to fly briefly back to Germany to finish his wind turbine job but the Icelandic dust cloud caused by a volcanic eruption happened, grounding flights, and Mark said he was stuck. He seemed really upset about being stuck in Italy. Things felt odd – his movements didn't make sense.

Italy, early July 2010

I eventually travelled to Italy and we had the most incredible week climbing in the mountains. It was super romantic. I still felt insecure, but Mark seemed to be pulling out all the stops to make things right.

'You're the love of my life,' he insisted.

It was just what I needed to hear.

At one point, Mark went off for a cycle ride. He had a fancy road bike with him and we'd passed countless cyclists who were slugging it up the hills. Mark wanted to cycle several mountain passes, along the famous Sellaronda route.

'I'll tell you what,' he said, turning to me. 'Why don't you drop me at the bottom of this mountain pass, drive around and then wait for me at the top of the last pass, and I'll do it all on my bike?'

He climbed out of the van and I drove up to the top and parked in a beautiful space on the side of the mountain pass. I was sitting there, waiting for him to catch me up on his bike, when I opened up the glove compartment. I don't know what I was looking for – my shades, I think – but really, I was looking for an excuse to have a root around. And that's when I found his passport. It was an old-style passport and had expired two years earlier. On it was a space for the number of dependents; next to that it said 'one'.

I felt as though the air had been stolen from my lungs. I glanced down at his name; it said Mark Kennedy, not Mark Stone. In my mind, I tried to explain away the different surname because of what he'd said about his dad or his dodgy past. But the dependent bit threw me. He'd always spoken about not wanting children, yet he already had a kid.

What the fuck?

I couldn't see straight; I was numb with panic. I rooted deeper through the glovebox and discovered an iPhone. There was no password protection; I scrolled through it quickly.

He's got a kid. Mark has got a kid.

I discovered photos of him and another woman in Berlin. I already knew about her.

That's not what I'm looking for – I know about that – I don't care about that right now.

A kid? He has a kid?

I frantically opened the emails, all the time checking the wing mirror so that Mark didn't creep up on me. The phone's battery was about to die and I was desperate to find something – anything – to explain this child.

My whole world had been flipped on its head.

Then two emails from two children popped up and both mentioned the name 'Dad'. The children were called David and Mairead.

Jesus Christ, he's got two kids. Who the fuck is this person?

I climbed out of the van and staggered up the mountain pass to sit on a rock in the steep-sided valley. I looked down but everything started to move – as though the ground beneath me wasn't solid. I felt as though I had motion sickness and wanted to throw up.

Who is this man?

No one else knows where I am. It's just me and him, and I don't know who he is. Am I in danger?

All these thoughts flashed through my mind.

Could it be something to do with his past, or is he just a lying shit with a wife and kids?

I didn't know what to do or if I was safe, I only knew I needed more information.

Suddenly, Mark reappeared back at the van, so I buried everything I'd just learnt and walked down to him. My instinct told me not to confront him there and then.

Keep quiet, don't say anything; not yet.

For the first time, I felt real fear.

Mark approached happily, still glowing from his bike ride.

'Can you take some pictures of me as I come up the pass?' he asked.

I took some photos. After a while, he strolled over.

'What's the matter? You're a bit quiet.'

'No, I'm fine.' I smiled.

But Mark knew something was wrong.

We climbed back in the van and carried on driving, looking for somewhere to go for dinner. As he sat behind the wheel, staring ahead at the road, I studied him.

Who the fuck are you?

I was frightened; I knew I had to tell someone where I was.

'I need to make a phone call,' I said casually.

Mark pulled up at a pizzeria and I climbed out of the van as he went in to order. I walked away from it to ring a close friend of mine called Jan who was also an activist. I told her what I'd just found, but her reaction frightened me – she sounded worried.

'Just be very careful and let me know where you are at all times,' she insisted.

'I don't know if I'm going to ask him about it or not.'

'Whatever you do, I'm here for you. But let me know where you are or I'll worry.'

Over the next two days, I regularly texted Jan to tell her where we were. I was steeling myself. I wanted to ask him, but I couldn't sleep.

I don't know who I'm lying next to.

Could he be an undercover cop? MI5? A gangster? It all sounds so ridiculous!

Mark was deeply asleep, so I climbed out of the van. We'd parked in a picnic spot on a mountain pass in the Dolomites; there was a bench outside so I sat down. The moonlight had bathed the cliff in a beautiful silver light. The sky was clear and full of stars. It looked incredible; I watched as a shooting star soared by.

I'm in paradise but I'm also in hell.

I continued to sit and watch the sun rise, painting the white mountains bright orange and red.

If this were a film, it would be too cinematic to be realistic.

I was surrounded by such vast beauty with my whole world falling apart.

The following morning was Mark's birthday, and the day after we were due to go to the animal rights gathering. My emotions were bursting at the seams. I didn't want to ruin his birthday but I needed answers. I was all over the place. I knew I couldn't go to the gathering if I didn't know who he was.

We went to climb a mountain route and he started taking selfies. He'd always been a bit of a poseur, but this was the first time it occurred to me: *Is there someone he wants to show these photos to and that's why he doesn't want me in them? Is he going to show them to his kids?*

'Why do you want pictures without me in them?' I asked bluntly.

Mark turned to look at me.

'Oh, I want to show my brother what a cool mountain I've just climbed.'

'Yes, but I could still be in those pictures.'

I'm certain Mark thought I was jealous because of his other relationships.

As we reached the top of the mountain, he pulled out a bottle of expensive whisky for us to drink. I felt utterly torn; we were having the most amazing time but inside I was in total turmoil.

We called in at a nearby bar to get a drink. The next day we were due to leave for the animal rights gathering. I was running out of time – it was my last chance. I had to confront him.

As Mark walked back from the bar with two beers in his hands, I looked up.

'Who's David Kennedy?'

His face blanched and he swayed a little as though he'd just been punched.

'I don't know what you mean,' he said, trying to compose himself as he settled the drinks down on the table. 'What are you on about?'

I stared at him.

'You know there's been something up for the last few days; well, I looked at your phone and saw messages from someone called David Kennedy, who calls you Dad. So, who's David Kennedy?'

Mark began to shake; *all* the blood had drained from his face.

'You have to tell me.'

He nodded and I noticed his hands were trembling.

'I will tell you, give me a minute,' he replied. 'I will tell you, just not here. It's too public.'

'All right then,' I said, scouring his face for clues.

Mark took a sip of his beer.

'Let me just finish this. We'll go back to the van and I'll tell you everything, I promise.'

I knew he was trying to buy extra time, so I drank my beer quickly and walked back to the van. Mark followed soon after. He began to cry, so we climbed inside the van, and he told me things he'd never spoken of before. He wept as he explained this was all to do with his chequered past.

'It's about those days and I want to tell you. I know I've not been honest about my past and now I'm going to come clean.'

At last, this is what's been wrong all this time. Now, finally, he's going to open up.

I waited.

'I had a partner, who I used to do all the drug smuggling with. We had a van ...'

I nodded – a signal for him to carry on.

Mark explained his 'work' partner had been the only person, besides his brother, who he trusted with his life. They'd been trafficking drugs from Pakistan and from Morocco.

'There was this drugs deal that went wrong.'

He said someone had pulled a gun on them both. I remembered he'd once told me someone had pulled a gun on him, but I'd never heard the full story, until now.

'... Anyway, they pulled this gun out, and my friend, he ...' Mark broke off again – his whole body racked with sobs. 'H ... h ... he was shot, right in front of me.'

I waited for him to compose himself. Finally, he did.

'They let me g ... g ... go, so I came back to the UK and then I went to Ireland and told his wife Mary that he'd been killed.'

But it didn't explain the children.

'What about them?' I asked.

'Before he was killed, I made a promise; a promise I'd look after his kids, and I have.'

So, the children weren't his, but his best friend's.

'This all happened when they were little so they've grown up believing I'm their dad. They even call me Dad ...'

And they'd even taken his 'other' surname of Kennedy, it seemed. He told me it was his mum's name, but that he'd had to change it after this incident and that Stone was his father's surname. Mark began to crumble as he explained how badly he'd done in his life.

'I've been a terrible father to them,' he admitted. 'But I've tried my best, I really have ...'

There was enough detail for me to believe him. But he seemed so distraught that I felt I couldn't press him further. Instead, I held him in my arms as he cried through the night and told me how much he'd loved his friend. He poured his heart out.

'The thing is,' he said, looking up at me, his eyes raw from crying. 'I always knew it would catch up with me and one day these kids are going to be told I'm not their real dad. I've been a useless, absent father who hasn't been there for them and I hate myself ... I really do, because that's what my dad was like.'

I nodded; I believed everything because Mark had finally opened up to me about the secret trauma from his past. I'd got to the bottom of things and now we could move forward. The raw emotion of his confession had affected me deeply.

If anything, now the truth was out, it would only bring us closer.

The following day, I rang my friend.

'It's all okay, Jan. I can't tell you all the details now, but it's okay – there's an explanation, and I think it's going to be all right. He's not a bad person.'

We later attended the International Animal Rights gathering and had a good time. I met some lovely Italians, who became our friends and we all went climbing together in some beautiful places. We told them we'd both be back soon so we could all go to the Alps.

I pushed my questions away. I'd been so silly to doubt him. I knew him better than I'd ever known him. I felt relieved and happy.

Nottingham, August 2010

We returned home and life continued. At one point, Mark went off on his own in his boat, but weirdly he bought new bedding and huge bags of shopping before he left.

'Blimey, how long are you going away for?' I teased.

He said he wanted to practise doing locks and get to grips with canal life so he went off in one direction, and I went in the other. After a week, I contacted him.

'I think there's still so much we need to talk about,' I began.

'Okay, I'll be back, just give me a couple of days.'

Eventually, I went to where his boat was moored – on the Trent and Mersey canal. But as I boarded it, I spotted a bottle of gin on the side. He didn't drink gin.

That's weird.

Then I noticed a bottle of tonic.

Someone's been here.

I thought it might have been the other woman, so I asked.

'No,' he told me.

'Why have you got gin and tonic then?'

'Oh, I just fancied one.'

I didn't believe him. I stood up and went over to the bottle.

'Well, I fancy a G&T so that's handy,' I said, pouring myself a large one.

Mark went off to make a phone call, leaving me alone on the boat, so I began to search through the drawers, looking for clues. As I rummaged, I discovered an old Nokia phone. Again, I thought it weird because Mark had an iPhone and a BlackBerry. I opened up the messages but there was only one in the sent file; it was to someone called Edel. The message said he was trying really hard to make everything work and to keep everyone happy. But he said it was hard because he was juggling a lot of things. He'd signed off with:

Bear with me.
Mark

The 'juggling lots of things' was a phrase he'd often used with me, so it immediately stood out. I decided not to mention it but bank it along with all the other things that were slowly adding up but leading nowhere. However, it wouldn't go away. Instead, a few weeks later I turned to ask him.

'So, who's Edel then?'

Again, his face blanched.

'Oh, that's the kids' mum. I told you about her.'

'Yes, you did tell me about her ... but you told me she was called Mary, so why is she now called Edel?'

He's lying.

Mark was evasive, saying that he found it all hard to talk about, and that he was protecting himself because the secrets he held could still get him into serious trouble. I didn't know what to think. I so desperately wanted things to be okay.

'Let's go to Italy again,' he said. 'Everything was brilliant when we were in Italy, but this time we'll have lots more mountain adventures. We'll go and see our animal rights friends in Milan ... we'll take them off climbing. You mean the world to me, and I want to do everything I can possibly do to make things right with us.'

He also explained he wanted to knock things on the head with the other woman.

'She wants more than I can give her. We could go back to Italy and do all the things we wanted to do in July but ran out of time for. I'll prove to you how much you mean to me.'

Maybe all my doubts are unfounded. Maybe it's just me being jealous. Only deep down, I knew it wasn't.

Helen

(Officer: John Barker)

London, summer 2010

It was a warm summer's evening when an old friend, Brian, called round. He had a letter for me from a woman called Rosa. I'd known her years before, initially through the Legal Defence and Monitoring Group, but mostly through a protest group, Reclaim the Streets (RTS). She had been in a relationship with a fellow RTS activist called Jim Sutton, but then he had disappeared in summer 2000. Later that year I had bumped into Rosa near Kings Cross and she'd told me she was very worried about Jim; his mental health hadn't been great and he'd set off travelling alone from Turkey to South Africa, but had gone missing. I'd been alarmed by the similarities with John's story. Around the time of his disappearance, a few people had speculated that maybe Jim had been a cop, but that rumour was dispelled a couple of years later when Jim and Rosa were seen together with a baby at the Kingston Green Fair.

Brian handed me the letter and we talked. It turned out that he now lived in the same region of the country as Rosa and had bumped into her. She and Jim had moved there a while back with their two children, but then later Rosa had fled with the kids to a women's refuge to escape Jim. She wanted to meet up with me, but most importantly she wanted people to know that Jim had been an undercover cop when he was in Reclaim the Streets. She had been trying for a long time to find a safe way to let me know.

Lisa

(Officer: Mark Stone)

Shambala Festival, Northamptonshire, end of August 2010

I went to the festival with my friend Jan – the one I'd rung from the Dolomite mountains in Italy. At Shambala, I heard a story about a man called Jim Sutton, who had been part of the Reclaim the Streets group and had had a relationship with a fellow activist.

It had transpired Sutton had been an undercover police officer with something called the Special Demonstration Squad – an undercover unit within Special Branch and part of the Metropolitan Police. An activist called Helen Steel had told a few people and word had spread. A friend called Greg knew Jim Sutton and had been utterly flabbergasted by his deceit. Everyone was talking about it. The main thing that stuck in my brain was the fact that Sutton had been in a relationship with a woman activist. It was the first time I'd heard of an undercover cop being in a close relationship with a campaigner. I'd heard of undercover police on demos or infiltrating meetings, but I'd never heard about one of them being someone's long-term partner.

Not just a one-night stand, but a proper relationship. And this hadn't happened during the Cold War but recently, in my familiar environmental activist scene. I found it utterly chilling.

Jan and I had an all-night conversation and she planted the seed that Mark might be the same. I was still resisting the possibility, although deep down I was sharing her questions.

'I'm busy trying to repair my relationship, not destroy it,' I insisted. 'This can't be what's going on with him. He's not a cop.'

'Please, Lisa, talk to someone else about it, tell them what you've found. I don't think Mark's a cop either, but wouldn't it be good to know for sure? You'll never be able to relax until you know what's going on.'

Jan's advice was sensible but, at the same time, I felt so close to working things out with Mark. We'd been through some tough times, but now we were slowly coming through it. I was deeply in love, and the pain it had been causing me that year, combined with the intense highs of our amazing trips to the mountains, had clouded my thinking. I doubted my ability to be rational, I lacked self-confidence and was clouded by the confusion Mark had sown in my mind. I felt like my brain had been slowly torn apart and I couldn't think clearly or make a decision.

Above everything, I wanted me and Mark to be okay; I was just desperate for everything to go back to the way it had been.

Italy, September 2010

Mark joked that this time he didn't need to hide his passport – he could be Mark Kennedy in front of me.

'You're the only one who knows my real name,' he remarked, after he'd booked us into a hotel on our return trip to Italy.

He made it feel like it was our secret – a bond between us.

We had an incredible time, and went climbing alone as well as with our friends. We scaled the highest mountain in the Dolomites – the 3,343-metre Marmolada. We went for three weeks but, by the end of the trip, Mark seemed stressed again. He was exhausted but we had to walk up to a high mountain hut where we'd planned to stay the night with our friends. On the way up, he began to struggle. I offered to carry some of his stuff but he refused. Then he stopped and sat on a rock.

'Just leave me here. I'll sleep here,' he insisted.

I was puzzled.

'Don't be daft, you can't sleep here. You'll die of exposure.'

I had to give him a pep talk just to get him to climb the rest of the way to the hut. Mark had no energy, which was weird for him. We had a gorgeous night with an amazing sunset and full-moon view over the high mountains. It was the most incredible location I'd ever spent the night – I was elated. The following day, my friends and I wanted to climb to the summit. But Mark didn't want to.

'I'm going to stay here. You guys go.'

Again, it was odd.

However, the following day, he woke early and seemed raring to go.

'Right, let's get down off this mountain,' Mark said, trying to hurry us along.

It was strange because he'd not mentioned we'd be leaving, especially not so quickly. With Mark at the front, he seemed to rush down. Once we'd reached the bottom, he said we had to drive home immediately.

'But we're in the Italian Alps,' I replied, a little lost for words.

'No, I've got to get back.'

I turned to face him.

'Why are you in such a hurry?'

'Work, Lisa. I've got work, and I've got a job starting on Monday.'

Today was already Saturday.

'That's crazy; you didn't say when we set off up this mountain that you had work on Monday.'

But Mark wouldn't listen or explain properly. Wearily, I climbed inside the van and Mark drove sixteen hours straight on the way back home, stopping only for a few hours' kip in a service station in the van. Once we'd reached the boat, he crashed out; he was up early the following morning, saying he had to leave because he had a three-week job to go to.

It had all felt so sudden and I crashed down to earth with a bump. I knew it wasn't normal; something wasn't right.

Leeds, late September 2010

I had some time with my thoughts after Mark left for work, trying to fit things together, but nothing made sense. The distance from Mark helped me realise things hadn't hung together. Late at night, I would pull out my laptop and start trawling the internet, looking for clues. The only thing I found was an entry for 192.com of a Mark and Edel Kennedy, living together in Orpington, Kent.

Did I have the right Mark? Was he married to this Edel, even?

Confusion reigned.

*

Not long afterwards, I visited Merrick at his house in Leeds. He was in the middle of a research project and was on a website called ancestry.co.uk. Merrick was helping his brother, looking up the names of First World War fighter pilots from their hometown. I watched as he searched.

'Can you get people's birth certificates up on there?' I asked, looking over his shoulder.

'Yeah, I can look up anything you like.'

'Do you think you could look up Mark's details?'

Merrick turned to me.

'Umm, yeah, I can, but why? Is there something you're not telling me?'

'I don't know,' I replied honestly.

Merrick put in Mark Stone's details but we couldn't find any records that matched.

'How about Mark Kennedy?' I suggested, remembering the passport.

He typed it in and a few different ones came up. We found one that seemed to fit because it had the names of his parents and his brother, Ian.

'How old is Ian?' Merrick asked, trying to cross-reference the dates.

I recalled Mark saying his brother was two years younger than him, which meant Ian would've been born in 1971. Merrick checked the details of the Ian who was linked to Mark Kennedy and the dates matched. I also knew he'd been born in South London, and this said Camberwell.

'Lisa, what's all this about?' Merrick asked as he clicked on the birth certificate.

We scrolled down and, written in black and white on Mark Kennedy's birth certificate, in the space where it said 'father's occupation', were the words 'police officer'.

What the fuck!

I looked at Merrick, as his eyes shifted from the screen to me.

'I think I need to tell you the whole story.'

I explained about Edel Kennedy and how I'd found an address in Kent in which she was listed as living with a Mark Kennedy. I retold the story Mark had shared with me about the kids and his friend and, as I said it out loud, I thought how implausible it suddenly sounded. We were both deeply concerned about the possibility that Mark could be some kind of undercover cop. 'But I still don't believe it,' Merrick added after I'd finished speaking. 'International drug smuggler sounds more plausible than police officer.'

And it was true; being a cop was so far removed from the Mark we all knew. We decided not to say anything until we knew for sure; to accuse someone of being a police officer in our circles would be so serious because mud, even if untrue, would stick. Instead, we decided to dig deeper. I knew it was such a potentially explosive thing to suggest and I needed to be sure before saying something to anyone else. The information on the website was limited, so we had to send off for a copy of one of Mark's children's birth certificates.

'This isn't looking good, but it's not conclusive', said Merrick about Mark's birth certificate on the screen. 'All it says is that Mark Kennedy's *dad* was a police officer.'

And it might not even be the right Mark Kennedy. I was trying to be as methodical as I could and think it through. His dad might have been a police officer but that didn't stop Mark being a drug dealer. The bit that was looking most likely was he'd lied about the two children. Now, everything pointed towards them being his own.

All we could do now was wait for the information to arrive in the post. I was off to a circus performance and a party with Naomi in Bristol. It was a really spectacular night in a disused police station in the middle of the city, which was very surreal, but a distraction I really needed. At the same, time I didn't want to share anything I'd found just yet. It was too soon. I tried to pretend things were normal, but she knew me well and I'm not sure I managed to hide my feelings.

Naomi

(Officer: Mark Stone)

Bristol, October 2010

When Lisa and Mark had left for Italy that summer, I felt relieved. I hoped it meant things had moved on for them both. However, when she returned, Lisa and I met in Bristol, and she was hugely unsettled. She said she had things to work out and questions to answer.

Oh no, what's he done?

I remembered what my friends had said about him possibly being a cop. By the autumn, things hadn't improved and there was a question I had to ask. One evening, before we went out, I managed to say it.

'This is going to sound really strange, but a couple of people have already asked me and I'm worried about what's going on.'

'Go on,' Lisa said.

I braced myself because I desperately didn't want to offend or upset her further.

'Do you think Mark is a police spy?'

The words had sounded ridiculous as they left my mouth.

Lisa looked across at me.

'Well, that's what I'm trying to prove, that he isn't,' she replied.

My stomach dipped and fell away.

Lisa

(Officer: Mark Stone)

Nottingham, October 2010

Mark was still away with work and afterwards had arranged to go to America to see his brother. So, when he rang, although all the questions about him were going through my head, I had to act and sound as though nothing was wrong. To do it, I tried to keep any phone conversations short. In the meantime, Merrick and I continued to search his true identity. Emotionally, I was in pieces – torn into fragments – but I was holding all the pieces together. However, when I was alone at night, I'd scream into my pillow. I felt split into three. There was part of me that was with the love of her life, having just had an amazing holiday in the mountains. The next person was going over the facts and trying to find out who the fuck this was and what was going on, and finally, the third person was just in a total blind panic. I needed to control that person as much as I could, and it took an immense amount of energy.

I was studying, long distance, at a uni in London, and I was also life-modelling at a college nearby. One day, around a week after looking up birth certificates with Merrick, I went to the class and took up my pose as the art students gathered around. My mind was racing with all I knew – or thought I knew – about Mark. After forty minutes there was a break, so I went to check my phone and found several missed calls from Merrick. He'd also left a voicemail, asking me to call him.

'Merrick, it's me, what's wrong?'

He took a deep breath.

'Mark's son's birth certificate has just come back. Lisa, it says the father's occupation … It's police officer.'

I gasped and lifted a hand to my mouth.

'I can't talk now,' I managed to say. 'Look, let's not get ahead of ourselves. Please don't talk to anyone else before you speak to me.'

'I won't,' Merrick promised. 'I'll come to meet you in Nottingham in the morning and we'll talk about it.'

I felt so grateful to him but I also knew it was too big for us to deal with on our own.

'We need to speak to someone else.'

I had to go and finish the life-modelling pose. I kept my body still while my mind raced at a hundred miles an hour. It was incredibly hard not to just slump on the ground or scream; I had to hold it together. After the class, I bought some cigarettes despite having given up smoking years previously. I sat waiting for my train home, smoking to numb the pain. I felt like I was in an altered state and the world looked unreal, like a cardboard cut-out.

Nottingham, 12 October, 2010

The following day, Merrick looked anxious as I met him off the train.

'Right, okay, what are we going to do?' he asked.

He'd brought the birth certificates with him – Mark's, his brother's and his son David's – and had come prepared. We had everything, now it was time to bring someone else in. Then I remembered Greg, Jan's friend, the one who'd heard about the deceit of undercover cop Jim Sutton. We needed to tell him.

Greg seemed a little surprised as he answered the door and found us both standing on his doorstep.

'Come in.'

As we passed, I turned to him.

'Look, I've got some quite full-on stuff I need to discuss with you.'

He took us to his room but before I began to explain, he told me he'd already spoken to Jan.

'She said you might come and speak to me because you might have found something out about Mark, but that's all I know – I don't know any details.'

Greg's face changed as I told him everything. Then we showed him the birth certificates. I explained there'd also been a reference to Mark's daughter's birth certificate. 'But we haven't got that yet,' I added.

To say Greg was shocked would be an understatement; he glanced in disbelief from me to the certificates laid out in front of him. He was totally overwhelmed.

'Okay,' he said, still trying to digest the news. 'Would it be all right if we had a few more minds on this? This is potentially massive, and we can't deal with it, just us alone.'

The three of us chatted about who we should ask. We agreed we needed a small group to look at it together but I was conscious I didn't want it to get out until we knew, without a doubt, that what we had was right. We had a lot of proof and it didn't look good, but it wasn't conclusive, especially if we didn't have the right Mark Kennedy to begin with.

All the pieces slotted together neatly, but what if we had the wrong jigsaw?

Also, it seemed far-fetched but what if Mark *had* been a drug smuggler and for a joke had written 'police officer' down as his occupation? I couldn't discount anything right now. There were far more questions than answers; the whole situation was mired in confusion. And fear. I was desperate to believe that we had it wrong, but I feared the worst.

We decided to speak to another old friend, Tim, who lived in a big housing co-op called NEDS, not far from Greg's place. Tim was one of my closest friends, so I trusted him. We all disappeared up to his bedroom for privacy. I shared my story once again. Everyone was mindful of the fact that I'd brought this to them and not the other way round, so they allowed me to tell it. I'd only just started when Tim reached out and covered my hand with his. Then he looked me straight in the eye.

'Before you go any further, I just want you to know I'm absolutely here for you. Whatever happens and however this turns out.'

His kindness made me want to weep. The level of consideration from all of them, but especially Tim, floored me; they'd all responded exactly as I needed them to. I felt a huge relief that I had my friends by my side – I knew they'd all got my back. We had asked another friend of mine, Steph, who lived in the same shared house, to join us as part of our growing team. I totally trusted her. Her reaction to the story – how Mark was possibly an undercover cop but had told me he'd been an international drug smuggler – was similar to my initial instinct. Steph shook her head.

'The international drug smuggler story is way more plausible,' she concluded.

I was so grateful for that because, whatever the truth, I realised I hadn't been the only person taken in by Mark's lies. He'd projected this 'bad boy turned good' persona so successfully that everyone had believed it and him. Mark had lived in Nottingham for seven years and everyone thought he was genuine. Greg had even lodged with him when his house had been raided by the police, so we'd all been invested in him in one way or another.

Over the following week or so, Merrick sent off for Mark's daughter's birth certificate and we searched for Mark's marriage certificate, but there was nothing on ancestry.co.uk. Then we remembered the Irish connection – his partner's name was Irish and so was his daughter's. We wondered if he'd got married to this woman Edel in Ireland. Merrick picked up the phone, called a mate in Dublin, and asked if he'd go to the records office to look for a marriage and birth certificate for Edel. He didn't tell him what it was about but asked his friend to trust him and not tell anyone.

The friend in Dublin came back with the goods after a few days. The marriage certificate also had the words 'police officer' under the occupation for Mark Kennedy.

Things were really stacking up and looking undeniably bad. Once my friends had the certificates, they were able to get an address and phone number for Edel's parents. Greg rang the number and recognised the voice immediately.

It was Mark.

Greg blurted out something about having called a wrong number and put down the phone. No one had been expecting Mark to answer.

While this was going on, I was in a uni seminar down in London. I was grateful for the break and the distraction. The next day, I returned to Nottingham, where the group met me off the train.

'We've had some developments,' Greg began.

They suggested we go to the pub so they could explain. Once there, they told me everything: the marriage certificate, the phone call, everything. We'd uncovered it all within just three weeks of that first internet search; it was so overwhelming that I was barely able to function.

'He told me he's in America, not Ireland,' I said, still in shock. 'He texted me just now ... on the train.'

Mark had sent me a text, saying he wished I was over there because he was having a 'cookout' and beers with Ian. He'd even said they were having baked clams and I remembered thinking how cheesily American it had all sounded. But he'd been in Ireland all along with his wife and kids.

Anger came; the evidence we'd gathered was now pretty conclusive. Perhaps he'd been spooked by hearing Greg's voice and tried a little too hard with his texts to convince me he was in the US.

'I need to hear it from him,' I decided. 'I won't accept it unless I hear it from Mark. I'm going over to Ireland.'

Merrick had already returned to Leeds, so the others rang him because they were worried about me. I was so determined that I started googling flights that same day. If I went, they all said they would come too. However, everyone thought it was a bad idea because it was too dangerous. I didn't care; I went and packed my bags. When I returned, the group had been discussing it.

'Look, if he's a police officer, and a British police officer in Ireland at that, we don't know what that means. If we turn up on the doorstep of a serving police officer, we don't know how far away the armed response unit could be, or the Army even. It just feels dangerous. If it's what you want to do, we'll support you, but we don't think it's a good idea.'

'Okay,' I replied, feeling deflated. 'I can see what you're saying and I know it's sensible, but I can also see my chance melting away of asking him to his face. I just don't want him to run; I really need to see him in person.'

We reached a compromise. I'd ring Mark and ask him to come back, talk to us and face me. If he refused and ran, then we had our answer, and if he came then we would get an answer directly; either way we'd get something. Part of me was still desperately trying to cling to the fact that, somehow, we might have the wrong person.

Picking up my phone, I called him and, for the first time, his voice sounded different.

'I know you're in Ireland and not in America,' I said, cutting him dead. 'You've got to come and tell me what's going on. I know you're not who you say you are.'

His voice changed again; now he sounded scared.

'Tell me what you think you know.'

Christ! What I think I know?

'No, I'm not talking about it on the phone. You've got to come and tell me to my face.'

There was a pause.

'But I've got the kids; I can't get away.'

The word 'kids' sliced against me like a blade. Steph saw me flinch and wrapped a kind arm around my shoulder for support while Tim held my hand.

'You've got to come and tell me, Mark; I want you to tell me to my face.'

He knew he couldn't get out of it so he changed his tune.

'Okay, I'll look into flights.'

I hung up and began to cry. A few minutes later, my mobile bleeped with a text – it was from him.

'I'll get to you by one in the morning.'

He told me he was flying into London, but would have to get a car to drive up to Nottingham.

Merrick checked the Irish flights.

'There's not a flight that lands that late. He must be catching an earlier one, but there's still a few hours missing.'

Who was Mark going to see before he came to see me?

Nottingham, 20 October 2010

We returned to Tim and Steph's house, which was shared by ten people. They'd already warned their housemates someone was coming and, if they heard an argument, to stay in their rooms; we would explain in the morning. People were confused, but everyone agreed. We didn't want Mark to be confronted by a mob because we didn't want him to run. Also, if we were wrong, we knew we'd have to contain it, and part of me was still clinging to this possibility.

In the early hours, there was a knock on the door. Steph went to answer it. We had already prepared the room; we didn't want to put ourselves in danger and provoke an armed police response but we also wanted to get as much out of Mark as we could. The group didn't know if he'd bring a handler or if there might be police vans parked outside; he'd been somewhere first and we didn't know where. Someone lit the log burner and the place felt warm and cosy, not intimidating. At this point, I suppose, Mark was still our friend and we wanted to give him a chance to explain, and to give ourselves the best chance of getting to the truth. Steph led him through into the living room and he sat down to answer our questions. I allowed the others to speak as I scrutinised his face.

Who the hell are you?

Although I remained silent, I knew that it must have shown in my face just how devastated I was. At one point, Mark looked over at me and then down at the ground. He seemed utterly dejected.

'Where have you been?' the others asked. 'Why are you over in Ireland? What do you do for a living?'

Mark looked at them all.

'I'm a delivery driver. I was over there delivering stuff. But I used to smuggle drugs.'

As the questions mounted, he began to stutter and I knew he was scared because his speech impediment always got worse when he was stressed. Then he started to trip over his words, but stuck to his original story as he danced around each question. We weren't getting anywhere. We gave him every opportunity to come clean, but he wouldn't. This went on for ages, until finally Greg asked in a quiet and gentle voice.

'So, what year did you join the police force, Mark?'

He looked up and visibly crumpled because he knew the game was up. We'd given Mark every chance and I was desperate for him to come up with something to prove us wrong; but he couldn't because we'd got it right.

Mark was an undercover police officer.

There was a pause, and then he began to explain as my brain went into freefall. I felt numb as he spoke. He told us everything I'd expected, and everything I'd hoped wouldn't be true. Mark explained he'd been working for the NPOIU – the National Public Order Intelligence Unit. The awkward acronym rolled off his tongue seamlessly as though it was second nature to him. I'd never heard of NPOIU before. I'd heard of the Special Demonstration Squad, that one was part of Special Branch, but not this. Mark told us he'd joined the police force straight out of school at nine-teen. As he spoke, it was as though his personality had completely changed and he'd morphed into something else before my eyes; the only thing that remained was his fragility – he looked broken. But as he spoke, he became something I didn't know – he'd shape-shifted into something else. He described how he'd got married in his early twenties and had had his first child by twenty-four. I'd always known him as a rebel – a lone wolf – who'd forged his own way in life. But all the adventures he said he'd had before he met me were bullshit. In fact, all the adventures he'd had in his life had been *with* me.

'I was always on your side,' he insisted. 'I was feeding them false information.'

We asked about Lynn, the woman who'd insisted on buddying up with me on the demo when we'd been arrested. She'd always been sarcastic and scathing and had this 'too cool for school' vibe about her. She'd supposedly left the country in strange circumstances a year previously and lost touch with her friends, but then someone had bumped into her in a pub in Dorset that summer and she'd behaved really weirdly. While Lynn had made some very close friends, and even had a one-night stand, she hadn't sought any kind of romantic relationship with activists.

In a moment of inexplicable candour, Mark confirmed our suspicions that Lynn had indeed been an undercover police officer. Then he laughed.

Why are you laughing?

He stopped and explained.

'The thing about Lynn was, she didn't like you guys as much as I did; she didn't have good things to say about you.'

I knew then; I didn't recognise the Mark I'd known and loved.

I glanced over at the others and asked if I could have time alone with Mark; they all left the room. I'd spoken to them before he'd arrived and warned that when the time came, they shouldn't leave me with him for too long because I *still* didn't emotionally trust myself around him.

I was sitting on the floor by the fire; Mark had kept on his coat – a Gore-Tex waterproof – the whole time, even though the room was very warm.

Was he wearing a wire?

However, when the others left, he took off his coat and sat down on the floor next to me. I don't remember much about what was said because I was so upset, but Mark insisted he'd never informed on me and had protected me the whole time.

'I'm not a police officer any more. I love you – I still love you. All the best things I've done in my life have been with you. No one else has shown me the love and care I felt from you.'

But I could barely take it on board because I was sobbing. I knew the others would come in, Mark would leave, and I'd probably never see him again. I also realised the man I loved didn't exist any more. It felt as if I were holding onto the hand of someone who was dying. Only he wasn't dying, he was fading – fading away to nothing. It was wrong, but I didn't want the moment to end, the others to come back in, or for it to be over, because that would be it. But the group did return and soon it was done. I felt like I'd fallen into a black hole.

Mark stood up and turned to face us.

'I'm going to make amends; I'm going to make it okay – I'm going to blow the lid on all this. Whatever you need me to say, I'll say it.'

Of course, we couldn't trust a single word he said. By trusting him, we'd only give him power. If we allowed it, he'd manipulate us all over again. Instead, we told him we'd be in touch, and then he left. It felt like an anti-climax but there was nothing else we could do. He said he'd left the force by now, but how could we know if that was really true, or if he was just going to be picked up by a cop car around the corner?

I stood at the front door and watched him walk away.

Naomi
(Officer: Mark Stone)

Bristol, 21 October 2010

I was due to give a teamwork presentation. I'd been planning it for weeks so I didn't take a call from a friend who rang early that morning. He called again but I knew I'd be running late if I answered. I decided to call him back afterwards. I arrived and saw he'd left a message.

'Please call me.' Something shifted; an alarm bell rang. I went outside and rang him.

'Hi, it's me ...'

'Naomi,' he began, his voice sounding both tired and serious. 'I've got to tell you that Mark Stone is an undercover police officer. His real name is Mark Kennedy.'

Suddenly everything went very still and the world recoiled. The railings in front of me pulled into the distance as though I was looking at them through a pair of binoculars the wrong way round. Then they zoomed back in at speed. The news hit me and I became aware of many things all at the same time, yet somehow I couldn't take it in.

Mark Stone was a paid police officer? No, Mark Kennedy was a police officer. Mark Stone was fictional, created by the police? How had he managed this for seven years? Why hadn't I realised? Who else was involved? Other people had voiced their suspicions so shouldn't this just feel like merely confirmation?

But it felt far from that.

Who else could I trust?

It was a shock like I've never had before or since.

My friend spoke a little more and explained how Lisa had exposed it, how they'd confronted Mark, but I don't remember the rest of the conversation; I pieced the facts together later. At this stage, only a handful of people knew but very soon a lot more people would. He asked if I could tell a few others face to face. Thankfully, it gave me a sense of purpose over the next twenty-four hours – something to focus on. I abandoned the presentation and walked out into a different life.

The more people I told about Mark, the more the whole thing sounded like one long crazy story streaming out of my mouth. I'd already planned to go to London that evening so I went. However, I was constantly on the phone explaining what I'd been told and everyone was in complete and utter disbelief. I recalled moments from my life over the last seven years and had to re-evaluate them. I found I had to re-remember so many moments with the new information I'd been given. So many happy and joyful memories; they all had to be re-thought, and they all became tainted and unsettling.

I travelled to Nottingham to see Lisa. She seemed traumatised and grieving, finding resilience from somewhere, supported by an amazing core of people who I could still believe in, despite everything.

I thought back to the day, five years earlier, when Mark had cried in my kitchen. I'd ended the relationship and he said he felt he'd let me down. It seemed impossible to think he hadn't known the double meaning of what he was saying. It made me feel sick.

Yes, Mark, you let me down. You let us all down every single day of the whole time you knew us. You let us down every single day you woke up and decided to lie to us all over again. You were never even really with us.

Following the discovery, I struggled for a long time. I was so angry I didn't even read it as anger: I turned it inward and it became depression. The guilt and shame of feeling I should have known earlier were paralysing. I didn't want to go out or see anybody, apart from friends I knew well. I felt very fearful in public places. The whole thing left me completely disorientated.

Lisa

(Officer: Mark Stone)

Nottingham, winter 2010

In the days that followed, my brother rang to say Mark had called him in tears.

'What's going on? He said he's going to do himself harm.'

My brother was in the dark because my story hadn't immediately become public and he'd been counselling Mark over the phone. Mark had also written to my sister-in-law, so I had to explain to my family, way before I was ready to do so, what had happened. At the same time, I had to keep Mark at arm's length and it took me a while to push him out. My brother asked Mark not to call any more.

It felt as though a bomb had gone off and I'd been at the epicentre, but the effects were wide-reaching.

As the days passed, I tried to make sense of the last year. My mind was manically racing around, reliving moments and trying to put together a picture. I was certain that, even though Mark was a police officer, he must have been coming apart at the seams towards the end. Much later, I discovered he'd left his undercover role in October 2009 and had travelled to America. He'd actually left the police in March 2010, which was why, without back-up and support from a team of handlers, he was unable to keep his story straight and his emotions in check. He'd effectively lost his support team – a whole back room of officers behind the scenes. He'd been telling the truth when he said he wasn't a police officer any more. Instead, it turned out he was working for a private intelligence-gathering company as a spy. Even though he'd left the police, he'd kept up his undercover persona. It was as though Mark didn't want to leave his old character behind; but he'd spun out of control and his story had started to unravel.

That's why he'd been in such a rush to get off the mountain in Italy; he really did have to be back at work. He had to report back to his bosses.

Slowly, things began to slot into place. Subconsciously perhaps, he'd been leaving me a trail of clues.

That's why I'd found his real passport; he'd probably had to surrender all his fake ID when he'd left the police.

Everything came crashing down and I don't remember much because I mentally collapsed and slipped into a dark place. It felt as though all the colour had been bleached out of the world. I was in a state of almost permanent flashback as events of the last six years replayed over and over. I was in pieces so Tim and Steph offered me a cosy box room in their house, nicknamed the broom cupboard. Everyone surrounded and cared for me.

There was a website called Indymedia that was used for posting alternative and protest news and information. The group had put up an article about Mark to warn others what the police had done. I was asked for a photo of him. The last thing I wanted to do was find a photo but I knew I had to. He was wearing shades in almost all of them – but I found one on my phone; it pictured him looking up, smiling at the camera as we brought his narrowboat home. Part of me didn't want to share it because I didn't want the world to have my memories – to have the image of him smiling at me in a private moment – as evidence of his treachery. But people wouldn't know what he looked like because he almost always wore Oakley shades, so I had to give the photo over.

From the start, I was adamant we didn't bring his kids into it even though our strongest evidence was their birth certificates. In my opinion, his kids and his wife had been victims too.

In the first few days, the biggest reaction we got was disbelief; some even questioned how we could spread such malicious lies about Mark. The group rang around people and visited them because everyone was so bewildered. Mark himself was in touch with some people and it was messy. Everyone started to comment online; I felt

I'd been cast as the 'unsuspecting girlfriend'. Their comments stole my agency. It wasn't healthy, but I read all the comments. Some suggested I'd known all along or had even facilitated it. There was a mass outpouring of confusion and people lashed out. I wanted to hide from the world. It took a while for people to realise I'd been the one to find it all out and it had been my suspicions that had initiated the whole investigation. There was a lot of criticism online, and I felt very judged.

I wanted to stand up, and scream and shout: 'If it weren't for me, he'd still be going to all your demos and meetings.'

Every single comment felt like a personal attack and, although friends told me not to read them, I couldn't stop. A week later it was my birthday and Steph told me people wanted to reach out to me.

'Well, maybe someone could send me some chocolate in the post,' I said glibly.

On the day of my birthday, I received dozens of cards, letters and presents from people – some I'd not heard from in years. I was sent hampers and treats to cheer me up. It was lovely. It made me realise just how much love and support I had from my friends.

It was also a reminder for me that I wasn't alone in a personal turmoil, there was also a collective grief in the whole community for the loss of someone thought to be a friend.

Among the cards and letters was one from Helen Steel; I knew of her because we had friends in common and had been to the same demos and gatherings over the years. Inside a card she'd written:

I really wanted to get in touch; I realise you're probably dealing with a lot right now and you're probably not ready to talk but, when you are, I'd really like to talk to you about this because something very similar has happened to me. So, when you're ready, please get in touch.

Helen

I thought it was lovely of her but I didn't believe anyone else could possibly understand how I felt. I had no idea of the extent to which she would understand, or just how similar her story would be.

Alison
(Officer: Mark Cassidy)

Hackney, London, October 2010

My partner David was watching TV while our two children, aged three and six, were asleep in bed. I tried not to search the internet for information about Mark Cassidy too often but occasionally allowed myself a 'lucky' dip. This was one of those evenings.

Despite the new life I'd managed to create with David, the gnawing feeling of unfinished business had never fully disappeared. I searched the name Mark and undercover police officer and the name Mark Stone/Kennedy popped up on a site called Indymedia. A man with a goatee beard and a wonky eye. I froze for a moment then scanned the comments beneath the article and it became immediately clear there were other women. Just as we'd suspected.

Lisa

(Officer: Mark Stone)

Nottingham, October–November 2010

I was on my laptop reading internet comments about Mark's story, when I spotted an email from him waiting in my inbox. My heart stopped. I clicked on it and began to read his emotional outpouring.

He wrote that he felt overwhelmed with his betrayal and guilt but was trying to make amends. He talked about 'Mark' in the third person and said how I'd been the only one to see his true character. He said he was crying every day and that he loved me 'with all his heart, body and soul'. He seemed to be under the impression that he could make things right between us, that if he convinced me he was being truthful, we could pick up where we left off and I could meet his family and friends. He was finally telling his mum about me.

It all felt so raw and unbearably painful. I'd never before experienced this sensation of simultaneously yearning to hear such words of love while also recoiling from them.

I spent time trying to compose my thoughts to reply.

Date: Wed, 3 Nov 2010, 19:06
I'm not sure I can begin to know what to say! A bomb has exploded in my life, blowing it apart and also affecting dozens and dozens of amazing people who considered you a friend. Quite frankly I'm still numb with shock.

I don't want to start a dialogue with you but I think I should probably put you straight ... there is no way to put this right and it's naïve to even hope this story could have a happy ending for us.

As for questions ... there are thousands! I wouldn't know where to begin and each one I've asked so far has only brought up more questions. Such a large part of my life has been based on an incredibly complex tangle of lies I don't think it's going to be possible for me to believe I'm now getting truth. I'm not sure I believe you know what truth is ... it's all far too tangled to unravel and I don't have that kind of energy.

Events and times, I may have questions about going back so far that the questions aren't just about who you are but who the fuck am I? Who would I have become over the last six years? Who might I have met and got together with? What paths might my life have taken?

And as for what you told me at NEDS and the 'all of it' that was true, does that include the part where you continued with your cover story right up to the last minute possible? Or the part where you wouldn't tell me how long you'd been a policeman? Or the part when you told me that undercover cops were getting involved with anarchists all over Europe just for fun?

Many times, I've thought you were sharing deep emotional truths with me as I held you in my arms and you cried ... yet I was being told a lie, so why are these tears now real? You've told me before that you'd shown your mum my picture and she thought I was beautiful! I once thought that you made so much sense to me, but now you've turned my life upside down and none of it makes sense ... you can't make up for it now, it's too late.

This last year and its lead-up to the dramatic, traumatic ending makes even less sense than the rest of it. Before that feels almost like a distant fictional love story. I'm not surprised you had some kind of a breakdown but I have no idea why it didn't happen earlier or why you came back. If you really loved me then you should have left me years ago. It's not good enough that you were enjoying yourself too much, or that our life together was better than your other life/lives, that you would risk my sanity because you were having fun being in love. It was incredibly selfish.

And if you did come back after your breakdown because our love was so important, why did you treat me with such disregard? Do you realise how traumatic the gradual unravelling of my life has been? The slow dawning realisation that I had reason to doubt my own boyfriend, being absolutely convinced it wouldn't be true yet finally being unable to ignore the unravelling lies. We will never know what may have happened if you'd told me first. I might have at least had more reason to believe your version now. And I've barely even begun to process how you may have risked mine and my friends' liberties and worked against our passionately held beliefs.

That last bit was more of a rant than I was planning on writing but I don't feel like deleting it. Be clear though that I'm not asking for answers because you've given me no reason to believe I can rely on them. I have to just accept there are a thousand unanswered questions and move on.

After all that, I believe I may have glimpsed the real you during all the incredible times we had. That person had the potential to be amazing. I really do hope that one day you can make sense of the mess that you are, learn to live truthfully and be that amazing person. That isn't going to be with me though.

I'm afraid there's no fairy-tale ending to this story. You might have thought you were living life in a film script, being the exciting double agent, but I'm sorry you don't get to run off with the girl in the end.

I'm being shown such a huge amount of fiercely true love from so many incredible people that I can't let down.

I choose them.

Lisa.

Mark's reply soon followed. He repeated that he loved me so much, that it was all his fault and that he had been foolish and cowardly. He said that having lived in both worlds, he knew where he would rather be. The emptiness he felt was, he said, all consuming.

I could feel a hollow numbness surrounding me and I felt empty too. I was heartbroken, stripped back to the core. It was as if the friends holding on to my loosening strands were the only thing that stopped me unravelling entirely.

Helen
(Officer: John Barker)

Wales, 13 November 2010

I was working as a gardener so it wasn't easy to get time off during the summer, and – coupled with endless battles as a union rep while a new grading system was implemented and management sought to down-grade us – somehow the summer seemed to have passed me by. It was late autumn by the time I finally managed to travel to Wales to see Rosa. I caught the train with a friend who had also known Jim Sutton.

We met up in a café to discuss what she knew. What Rosa said horrified me. Jim Sutton, or Boyling as she'd later discovered he was really called, had been working as an undercover cop all the time we'd known him. In 2000, he'd feigned a mental breakdown and said he had to go travelling, just as John did. When he then went missing abroad, Rosa tried to find him by following the leads of what he'd told her about his life and family. But everything crumbled upon investigation and she discovered that so much of what he'd said was false, just as I had about John.

Some months into her search, Jim had begun sending cryptic emails claiming that he wasn't coping, that he hadn't been acting freely, that she should trust no one and that her phone wasn't safe. Any attempt to obtain any sense from Jim was met with mixed messages and riddles.

Despite severing contact with him for her own mental health, Rosa kept up her search for the truth. In desperate need for under-standing and closure, she had even gone to South Africa, where Jim had said he was going for work, to try to track Jim down, but she couldn't find him. Eventually, many months later, evidence indicated that he was actually in the UK.

Rosa had returned to the UK deeply distressed, in poor health and down to the last of her savings. She feared she was being tracked and didn't dare contact her old friends or family, feeling she couldn't be sure who people really were or who was being watched.

Continuing her investigations, she found a government address through phone records related to Jim, but when she checked the place out on the ground, it appeared to be a secret government building and she feared for her safety. Since she had found out, a year before, that Jim didn't exist as the person he originally claimed to be, she had been trapped in a twilight zone world, absent of the reality she had known before his disappearance. She survived in a state of hypervigilance where all the rules of society had changed and she now feared being disappeared. She believed she had uncovered secret spying operations, which were not public knowledge and which presumably the state would not want people to learn about.

Rosa had also discovered Jim was spending time in the Kingston area. In urgent need of money, when she saw a job advertised for a newly opened bookstore in Kingston, she took it, despite her ongoing fear that she could be traced through her National Insurance number. She felt it would give her a good position to observe the public coming and going and increase her chances of spotting Jim.

On her first day in the store, Jim walked in. He told her she wasn't allowed to be angry or he wouldn't explain anything. They met up again after the shop closed. When Rosa probed some of his lies, Jim admitted that he'd been an undercover cop, but then spun her more lies, claiming he'd been placed as part of a criminal investigation that the police thought involved someone in Reclaim the Streets. According to him, the police had then realised this had all been a case of mistaken identity and had pulled him out. He told her it would be ludicrous to think the police would keep long-term spies in protest groups and even mocked her for considering it; this had just been an isolated incident based on a misunderstanding, he claimed. He then switched to displaying empathy for how the ordeal had clearly affected Rosa's sense of reality.

Jim told Rosa he had always hated the police since joining, he still loved her and that from day one of being in the group, he'd realised that he actually shared their politics and values and felt he'd found where he belonged in life. He now wanted out of the police, he said, but he was afraid they would try to stop him if they knew. He claimed he was trapped in a life that held no meaning for him and that he had tried to protect the movement from his superiors. He was terrified his work would find out who he really was inside and 'have him destroyed'. He insisted the movement was now safe and asserted that telling anyone would only spread paranoia and distrust within it – *he* was the one left at risk from the police.

Having lived in an upside-down world where for a long time nothing had made sense, the new lies Jim had spun to Rosa seemed more believable than what later turned out to be the truth and he seemed to be the only bridge to the firm ground of her past life. Jim said he wanted nothing more than a free and ethical life and to be with Rosa, but that he lacked the strength to escape the police alone. He needed her help. They discussed leaving the country under the passport radar and obtaining new ID. Heavily traumatised and deeply manipulated by a man who knew all her psychological triggers for solidarity and responsibility, within two weeks Rosa was pregnant. Jim then used his training in deception and manipulation to control her. He made Rosa change her name by deed poll and destroy her own address book, claiming they may be raided at any time and this would be used in evidence against him by the police for being a turncoat. She then had no means of contacting old friends and he began to isolate her further. He forbade her from talking to other people about her background, her interests and who she really was.

Despite Jim's promises, he never left the police. Then, blaming her supposed lack of commitment to him as the reason he had not had the courage to leave the police yet, he pressured her to sign marriage documentation.

Jim smoothed over the contradictions in his claims with gaslighting. Rosa was still reeling from Jim's announcement that he was unilaterally cancelling their long-awaited escape plan for him to leave the police, when she discovered she was already pregnant with a second child. Later, heavily pregnant and with toddler in hand she did make an escape attempt alone, but her hopes were dashed mid-train journey when she was persuaded that she wasn't thinking clearly and must return home with her daughter at once before social services viewed her actions in a dim light, having fled with nowhere to go.

Some while later, after concerns about the children's development, they were diagnosed with a profound and life-limiting genetic disability. Rosa was already in touch with Women's Aid at that point and the diagnosis was an added wake-up call; the children did not have time to waste being trapped with their abusive father. All the same, in practical terms their condition made leaving even more difficult. Eventually, Rosa managed to escape to a women's refuge with her children.

I found it hard not to cry at what I was hearing, and broke down several times. It was a terrifying and heartbreaking story, and even though I recognised some of the patterns of lies from my relationship with John, hearing it from Rosa made it all so much more vivid. I initially didn't grasp the extent of some of the manipulation and I said Jim must have loved her to come back. But Rosa was adamant that it wasn't love; it was about power and control. She had only come to realise that over time and through the help and insights she gained through Women's Aid.

Rosa went on to tell me that during the time they lived together, Jim had told her that John had also been in the Special Demonstration Squad and that I continued to be monitored after John left. One of the stories he told Rosa to control her was that when I travelled to New Zealand, the police had searched my rucksack without me knowing and had found the *True Spies* videos. He used this to instil fear into Rosa that whatever she did, the police would find out. His work would pick her up before she ever got to me. She had been trying to find a safe way to reach me with the message for years. The nearest she got was to persuade Jim they should attend Kingston Green Fayre together and hope she might find me there, but it didn't work out.

I felt utterly sick. There was no way she could have known of the contents of my rucksack without the police having spied on me, and it was chilling to hear how Jim had used this to control her.

But there was more. 'Helen, when I was living in Kingston with Jim, he told me that he felt sorry for you,' Rosa said, holding my gaze. 'He said he was the third officer who had spied on you. The other was Bob Lambert, do you remember him?'

I didn't recognise the name so Rosa said she'd try to find a photo of him.

I mentioned to Rosa that I thought we needed to take a legal case against the police to challenge and expose what had happened and try to prevent it happening again. She immediately questioned the likelihood of getting anywhere.

'Do you really think anyone cares about what happens to us? How can we complain to the state about what the state has done? What are they going to say about it?'

She had come to believe that she no longer had any human rights, that they could do anything anytime they wanted. She told me she would have laughed if it had been anyone else who had suggested it, but given our friendship and above all our shared realities, she was willing to hear me out.

Rosa explained that she had been exhausted by the divorce, which had only finally finished the previous year, and that she was midway through a case for her children's disability rights with the local authority. She wasn't sure how much more she could deal with on top of meeting her children's daily needs, but if I was sure it was worth it, she would join a case.

We later went to Rosa's house, where she showed me a photograph of Bob Lambert on the internet, but I didn't immediately recognise him.

She explained that he had since left the police and become a lecturer in terrorism studies at Exeter and St Andrews universities. He'd been very busy since leaving the Metropolitan Police.

'Is this definitely the same man who spied on me?' I asked.

'Yep, I've met him, Helen. He paid a visit to my home a few years ago with a man called Noel, just before I escaped to the refuge. They called it a "welfare visit". He was sitting in my children's playroom as clear as you are now, but he wasn't very friendly. I didn't know who he was back then, but Jim said he was close to you. You knew him,' Rosa said, urging me to remember.

Later that day, I suddenly thought of Bob who used to be in London Greenpeace.

Could it be him?

Haringey, London, 27 November 2010

I'd read the story about Mark Stone on Indymedia; it was big news in activist circles. I'd met both him and Lisa at Earth First! gatherings and political events, and knew they'd been in a close relationship. I felt sick to the pit of my stomach, thinking how Lisa must be feeling. I met up with a friend – one who'd helped previously with research on John after I'd found his marriage certificate. I asked if he'd seen the article. He had, but he said he couldn't believe Mark would have been a cop.

'They wouldn't put someone in the movement for seven years, that's ridiculous. There must be some other explanation.'

I knew then we had to bring a legal case; it was the best way to expose the truth. Without legal action no one would believe the state was going to these extremes. This abuse had to be stopped.

A few weeks later I saw a potential opportunity. About a mile from where I lived, a hostel for the homeless was to be opened and the renowned human rights lawyer Gareth Peirce would be giving a speech. I always assumed phones might be bugged and mail intercepted so I knew that if I wanted to get legal advice without the police finding out, I had to meet her face to face. I went to the launch event and, after Gareth had spoken, I found a moment to ask if we could have a private chat. I explained there were at least four women who had been deceived into relationships with undercover policemen with devastating consequences and did she think it would be possible to bring a case against the police to stop it happening to any more women? Gareth seemed shocked. She said she didn't know for sure what would be possible but she would certainly help us find out if we wanted to come to her office for a proper chat.

As I left the venue, I felt like a weight had been lifted from my shoulders. Finally, there was someone who believed this and was willing to take it seriously.

Lisa
(Officer: Mark Kennedy)

Nottingham, December 2010

Friends of mine involved in the Ratcliffe-on-Soar court cases began turning up in the city because of their impending hearings. It was great to see friendly faces, but it was also a lot to take on board everyone else's responses to the news about Mark.

There were twenty-six people, split into two groups, who were charged with conspiracy to break into the power station. The first group of twenty were people nicknamed the 'justifiers'. They were running the defence of 'necessity'. This involved calling in experts to argue that shutting down the power station was justified and necessary to save the lives being lost through global warming. They were found guilty, but spared jail. They hadn't brought their knowledge about Mark's identity into the case, so the story was still under the press radar.

The second group had a different defence, and their trial was still to come. They were nicknamed 'the deniers' because they denied being part of any conspiracy; they said they hadn't decided if they wanted to be part of the full protest or not, having not known the details in advance. They had been arrested before making their decision. The fact that Mark would have known this was crucial to their defence.

Mark had promised to one of them that he would give evidence to 'help his old friends'. He went back on his word, but the conversation had been recorded.

Nottingham Crown Court, 10 January 2011

The six deniers were in court. Mark's admission to us that he'd been an undercover officer and the recorded conversation had been enough to undermine the whole case. When the defendants asked to see Kennedy's secret evidence, rather than disclose it the Crown Prosecution Service (CPS) dropped the charges.

The same morning, the *Guardian* went public with the story about Mark and the court case, after interviewing activists and defendants in the case. The story didn't include me yet. I was still trying to keep my heartbreak private, which worked initially, but then the story began to blow up.

A few months after the deniers had been found not guilty, the justifiers also had their convictions quashed. The court ruled that the evidence gathered by Mark would have exonerated them had it not been withheld by the police.

Eventually, two reports were commissioned into the withholding of evidence from the court, one by the Independent Police Complaints Commission, another commissioned by the then-head of the CPS, Director of Public Prosecutions Keir Starmer.

It was a disaster for Mark's bosses at the NPOIU because not only had the actions of one of their officers become public knowledge, but the whole operation had cost millions of pounds – for nothing. The case had collapsed and the unit's future was in question.

Nottingham, January 2011

For around two weeks, the source of my greatest heartbreak and the events that had caused the bottom to fall out of my world were out there on the front pages for everyone to devour. My story was featured in every newspaper and TV news programme.

On the Thursday of the first week, I was due to head down to London for an exam, but my studies felt like the last thing on my mind. Instead, I felt compelled to read every single word printed. I endlessly picked away at the scab.

'How could she not have known?' one person asked in an online comment.

'It's a waste of taxpayers' money!' stormed another.

Someone else remarked 'the greenies' should all be strung up. We deserved it all and more, apparently.

I couldn't help myself; I searched out every single nugget of information to try and make sense of it. I felt I was watching a gory scene in a film; I hated every minute but was unable to turn it off. My heartbreak was now public property, and my devastation a matter for general debate. Mark's relationships had been discussed and everyone needed to know who I was. The world wanted to get a good look at me, but I didn't want to join in the circus. I felt far too bruised and I needed to preserve what little I had left of myself. I'd already spent years unwittingly on display without consent, and now they wanted even more.

Following my exam, there was a media storm raging, and friends told me journalists were in Nottingham, looking for me. I felt really under attack. I had even been worried that journalists would be waiting for me outside the exam room as I'd told a college friend my story and her husband worked for *Newsnight*, but she had thankfully kept my identity secret. Together with Naomi, I left London and caught a train down to Brighton. I've no idea why we chose Brighton, but there was fresh sea air, and nobody was searching for me there. The seaside town felt surreal but strangely comforting. We were on holiday but also on a break from reality. I didn't even know what reality was any more. We weren't on the run, except we were in hiding, trying to find somewhere safe. I strolled down to the pebble beach and spent time with the sea air blowing against my face and hair. The song 'Terrible Love' by The National played loudly in my headphones with the lyric 'It takes an ocean not to break', and as the waves crashed on the shore I felt determined not to break myself. I didn't want to give the police the satisfaction.

Following the collapse of the trial, and the *Guardian* exposure, the full story began to break in the news, including the details about Mark's relationships. Everything was about to explode all over again and it was very hard to hide.

Brighton, January 2011

We discovered Mark had got himself an agent.

His name was Max Clifford.

Mark had sold his story to the *Mail on Sunday* in an exclusive interview. He'd mentioned having a 'beautiful Welsh red-headed girlfriend'. Naomi and I watched a video but we barely recognised him. In it he was clean-cut and clean-shaven. I could hear his voice, but the man looked nothing like the Mark I'd once known. He didn't even look like a real person. He looked like a caricature – a cardboard cut-out with the right image to project the media narrative and further his own ends, tell his side of the story. I didn't feel any closer to knowing who he was now or who he'd been before.

It was clear Mark didn't know either.

The stuff in the papers was a strange mix of things I recognised and some absolute nonsense. Mark had cast himself as a James Bond-type character with me as the love interest. He'd even told the reporter how he'd once saved my life in Iceland. He painted a picture of activists being scavengers, telling the journalist that he found 'the dirt' difficult to live with.

> *They should have known I was a cop as I was the only one who ever cleaned anything … and they had no respect for other people's property. They put rubbish everywhere.*

I was angry but also devastated. A part of me was still clinging to the idea that he might act with integrity in the face of everything coming undone, but everything I read attributed to him in the press made me realise he was just trying to save his own skin. Looking out for number one, as he'd always done. Mark explained how he'd had to withdraw from his role following the arrests over Ratcliffe-on-Soar. The article also revealed that he'd resigned from police work to take a job with a private company called Global Open, advising corporations on activist movements. He'd taken all his police training, his legend, his entire undercover persona and all his contacts and used them to further a new career. We were his assets, our friends and me.

I was a hollowed-out husk as I walked through the narrow and unfamiliar streets in a daze. Lots of friends called me to see how

Naomi and I were doing. At one point, I started to speak in Welsh to an old friend as we walked along. Naomi was worried people might see a red-headed woman, speaking in Welsh, and realise I was the one in the papers. It was crazy; as though we were both living in a film. Nothing felt real.

Naomi
(Officer: Mark Stone)

Brighton, January 2011

The Ratcliffe-on-Soar case had collapsed and Mark was in the news. The press was desperately trying to find people who knew him and had turned up in Nottingham, doorstepping the house where Lisa was staying. I went with her to a hotel by the sea to get away from it all. While we were there, Mark gave an interview to the papers and then on TV. He said he wanted to tell his version of the story, except his version of the story changed all the time depending on who was listening and what the agenda was. Mark had already left the police force but his training had stayed with him; he still knew how to lie professionally.

As I watched the interview, a picture of a man in a smart suit appeared on screen. For a split second, I thought it was the inter-viewer, then I realised it was Mark. He looked completely different – short hair, smart suit, tie. His real self had been exposed. It felt like receiving the phone call – the one that had told me he was a cop – all over again.

Helen

(Officer: John Barker)

London and Wales, January 2011

With the collapse of the Ratcliffe trial, suddenly the media seemed awash with coverage of Mark Stone and undercover policing in protest movements. Through a friend I was told that the *Guardian* also wanted to print a story exposing Jim Sutton as another spy in the environmental movement. So far this had not been reported in the mainstream media. I travelled again to Wales to see Rosa to forewarn her and discuss what she wanted to do. I also asked her if she would be up for joining a legal case against the police now that Gareth Peirce was willing to meet and give us advice. I had floated the idea of bringing a case when we first met up in November, but now the idea was solidifying.

I explained that I'd spoken to Gareth and she was willing to look into how we might take a case. I said it would be taken far more seriously if the case involved more than one woman and more than one officer. It would be too easy for people to dismiss the case as an isolated rogue officer if it was just one person on their own, as the police and the media had already done with Mark Kennedy. I said I was intending to talk to other women affected as well, so hopefully there'd be a whole group of us. I knew I didn't have the strength to do it on my own. I'm a deeply private person and this was about the most intimate aspects of my life. There would be strength in numbers.

Rosa also expressed concerns about taking a case – she too felt vulnerable – but reminded me that she had already agreed when I first suggested the idea in November and she wasn't backing out now.

I was so relieved. It wasn't that I had great faith in the British legal system to make everything all right. But I knew the serious harm that had been caused to us and I wanted to stop it being inflicted on other women in the future. From my experience with the McLibel case, I knew a court case might be the only way to expose the extent of what had been done to us and hold the state to account. Somehow the existence of a court case makes the events more real to outside observers. The hearings themselves become news and provide a hook to get publicity about what happened and a focus to campaign around. Where the media might be reluctant to print an interviewee's story in case it was made up, once it becomes a court case, people start to treat it more seriously.

I also hoped we might gain some answers through the standard disclosure process involved in bringing a legal case, where the police would have an obligation to give us copies of documents in their possession relating to what they knew about the relationships. I hoped this might provide answers about how the abuse had been allowed to happen and who knew about it.

The following weekend I went over to Alison's flat. Seven years had gone by since we first met up to discuss our respective experiences and with all the recent media coverage of undercover policing there was a lot to talk about. I told her I had spoken to Gareth Peirce and asked if she too would be willing to get involved in a court case if the lawyers said it was possible. Alison also felt vulnerable at the thought of having to talk about her relationship in a court case and she still had no hard proof that Cassidy had been a cop either, although we were both convinced he was. But she said she would think about it. We chatted for hours about the possibilities for raising awareness both through the courts and the media of the impact of these state-sponsored deceptive relationships. It was after midnight by the time I cycled home to Tottenham, running high on adrenalin.

New Scotland Yard, London, 24 January 2011

Two days later, a women's blockade of New Scotland Yard had been organised by women who had been appalled to learn of the state abuse of female protestors by undercover police. I didn't know who had organised it and at this point I had still not gone public with what had happened to me. When I arrived, there were already at least forty or fifty women sitting down outside the main and side entrances. I sat down between my friend Jax and Alison's friend Jude, who by chance were sitting beside each other, then introduced them.

Although there were photos of Mark Kennedy and Jim Boyling with question marks over their faces, I couldn't see any leaflets or posters explaining what the protest was about. I decided to do a handwritten one on a piece of cardboard: '*Stop State Sexual Abuse*'.

As we were leaving, I noticed a couple of women had awful placards that read: '*You told me the handcuffs were kinky*' and '*Keep your truncheon in your trousers*'.

I was upset by this, as were other women. Someone told them the placards were inappropriate, but it was too late, the protest was over. I worried who these women were and why they would turn up with placards like that.

Of course, those were the pictures that made the press – as though this was all a joke.

London, early February 2011

Jax messaged me and said she needed to see me urgently. She came round and told me she had bumped into Mark Kennedy at a train station. She wasn't sure what to do; she needed to let Lisa know, but didn't want to talk about it over the phone in case the police found out.

They had both been shaken by the surprise encounter. He had cried and apologised for betraying activists, saying they were his true friends and he promised to answer any questions honestly. But when she did then ask him questions about anything significant, he kept replying 'I'm sorry, I can't tell you that.'

Jax was the first person to see him since he was outed and it was a big shock. Everyone had thought he was in the States. We wrote down as much as possible about the meeting while it was still fresh in her mind and then the following day she went to Nottingham to let people know what happened.

A couple of days later, Jax invited me for a meal with Lisa. It was the first time I'd seen Lisa since the story first broke on Indymedia in October and we talked long into the night about our respective experiences, what I had learnt from Rosa, and what we might be able to do about all of it. I asked if she might be up for joining me and other women to take a case against the police, but she wasn't sure she could cope with that, nor whether any good would come from it. I could see it was all still so raw for Lisa. Unlike me and Alison she had still been in a relationship with Mark when she'd discovered he was a police officer. And so little time had passed since then. I remembered how I'd found out the truth little by little and how I'd thought it was maybe just as well, as it had helped me adjust to reality gradually. And I also knew how long I had continued to have feelings for John, despite everything he'd done.

Lisa

(Officer: Mark Stone)

Nottingham, 14 February 2011

Word reached me that Mark was working on a documentary for Channel 4. I knew that Jax had unexpectedly bumped into him in London. At that time, I was still regularly travelling there for uni so I knew there was a slight possibility I could bump into him too. Every time I travelled, I went over in my mind what I'd say if I saw him.

Jax was friends with Helen Steel, and she urged me to meet her. Jax cooked us both dinner and we discussed everything. I couldn't believe Helen had lived with the same situation for such a long time. We discussed the possibility of bringing legal action, but it seemed implausible.

'We can't complain to the state because the state did this to us,' I remarked.

By the end of the evening, I came to a decision; I needed to meet up again with Mark.

I've exposed Mark as an undercover police officer, but I still haven't split up properly with him, my boyfriend.

I called him. His old number still worked.

'I don't want to know anything about your life but you've bumped into Jax and I don't want to live in fear of bumping into you. This way is better.'

I chose a random train station outside London and told him to look for the nearest pub.

'I'll be on my own, but some friends will be there with me, sitting at another table.'

We met near Hemel Hampstead. It was only on the way there I realised what day it was.

I took Helen and Jax along to make sure I was on the train back to London with them later because – even now, despite everything – I couldn't trust myself around him. The pub was festooned with love hearts and Valentine balloons. It was filled with happy couples – and us. I spotted Mark; this time he looked more like his old self – whatever that was. He'd grown back his goatee and his hair seemed less tidy, as if he wanted it long again. I asked him lots of things, including about the gin and tonic on the boat. He explained it'd been his wife's. I also asked why he'd been in such a hurry to come down off the mountain in Italy.

'Because I had to report for work with the private company.'

I was basically asking for confirmation of the things I suspected. I didn't even know why, because I already knew the answers.

At one point, I looked up at Mark.

'Were you leaving clues for me to find?'

He looked at me directly.

'In a way, yes.'

I was absolutely livid, him toying with me like that.

'How dare you!'

I realised then that this was never about getting answers from him. I'd never know what to believe and what not to believe. It was about needing to say my piece to his face and show him what he'd done. It was to stop it circulating round my head day after day.

I said he was a terrible father because he'd missed his children growing up. I repeated all the things I needed to say while he hung his head. But once my anger had dispersed, I began to soften.

'I genuinely loved you, Lisa,' he insisted.

'What about your wife?'

Mark stared down at the table.

'She left me.'

'And the police?'

He shook his head.

'They've hung me out to dry.'

That was why he'd sold his story to a newspaper for a five-figure sum, he explained.

I stood up and walked over to Helen and Jax.

'I think I'm ready to go now.'

I returned to Mark, we hugged and cried. For a split second I could imagine none of this had happened, and we were the same people I'd thought we were a year ago. Nothing would ever be the same again, though. I didn't stop sobbing for the rest of the night. I was grateful Helen was there. Other people had judged me, but I knew she wouldn't. She knew what it was like to be me.

Naomi

(Officer: Mark Stone)

Bristol, spring 2011

With my new partner by my side, I tried to move on with my life. It was my fortieth birthday and my friends had organised a celebration, but I was still scared. The whole thing had knocked my confidence. I even backed away from campaigning – something which had always been at the centre of my life.

Helen

(Officer: John Barker)

Wales, March 2011

After the *Guardian* reported on Boyling, the Police Department of Professional Standards turned up at Rosa's home and asked her to agree to an interview about his conduct. She asked me to sit in on the interview. It was absolutely harrowing listening to her detailed account of how Jim had treated her. At the end of the interview it was clear the officers had also been deeply shocked by Rosa's account and they apologised to her on behalf of the police. They also asked me if I wanted to make a complaint about John. I said I would think about it, but in the end, I thought we were more likely to get success through the civil courts.

As we parted, I told Rosa I hoped to meet Gareth Peirce with Lisa later that month. Rosa was eight months pregnant, and with two children with a profound genetic disability to look after already there was no way she could make it to London to join us, so I promised to let her know how it went.

Lisa
(Officer: Mark Stone)

London, April 2011

I'd been quite resistant to the idea of a legal case when Helen first raised it over dinner with Jax, but now I agreed to meet up with Gareth to discuss it. I was still nervous because the narrative at the time was very much that Mark Kennedy was a rogue officer, and I didn't want a criminal case against one officer. I wanted to show that this was a deliberate tactic across the police. Also, on a personal level, our relationship was still so fresh and raw for me. The thought of banding together with his exes while I was still devastated from our break-up was horrible. But going with Helen felt easier somehow, because she had a very similar story to me and understood what I was going through but wasn't connected to Mark in any way.

It was towards the end of the day and was starting to get dark. Gareth's office was in an old building in Camden and we had to climb up these narrow, rickety stairs to the top floor. It was after hours so there was no one else around and there was such a cloak-and-dagger atmosphere.

I hadn't met Gareth before, but I knew about her from her work with miners during the miners' strike, the Guildford Four and the Birmingham Six. She was such a big figure, and I thought I'd find her intimidating, but she was very softly spoken and gentle. It was the first time I'd spoken about Mark to anyone official. Even though it'd become a big media story, I'd refused to speak to any journalists. It had felt like a very private trauma at the time. I felt like there had been so much judgement from the press and from anonymous people online, but with Gareth it was different. She let me speak without assuming she already knew my story, and she made it feel like a safe space where I could tell everything from my perspective. As soon as I started speaking, I could see from the expression on her face that she was on our side. It was quite overwhelming and I found it hard not to cry because she was so kind.

When I'd finished, Gareth told us that this kind of case had never been brought to court before. No one had ever publicly exposed an undercover cop they were in a relationship with, so there wasn't any case law to base it on. But there wasn't a flicker of doubt from her. She said she wanted to take it on.

I was relieved that she took it so seriously, and I felt like I was in the room with two very strong, capable women. At a moment when I felt so vulnerable, there was a kind of validation that I'd done something strong by exposing Mark.

London, April 2011

I moved my boat down to London to finish off my studies. I still had my dissertation left to write, so I decided to throw myself into it. Being moored up in Nottingham only brought back too many reminders and I needed to focus. By this time, Gareth had referred me and Helen to someone in her law firm's civil claims department – a woman called Harriet Wistrich – who specialised in human rights cases and was a passionate advocate for women. Helen set about tracking down other partners of suspected undercover cops so that we could bring a collective case.

On my way to London, I had people with me on the boat to help sail and do the locks. My mum and sister were my crew as we passed near Milton Keynes. But the boat engine started to overheat and fail. I knew there was a boatyard up ahead so I decided to try and get as close as I could so I could ask them to look at it the following morning. We were still sailing along when I spotted a familiar boat moored up at the side of the bank – it was Mark's. I didn't want to stop, but the engine was struggling and pouring out steam in an alarming way. We limped on a little further, just out of sight, and moored up next to a bridge just two minutes' walk from his boat.

'It's him. That was Mark's boat back there,' I told my family. 'What do you think I should do?'

Mum looked at me.

'You should do whatever you feel you need to.'

I was flummoxed and we debated it into the evening. Finally, around 9.30pm, I called Mark to tell him I was moored up further along the bank. He'd just got back from filming in London, so we agreed to meet in a pub along the canal.

I'd not had time to prepare, and Helen and Jax weren't there for back-up, so it was a lot messier. But I needed to do it – to try to put some of this to rest, in the hope it would stop the constant thoughts of him, of us, of the past, consuming me. Mark asked about my family. I told him they were well. Then he began to open up.

'I'm trying to make it right, Lisa. I don't know what I'm doing, I've got no friends.'

'I need to move on,' I told him, getting up to leave.

As we stood on the bridge, looking down at the water below, Mark turned to me.

'I don't want you to go.'

I shook my head.

'My mum and sister are waiting for me.'

I said goodbye and gave him a hug.

Mark paused and then spoke.

'There's no one else, you know. I don't want anyone else.'

I held my resolve. For me it was a long way too late.

For anyone reading my story, the events may seem black and white but for me it was all confusing shades of grey. I know there were elements of our relationship that were real. I also clung on to the hope that I'd be able to recognise love again in the future, if I was ever lucky enough to experience it. I received a few messages from Mark after that last meeting, including one when Wales won at rugby. It always threw me into confusion, but I knew I had to move on.

I would still occasionally google him and, in 2012, I was saddened to discover that his brother, Ian, had committed suicide. I messaged Mark to tell him how sorry I was, and he replied saying he was devastated. That was the last time we were in communication and it was one line each. I stopped accessing that email account and changed the password to something I promptly forgot. All the small threads that once held us together snapped away one by one.

If we'd been in a cheesy Hollywood film, we would have ended up together, against all the odds. But life isn't like that.

There was no happy ending, not for anyone.

Helen
(Officer: John Barker)

London, May 2011

Her Majesty's Inspectorate of Constabulary (HMIC) had invited interested parties to a meeting about undercover policing in protest movements. I found out at short notice and went along. Weirdly, one of the judges from the McLibel appeal was on the panel and we ended up talking briefly before the meeting started, twelve years since I appeared in front of him in court.

The meeting was hosted by Bernard Hogan-Howe, an HMIC officer, who had been appointed to oversee a review into undercover policing after the revelations about Mark Kennedy. I was cynical about any positive outcome from the meeting, but as there might not be another opportunity I felt it was important to challenge him over the police abuse of women's autonomy and rights. I felt he deflected and avoided answering my question but I was still glad I had managed to raise the issue anyway.

Later that day, I met up with Ruth, another woman who had been involved in Reclaim the Streets, who had also been deceived into a relationship with Jim Boyling, prior to his relationship with Rosa. I told her about our planned legal action and was pleased she agreed to get involved too.

London, 29 June 2011

We finally had our first proper group meeting, with three lawyers present: Harriet Wistrich, Gareth Peirce and Phillippa Kaufmann. There were five deceived women present: me; Rosa, who came with her new baby; Lisa; Alison; and Ruth. It felt powerful and moving to be in a room full of determined women seeking justice. For most of the women apart from me, this was the first time they had met. As we each introduced ourselves and talked about our experience, we started to notice patterns emerge. We could see that what had seemed like heart-wrenching stories told by the officers at the time were so similar they could only have come through shared practice. It was chilling.

Rosa's perspectives were so helpful, too. The intensity of love we felt during the relationships had led most of us to wish we could go back to that time, almost hoping that even if the relationships had started with deception, maybe they had developed into genuine feelings and could be recovered via total honesty. But what Rosa told us of the reality when she did eventually find Jim was a stark warning about the impossibility of such dreams.

Harriet said she had never encountered comparable cases; we would be breaking new ground. She and Phillippa would investigate what was possible. They told us that action could potentially be taken against the individual officers, or if it was in the course of their employment the employer became 'vicariously liable'. All of us felt it was important to hold the police as a whole institution to account, rather than focusing on individual officers.

There was no way that all this could have happened so many times without the knowledge of more senior police officers. They should have put measures in place to stop it.

Lisa

(Officer: Mark Stone)

London, summer 2011

More women were starting to join the case. We each had an individual one-on-one meeting with the lawyers to tell our stories, then we had group meetings, all of us together in a tiny conference room at the lawyers' office in Camden.

When I turned up at the office, I felt like someone was watching me. I stood at the door waiting to be buzzed in and imagined someone with a big telephoto lens in the window of the flat across the road. I knew the police would hate that we were doing this and I wondered if they had us under surveillance. I only had to wait a few seconds to be buzzed in, but I could feel eyes on me.

The room wasn't quite big enough, so we were all huddled round the table. It looked out on a busy road and we couldn't open the windows because there was too much traffic noise, so it was very stuffy.

There were a lot of lawyers at that first meeting, which reassured me that they were taking our case seriously. They had an agenda and tried to keep us on track, but it must have felt like chaos to them. One person's experience would spark a memory from someone else and we'd all chime in. I was struck by the similarities in the way the officers behaved and the lies they told. It all seemed so similar and that was deeply unsettling.

The meetings went on for longer than planned, hours and hours sometimes. The lawyers had to keep bringing us back to the point as we'd get lost in anecdotes. We brought snacks to keep us going and we all kicked our shoes off and settled in. When we went for toilet breaks, we'd be padding through the lawyers' offices in our bare feet, past people in suits doing their very official work. I wondered what they made of us.

There was a lot of laughter and we really needed the jokes to get us through. It was as if the other women were the only people who had permission to take the piss out of me because they understood. There were things we could share with each other that we couldn't tell anyone else.

Afterwards, we needed to talk more, so we spilled out and looked for somewhere to eat. We went to a pub to have some food and wine, and to carry on sharing our stories. That was when we really bonded as a group.

Alison

(Officer: Mark Cassidy)

London, summer 2011

I had an initial meeting with Harriet Wistrich, the solicitor, so she could go through my story with me. My first question to her was, 'What are the other women like?' I didn't know any of them apart from Helen.

But when we had our first meeting together, I immediately felt a unique bond. I was reassured being around these women who I knew would believe my story, and hearing the similarities in theirs was chilling. The things they said made me reframe my own experience because I suddenly saw the patterns. It made me question how much Mark had ever really cared about me.

My overwhelming feeling was one of responsibility towards the other women, especially those for whom it was still so new. I'd lived with my story for ten years but, save for Helen and Rosa, these revelations were very recent. They were still in the throes of it and the emotion was raw.

My life had moved on so far by that time. I'd made my peace with the idea that I'd never get any answers. But now I could see that, together, we might actually find some. And even if we didn't get the answers we needed, we could shout and make a scene and get public attention; we'd do anything we could to stop it happening again to others.

Helen
(Officer: John Barker)

Belinda's house, August 2011

Even after watching video footage of Bob Lambert, I hadn't been sure whether he was the same person as Bob Robinson in London Greenpeace. But I knew that Belinda would know for certain and she had a right to know the truth about her ex-partner.

'Do you recognise him?' I asked, showing Belinda some film on my phone. 'Is that Bob?'

Belinda turned and then looked at me as though all the wounds she'd suffered years before had been ripped apart once again.

'Oh my God, it's him,' she said, her voice stolen by emotion.

She began to cry and her hands trembled as she lit up a cigarette and wandered over by the back door to calm her nerves. I had to break it to her that Bob, along with John Barker, my ex, who Belinda had also known, had both been undercover police officers – and they weren't the only ones.

I told her we were attempting to bring a case, and asked if she would be interested in getting involved.

Lisa

(Officer: Mark Stone)

Gower Peninsula, September 2011

The case was starting to gain momentum and a few other women had joined the group. I was still the only woman involved who'd been in a relationship with Mark, and I hadn't really mentioned it to his other exes. I was still feeling very tender about it all. In meetings, we were having to share intimate details of our experiences, and I was worried about how I'd feel hearing other people's memories of Mark. But I wanted to tell the full story, as he'd been in more than one relationship. I'd already talked to Naomi about her time with him, and she had supported me so well throughout the media storm, so I trusted her and felt safe asking if she wanted to join the case.

There was a group of activists going on a surfing trip to the Gower Peninsula, and Naomi and I both went along. One day I asked her to come for a walk with me along the beach. It was a blustery, sunny afternoon and we were walking arm in arm, admiring the beautiful coastline, when I started telling her about the case.

I'd kept fairly quiet about it up until that point, and hadn't told Naomi that I'd met with lawyers. She seemed quite surprised to hear how many other women and officers were involved, as she hadn't realised the full extent of the surveillance. I'd been worried about asking her to join the case, because I didn't feel I had the emotional capacity to support someone else through the process, but her immediate response was to make sure I was okay with it. I told her I was planning to ask Kate to join, who had been the first woman Mark had formed a relationship with when he went undercover in 2003. I suggested that Naomi and Kate could support each other emotionally if I wasn't able to hold it all together. By the end of the conversation, I felt really reassured that I'd have someone who was already a close friend by my side.

Helen
(Officer: John Barker)

TUC headquarters, London, 15 October 2011

Through my position as a union rep at work, I would often receive emails about trade union events. I couldn't believe it when an email arrived advertising a TUC conference on Islamophobia with Bob Lambert as a speaker.

I met up with a couple of people in London Greenpeace and asked what they thought we should do. The event was only a few days away so we had little time to plan. We had no idea what time Lambert would speak and were wary of discussing it over the phone, as we didn't want the police to stop us. In the end, we agreed to write a leaflet and meet at the beginning of the day to form a plan. We didn't want to disrupt the conference but felt people shouldn't be deceived about who Bob Lambert was. We decided we would hand out the leaflets and call on him to apologise for his actions.

Bob strode confidently onto the stage and spoke for ten or fifteen minutes. He was just heading back from the lectern to his seat when Dave Morris, who we decided had the loudest voice, shouted that Bob had overseen spying on campaign groups including anti-fascist groups and London Greenpeace. Dave also asked him to publicly apologise for his work as an undercover police officer. People in the audience gasped as Bob looked down, fumbling with his papers. For the first time in his life, he was lost for words. He took a gulp of water and slumped back in his seat.

A couple of burly security guards bounded over towards Dave to throw him out along with two other activists, who were busy distributing leaflets. Meanwhile, I quietly exited the room and then waited with Dave outside. We spotted Bob coming before he saw us. We were angry but determined. We wanted answers, for us and for Belinda and the others he'd deceived.

'Are you going to apologise, Bob? Are you proud of having deceived women?' I asked as Dave and I followed him along the street.

He was cornered and, for once, there was nowhere to hide. I continued to question him. When he refused to respond, I felt angry at his arrogance and took out my mobile and began to film. I knew I had to record it and get it out there for the whole world to see.

'Bob, we'd like to talk to you about your infiltration of London Greenpeace and your abuse of female campaigners, having relationships with them when you were undercover.'

Suddenly, he crossed the street and started to run, but we kept pace with him.

'Would you like to say sorry to Belinda for what you did to her?' I asked. 'Would you like to say sorry to any of the other women that had relationships with your undercover officers? Or are you proud of what you did?'

Bob said nothing. Instead, he remained stony-faced as he jumped into a cab.

As the car pulled away, we shouted back.

'Shame on you!'

The *Guardian* covered the story and Channel 4 later used our footage on the evening news. Bob was well and truly outed.

Camden, London, 17 October 2011

Two days later we had another legal meeting in Harriet's office, this time with me, Alison, Belinda, Ruth and barristers Phillippa Kaufmann and Charlotte Kilroy to give advice and discuss specific legal claims that might be possible. I showed them the footage of Lambert running away and Belinda remarked on what a coward he was.

Lisa and Rosa were unable to make it to this meeting, but Harriet told us that two new women were likely to join the claim: Naomi and Kate, who had both had relationships with Mark Kennedy. We now had eight women to bring the case, who between us had been deceived by five different undercover police officers over a period spanning twenty-four years. It would be impossible for the police to claim this was a result of the actions of one or two rogue officers. It was now obvious there was a systemic problem of officers exploiting women as part of their infiltration strategy. I was adamant that we needed to name those officers and highlight this as institutional sexism.

London, 15 December 2011

We finally launched our case against the Metropolitan Police by service of a letter before claim – a legal requirement aimed at avoiding the need for court proceedings by encouraging resolution of the dispute. The 'pre-action protocols' require both parties (claimant and defendant) to act reasonably in exchanging information and documents relevant to the dispute before actually filing a claim in the court. As well as the nature of our claim, the letter outlined details of our relationships and the harm that had been caused to us by the deception. We sought disclosure of any relevant documents in their possession, a declaration that the conduct was unlawful, damages and confirmation that the police had taken action to prevent such relationships from happening again. The press release explained the action:

Eight women deceived into long-term intimate relationships with five separate undercover officers commence unprecedented claim against police

Birnberg Peirce & Partners have commenced legal action against the Metropolitan Police on behalf of eight women who were deceived into having long-term intimate relationships with undercover police officers. The five undercover officers were all engaged in infiltrating environmental and social justice campaign groups between the mid-1980s and 2010 and had relationships with the women lasting between seven months and nine years.

The women assert that the actions of the undercover officers breached their rights as protected by the European Convention on Human Rights, including Article 3, ('no one shall be subject to inhumane and degrading treatment'), and Article 8 ('respect for private and family life, including the right to form relationships without unjustified interference by the state'). The women are also bringing claims for deceit, assault, misfeasance in public office and negligence, and seek to highlight and prevent the continuation of psychological, emotional and sexual abuse of campaigners and others by undercover police officers.

The press release went on to give a collective quote from us women:

We are bringing this case because we want to see an end to the sexual and psychological abuse of campaigners and others by undercover police officers. It is unacceptable that state agents can cultivate intimate and long-lasting relationships with political activists in order to gain so-called intelligence on those political movements.

A case about such serious violations of human rights ought to have been front-page news everywhere, but the story didn't even get covered. The *Guardian* had said they would cover it, but someone famous died and we were bumped from the paper. I felt frustrated that such a serious issue as tackling state abuse of women could be relegated in this way.

Lisa
(Officer: Mark Stone)

London, December 2011

I lost count of the number of reports that were commissioned into different aspects of the Mark Kennedy operation. The *Guardian* reported a total of twelve ongoing by now. It was as if the state were trying to parcel it off into multiple small packages in order to confuse us and hide the complete picture. Nothing was joined up, and everything was pointing towards an operation to minimise the damage. One of the first reports to make its findings public was by retired High Court judge Sir Christopher Rose. It had been looking into allegations that the Crown Prosecution Service (CPS) had suppressed vital evidence in the form of recordings made by Mark Kennedy in the Ratcliffe-on-Soar case.

Unsurprisingly, the Rose report concluded that 'the failures were individual, not systemic', even though to us it was clear that police and prosecutors knew full well about the involvement of undercover police. Just as other reports portrayed Mark Kennedy as one bad apple, this one blamed one person in the CPS as being entirely at fault for the miscarriage of justice in the case. Keir Starmer went on *Newsnight* to defend the report and reinforce that there was no institutional problem.

It was so obvious to me that we had to fight hard to keep it all connected. Our case linking the different officers seemed so vital, and I was incredibly glad to be part of a wider case and not on my own.

London, February–March 2012

All eight of us made common law claims against the police, but only those of us who had relationships with Mark Kennedy were able to bring claims under the Human Rights Act, because the other relationships predated October 2000, when the act became law.

This meant that Naomi, Kate and I were officially in one group and Helen, Alison, Belinda, Rosa and Ruth were in another, although we worked together as a group as much as we could to make the cases come together despite the slight legal differences. In February, the three of us received the first response to our claim from the police. It was brief, but significant.

In a letter dated 10 February 2012, the police stated: *'If it assists, I can confirm Mark Kennedy was a Metropolitan Police officer and did not serve with any other force. He left the Metropolitan Police Service in March 2010.'*

This confirmed to me what Mark had said about leaving his undercover role and working for a private firm, but I thought he'd left the police sooner. This was the first official piece of information I got that told me something new, and that felt important. It made me really hungry for more information, and I pictured the mountains of files they had full of things like this that would help me make sense of those years of my life.

They then went on to say that they wouldn't accept any 'vicarious liability' for 'Mr Kennedy's sexual conduct', as we had set out in our claim.

In a letter dated 14 March 2012, they stated:

> *I confirm that during most of the entire period from July 2003 to February 2010, Mark Kennedy was authorised under the Regulation of Investigatory Powers Act [RIPA] to engage in conduct of the sort described in section 26(8) of Regulation of Investigatory Powers Act.*
>
> *He was lawfully deployed in relation to certain groups to provide timely and good-quality preemptive intelligence in relation to pre-planned activities of those groups. The authorisation extended to participation in minor criminal activity.*

This shocked me; it seemed they were saying it was lawful, it was authorised and it implied they didn't have a problem with anything that had happened during his deployment. The RIPA section they referred to said that he was allowed to form a 'personal or other relationship' with people while undercover. Those words felt very loaded to me, like they knew exactly what was meant by 'other' relationships.

Naomi

(Officer: Mark Stone)

Rolling Stone magazine, March 2012

When I first heard of his deceit, I'd tried to process some of my anger by burning my photographs of Mark Stone. However, a photo I'd taken of him on holiday in Northumberland resurfaced in _Rolling Stone_ magazine; Mark had given an interview and the same photo of him beamed out from the page. It was a picture I'd taken and, I presumed, had also burnt. But Mark must have kept a copy – he obviously fancied himself in it and the image it presented to the rest of the world. Talking to _Rolling Stone_ played into some new 'rock 'n' roll' persona of his. Underneath the picture, using his old nickname, it said: _Flash in 2004._

It was incorrect. The picture was of Mark Stone in May 2005. I knew this because I'd taken it in a car park in Northumberland on the last day of our holiday as we packed up the car.

Rolling Stone had used another photo – one Lisa had taken from her tent in Iceland.

He must have kept all the ones he liked.

Later, Mark appeared in a documentary and another photo I'd taken was used in it. He seemed to be loving the notoriety and enjoying acting out his part. Although the pictures were part of the lie, he was still using them to represent who he was. He'd been exposed and yet he'd kept the photos because they were part of his 'identity', the way he wanted to see himself. In interviews he'd denied his connection to me and others by only ever acknowledging some of his relationships, but he'd used photos of mine, taken during our relationship, to promote himself.

Helen
(Officer: John Barker)

London, spring 2012

I'd wanted to bring the case to expose the police use of these abusive relationships and so to prevent them happening to anyone else, but we were told the legal system primarily sees money as the remedy for wrong, so damages had to be the focus of our claim. That meant we had to have psychiatric reports compiled on us, in order to prove that the relationships had caused damage and then to quantify that damage. All of us were uncomfortable with this; we felt our private lives had been intruded into far too much already. Why should we now have to give even more of our personal thoughts and experiences to a stranger who would then compile a report to be handed to the police? Hadn't they invaded our lives enough with the fake partners?

I argued we shouldn't have to go through these psychological interviews; there should be automatic basic damages for perpetrating such an extreme level of deception. There were set amounts for broken arms and legs, so why not broken hearts?

Irrespective of whether we all had recognisable psychological damage, I also wanted us to argue for compensation for the time we wasted in the relationships with entirely fake men and searching for the truth afterwards, including the loss of opportunity to form genuine close and loving relationships and have children. People can be prosecuted for wasting police time, so why shouldn't the police pay for wasting years of our lives? If they had bothered to consider the potential impact on us as women they would have realised that while men can potentially father children at any time in their adult lives, women only have a limited window of opportunity. They had stolen a significant number of these years from us.

But our barristers said that time-wasting wasn't a recognised complaint: only psychiatric or physical injury and loss of earnings and career potential were covered. We had no choice; we had to be interviewed for psychiatric reports.

In the end, most of us were diagnosed with serious psychological injuries – between us this included post-traumatic stress, extreme anxiety, depression, panic attacks, obsessive compulsive disorder, delusional disorder, paranoia and depersonalisation. The deception and abuse by these officers had clearly had a significant impact on our lives and mental wellbeing.

London, June 2012

Six months after we started our claim process against the police, we finally received a response. The police said the common law claims, which would have been heard in open court, should await the outcome of the first three human rights cases in the secret Investigatory Powers Tribunal. They went on to say that they could 'neither confirm, nor deny' (NCND) whether any of the men who abused us had been undercover police officers. It felt like this was adding insult to injury. For good measure the police also argued that our case was unfounded in law, that if it was allowed to go ahead then anyone who told small lies about themselves, for instance about their age, could be charged with rape – as if the deception they perpetrated on us was just a minor detail.

It was clear that the police were desperate to prevent our case going ahead. And if it did go ahead, they wanted it to be held in secret, without us or anyone else being able to hear or see the evidence. We had to fight this cover-up.

I was struggling with really bad shoulder pain at the time from my work as a gardener. Lying awake in the early morning one night I suddenly remembered all the times the police had already confirmed the identities of officers. I got up and fired off an email to our lawyers and the other women. I was fuming.

They had admitted that Mark Kennedy was an undercover officer in their letter just a few months ago. They had confirmed to the media that Mark Kennedy was a police officer when the story first broke in 2010. They had confirmed that Jim Boyling was a cop when they interviewed Rosa back in March 2011. No less than the commissioner of the Metropolitan Police himself, Bernard Hogan-Howe, had appeared in front of the Metropolitan Police Authority in October 2011 and publicly confirmed that 'Jim Sutton' was under investigation as a serving police officer. And after we outed Lambert that same month, he had issued a public statement confirming he had been an undercover police officer and apologised to Belinda for deceiving her. Surely, as one-time head of the SDS, Lambert would have known about it if there had been a policy of 'neither confirm nor deny'. And was it really credible that the top cop in the Met Police didn't know about the policy either? Were they taking us for idiots?

And if there really was a long-standing and active Metropolitan Police Service policy of NCND, why hadn't they immediately responded to that effect in December 2011 rather than waiting six months to tell us?

Camden, London, July 2012

At a legal meeting to discuss how we would challenge the latest police responses, Harriet told us that Jenny Jones, Green Party member of the Metropolitan Police Authority, had been in touch. She had been very concerned to read about our cases. She offered to raise questions directly with the Metropolitan Police Commissioner at a monthly 'Mayor's Question Time' she attended as part of her role. Harriet also told us that a variety of journalists and radio and TV presenters had been in contact, and we might want to speak to them in order to raise the profile of the case. We all had serious qualms about talking directly to the media; it felt terrifying to start talking about the most intimate aspects of our life in public. But we were pleased that people had been in contact to see how they could help raise the profile of the case and our efforts to stop these abusive relationships.

London, 2 October 2012

We'd decided that we had to start speaking publicly because so many people just didn't understand the nature and extent of the violation and damage caused to us. News commentators would say things like, 'Lots of people are lied to in relationships, what's all the fuss about?' There was only one way to get the harmful effects across, so we agreed to be interviewed for the radio programme *File on 4*.

Radio 4 broadcast a long programme on undercover policing, over half of which was concerned with our cases, and included Lisa, Belinda, Alison, Kate and I talking about our relationships and the impact the deception had on us. We were all interviewed together in Harriet's office, leaning on each other for strength. We explained that while deception in any relationship was wrong, the police deceit was on a totally different scale, and was carried out by the state, which has a duty to protect human rights, not violate them.

This was our first big media piece and it felt like a milestone given how vulnerable we had all felt about doing interviews. The police gave weaselly answers about whether or not sexual relationships were permitted while undercover, and it was clear they did not have a strong position to stop such relationships even now. Listening back, I was pleased the programme included me saying my key concern was that I wanted to prevent this from happening to other people. I wanted people to realise this was not some historical issue; there had been decades of abuse and it needed to be stopped from happening again.

Lisa

(Officer: Mark Stone)

Royal Courts of Justice, London, 21–23 November 2012

Our first big hearing was about whether our case should be heard publicly or not. The police had applied for the three Human Rights Act cases to be heard by the shadowy and secretive Investigatory Powers Tribunal (IPT). In the IPT the claimants are not usually allowed to see or even hear the evidence. We didn't want that, as it seemed like there would be little chance of getting the answers we were seeking that way.

Our lawyers argued that nobody had ever imagined undercover police should be allowed to form intimate sexual relationships with their targets. Parliament could not have intended to say that this would be authorised under RIPA laws when they were drawing them up.

The Metropolitan Police served a defence of 'neither confirm nor deny' (NCND), claiming that they couldn't be expected to defend the claims as it would mean revealing operational under-cover details. They tried to delay and deny as much as possible. They were constantly putting obstacles in our way, trying to get the cases thrown out for various reasons, saying it had been too long ago or we didn't have a case in law.

It was surreal, stepping inside the Royal Courts of Justice. The building was so ornate, all Gothic arches and white stone. Looking at the judges sitting on high, I felt like they were part of the establishment, and together with the police, were all on the same side. I had the impression that the police had unlimited resources to throw at the case, and I had no faith in the legal system. But still, I was confident that we had an amazing team of strong women on our side, and I knew we were doing something important.

We never got to give evidence in court ourselves – it was always the lawyers speaking on our behalf – but we were very engaged and wanted input on everything they said. Sometimes that led to arguments in the corridor, when we wanted to argue things that didn't have a precedent in law, whereas the barristers wanted to go for things they thought they could win.

The main thing we were fighting for was disclosure. We wanted to see the files that the police had on us. I wanted to know who'd been aware of my relationship with Mark, and who had been in that relationship with us. What conversations had been had, how closely Mark was being observed all those times we were together. *Were they coming on holiday with us? Were they reading our text messages? Had they seen intimate, personal photographs that I'd sent Mark on his phone?*

I had an image of a roomful of cops looking at them and laughing. For me, it was all about getting those answers. I needed answers to all those questions to feel like I could move on. But the police were doing everything they could to avoid giving us any details.

We held protests before the hearings to publicise what was going on – it was so important to get our message out to the wider public.

Alison

(Officer: Mark Cassidy)

Birnberg Peirce offices, London, December 2012

Harriet, Belinda and I had a meeting with senior officers from the Metropolitan Police Department of Professional Standards (DPS) to discuss making a complaint to Operation Herne about Mark and Bob. In return, since the DPS only investigated police officers, we'd expected they would confirm Mark was an undercover police officer. We sat down, with Harriet on my left and Belinda on my right. The room smelt of stale sweat.

'I need to explain at the outset that none of the names of people discussed in the room during the meeting can be confirmed or denied as employees of the Metropolitan Police presently or in the past,' the officer said.

It was like he was flinging up a brick wall in front of me. The police were refusing to confirm or deny that Mark had been working for them. I could feel my anger rising.

'I want you to know,' he continued, 'the police are investing a large amount of resources in terms of time and people into investigating the SDS and that it is coming from the highest levels within the force.'

He asked me to show them photographs, videos and letters from my time with Mark. Anything I had to 'evidence' the relationship. That was when I realised what was really going on. Mark was denying it had ever happened.

For the first time since he had disappeared nearly thirteen years earlier, I was in a room with someone who knew him, the real him. But they were refusing to tell me anything. I refused to co-operate or make a statement, and walked out.

Portcullis House, early 2013

I made an appointment with my local MP Diane Abbott to discuss
my case. I wondered if she might have advice about bringing the
scandal to wider public attention. I visited her with my mother,
we discussed the extent of the infiltration, and she said she would
raise it with the then-chair of the Home Affairs Select Committee,
Keith Vaz.

Lisa
(Officer: **Mark Stone**)

Royal Courts of Justice, 17 January 2013

After the three-day hearing in November, judgement was finally handed down on 17 January 2013.

The judge, Mr Justice Tugendhat, agreed with us that our cases should be heard in public in the High Court, but said that we would have to wait till the secret tribunal had reached its verdict first. It wasn't the decision we wanted, and we knew straight away we would appeal.

Incredibly, in his judgement he wrote that sexual relationships by police officers must have been contemplated by the legislators because *James Bond is the most famous fictional example of a member of the intelligence services who used relationships with women … fictional accounts (and there are others) lend credence to the view that the intelligence and police services have for many years deployed both men and women officers to form personal relationships of an intimate sexual nature (whether or not they were physical relationships) in order to obtain information or access.'*

We were astonished that the courts could rely on a fictional character to back up the law. I found Mr Justice Tugendhat's comments about James Bond in his judgement incredibly insulting, I couldn't believe he would say something like that.

The judge did, however, say that if the allegations were true they were very serious. He went on to say that physical sexual relationships that are covertly maintained may amount to inhumane and degrading treatment depending on the degree and nature of the concealment. This was an important concession because if they breached our human rights in this way then these relationships could not be authorised under RIPA and would therefore be unlawful.

Helen

(Officer: John Barker)

Tottenham, London, 4 February 2013

I knew the *Guardian* was covering my story, so I bought a copy
on my way to work, but I didn't have time to read it before starting
my shift at 7.30am. At my tea break, I was glad to find the council depot empty. I spread out the paper and saw, for the first time,
pictures of John in the national press with the story of our relationship. Although at that time I was using the pseudonym 'Clare',
seeing it in black and white felt like a milestone. Up until then it had
felt a bit unreal, as though it hadn't really happened, because there
was no visible evidence.

I'd told the *Guardian* about finding the death certificate for the
identity John had stolen and the impact it had had on me. The head-
line read: *'Woman's 18-Year Search for Truth About Police Spy Who
Used Dead Child's Name'*.

House of Commons, 5 February 2013

We were in the House of Commons café ahead of giving evidence to
the Home Affairs Select Committee investigating undercover policing, when a *Guardian* journalist told me that the real John Barker's
family had been in touch and had asked to pass on thanks to me for
exposing what the police had done. A wave of relief washed over me;
I had worried about the impact on them of finding out John had
been using their loved one's name. Images of the house where he
had been born came flooding into my mind and I became tearful
remembering all the times I had knocked on the door. I thought,
too, of what might have happened had they been there at the time.

Half an hour later, when we appeared in front of the Home
Affairs Select Committee, the politicians seemed more concerned
about getting us to agree that undercover policing was a legitimate

tool and asking us what we had done than they were in learning what the police had done to us, how they had done it and the impact it had on us. I was angered by their treatment of us.

We stayed to watch Patricia Gallan, then deputy assistant commissioner of the Met Police, give evidence. The chair repeatedly asked her to apologise to the families of children whose identities had been used by the police, but not once did he ask her to apologise to women who had been deceived into relationships by police officers.

It seemed like everyone was more bothered about the police using the stolen identities of children who had died than they were about the harm caused to us women. It felt like they assumed we were to blame for the abuses perpetrated on us.

Alison

(Officer: Mark Cassidy)

House of Commons, 5 February 2013

Helen, Lisa and I were all asked to give oral evidence to the Home Affairs Select Committee. When we walked in, I was struck by how grand the room was – with its Victorian wallpaper and gilt-framed oil paintings. Our evidence was taken in private to protect our anonymity, and we sat in a row facing the horse-shoe of tables behind which sat eight suited parliamentarians. The image of the crowned portcullis on the back of each chair was a reminder of where we were.

We'd agreed among ourselves that I'd start by reading out a statement I'd prepared. We didn't know the protocol but thought it was important to put on record the specifics of what had happened to us. We wanted these parliamentarians to be in no doubt that this was far more than a tale about lying boyfriends. The committee chair tried to interrupt me at first, but then he did grant me permission to continue.

After this, they started asking questions. They seemed to be suggesting that we'd brought the spying on ourselves with our radical politics. But we pushed back and said there were no circumstances where undercover police having sexual relationships with members of the public could be justified, no matter what our politics were.

After we'd finished, it was the turn of our lawyer Harriet Wistrich, whose evidence was recorded for the online parliamentary video stream. We sat behind the lawyers with friends in the public gallery. I could see where the cameras were in the room and tried to ensure I was never in full view. I knew this video would be made available on the parliamentary website and if Mark were ever to watch it, I wanted to look smart and together. I'd worn a black fitted jacket for the occasion and my hair had recently been cut and coloured. He hadn't destroyed me and this stake in the ground was a marker of that.

Lisa
(Officer: Mark Stone)

House of Commons, 5 February 2013

The Home Affairs Select Committee was the first time I'd spoken publicly about what had happened, apart from the couple of brief quotes I'd given to the *File on 4* programme. Other people had spoken for me and about me, but I had never spoken properly for myself. It felt important to get my own words out there so it wasn't just Mark Kennedy's version of events.

By this point Mark and I weren't in touch any more. I knew he'd be giving evidence as well and it was really spooky to think he was in the building somewhere. I kept wondering whether I'd be leaving the room as he came in and we'd cross paths. I felt like if I saw him, I might be able to tell if the person I knew was still there or not, now that some time had passed. He might have shed his old persona by now, which was still there when I said goodbye to him that last time on the canal bridge. How much of him was real?

It was quite intimidating, being questioned by the MPs. I wanted to share my story but I didn't want to be under examination. I felt like they were asking me what I'd done to deserve it. They wanted to know about our political activity and which groups we were involved in. It felt like the equivalent of asking someone who'd been raped if she'd been wearing a short skirt, as if some political activities deserved this kind of treatment. I refused to answer certain questions. It was frustrating that they didn't seem to understand the issues at all. But having Alison and Helen speak about other officers alongside me made me bolder. The other women who weren't giving evidence also came and sat in the room, so I felt like we had a lot of support.

As soon as we finished giving evidence, the House of Commons security ushered us out. We tried to hang around. I snuck off to the toilet, then tried to loiter in the foyer to see them bring Mark in, but we were herded out. It became clear that they were scared of there being a confrontation, so we were essentially evicted from the building very unceremoniously. It felt like he still had the protection of the state.

Helen

(Officer: John Barker)

London, March 2013

Although we had still received no documents from the police about our relationships or the files they kept on us, the time had arrived when we had to serve our 'Particulars of Claim' – a document setting out much more detail about our relationships with the officers, the impact of the deception on us and the nature of the legal claims we were making against them. We had to provide evidence of the psychological harm caused to us, and this was one of the most traumatic parts of the whole process. It felt like another layer of invasion and torment. We had no trust in the police but we were obliged to give them information that could be used by them to make us vulnerable, potentially to further abuse in the future. It seemed so wrong.

It also meant I had to make a decision on giving up my anonymity. Part of my claim concerned collusion between the police and McDonald's – we were together outside John's home when the libel writ was served on me; Bob Lambert was involved in writing the anti-McDonald's leaflet we were sued over; John was involved in the anti-McDonald's campaign, and in the McLibel Support campaign and our legal defence. It would be obvious to anyone reading that part of the claim that it was about me. I had to give up my anonymity, despite the fact that I had no desire at all to announce details of my private life and talk about my emotional heartbreak to the world. I was also glad that Belinda was giving up her anonymity at the same time. It felt slightly less scary with two of us doing it.

London, 7 May 2013

The police served their defence for the case of the five of us. It told us nothing, apart from that they viewed us with total contempt.

They pleaded 'neither confirm, nor deny' in respect of all the factual allegations in our claim. But for good measure, they stated:

'It is denied that the acts alleged constituted the tort of deceit. The Claimants have failed to identify the misrepresentation(s) which supposedly provide the foundation for their claims.'

It was incredible – it seemed they were trying to suggest that deceiving us as to their entire identity and into relationships lasting years was just not serious enough.

Rather than acknowledging that intimate sexual relationships while undercover would be abhorrent and unlawful, they instead required us to prove that *'officers foresaw that the Claimants would be damaged by a sexual relationship and/or were recklessly indifferent to the risk of such damage'* and *'officers knew that it was unlawful for undercover officers to enter into intimate sexual relationships with individuals, and/or were recklessly indifferent as to whether it was unlawful for them to do so'*. They also asserted that our consent to sexual activity had not been vitiated by the deception. It all felt so contemptuous.

For good measure they finished off by asserting that Rosa and I were out of time for bringing our claims because we had discovered the deception many years ago.

It was so insulting that despite our clear evidence that their officers had abused us and caused us serious harm, they were going to force us through a stressful and long-winded legal process rather than immediately apologising and attempting to make good the harm they had caused.

London, 24 June 2013

Channel 4's *Dispatches* broadcast a TV programme about undercover policing, coinciding with the publication of *Undercover: The True Story of Britain's Secret Police* by *Guardian* journalists Rob Evans and Paul Lewis. The programme was the first in-depth critical examination of the tactics of the Special Demonstration Squad on television. Belinda and I were interviewed and were shown meeting Peter Francis, a former Special Demonstration Squad officer turned whistle-blower. He revealed in the programme that Bob Lambert had been his manager and had advised the SDS team on how to handle relationships – essentially 'don't fall in love' and 'use condoms'. It was nauseating to hear directly what little regard they held for women's autonomy and right to know the truth about who we were in relationships with. The programme revealed that in fact Lambert himself had fathered a child with another woman activist he had deceived into a relationship, leaving her to bring up the child alone when he disappeared at the end of his SDS posting. She was devastated by the deception.

Peter Francis also revealed that while undercover he had been tasked to find information that could be used to undermine the campaign for justice by the family and friends of Stephen Lawrence, a black teenager murdered in a racist attack in 1993 in London.

The revelations were deeply shocking to many people, who simply hadn't been aware until then of the nature of the long-term police infiltration of political campaigns and protest groups in the UK. An investigation was announced in parliament into what the programme had revealed.

London, 5 July 2013

Channel 4 News broadcast a long interview with Bob Lambert in which he was forced to apologise for his actions undercover. He admitted he understood why a victim deceived into a sexual relationship by an undercover officer would feel that they had been 'raped by the state'.

Royal Courts of Justice, London, 6 August 2013

We had pushed for a hearing to set dates for all the formal pre-trial procedures to take place. Usually both sides are supposed to fully set out their position in writing so that each side, and the judges, know what is accepted and what is disputed. Each side is also supposed to disclose any documents in their possession that are relevant to the claims or defence. The police were refusing to do either and seemed to be dragging their feet endlessly. We needed the court to set dates so this couldn't drag on forever.

Shortly before the hearing was due to start, I met Alison by the back doors of the Royal Courts of Justice only to discover they were locked. We had to run round to the front of the courts, wait in a queue to pass through the metal detectors and bag X-rays, before trying to find our way through the labyrinth of passages in the Royal Courts of Justice, up past the 'Bear Garden' (a big hall with high ceilings and huge tables, apparently named in response to Queen Victoria's description of the noise of barristers talking to clients) to the 'Master's Rooms'. These were where 'Masters' made directions in the early stages of a court case, long before you ever had a hearing in front of a judge.

We arrived outside Room 116 just before the arrival of Master Leslie, and were soon ushered in. Our solicitor, Harriet Wistrich, was making the application on our behalf and the police had their solicitor present to oppose it. Alison and I sat on cushioned chairs at the back, notebooks balanced on our knees, listening to the lawyers speak. Our eyes explored the room as the lawyers spoke, scanning the numerous pictures on the walls and books on the shelves. There was even a fireplace complete with mantelpiece and clock. It was more like someone's living room than a courtroom.

Refocusing on the legal arguments going on, we struggled not to laugh as Master Leslie kept interrupting to ask, in a very posh voice, what various acronyms meant. 'I've heard of CND, the Campaign for Nuclear Disarmament, but what's NCND?' He also said that in his day the men would have been called 'cads'.

We kept hearing a trolley squeaking up and down the corridor outside and at one point Master Leslie got up from his seat, strode purposefully across the room and out of the door to exasperatedly ask the person with the trolley to oil the wheels. It was all a bizarre and surreal experience.

By the end of the hearing the Met weren't happy. Rather than keep prevaricating, they were ordered to make their long-threatened strike-out application within a month and to provide supporting documents by then, otherwise they would have to make disclosure to us of any relevant documents by October.

As we left the hearing we felt elated that finally the case was moving and hopeful we might soon get some answers to the questions we had been left with years before.

When we met as a group again a few weeks later, Alison performed a re-enactment of the hearing and we all fell about laughing. It was good to have a release from all the stresses of the case.

Royal Courts of Justice, London, autumn 2013

A month after the August hearing, the police applied to have our entire case struck out, on the grounds that their 'NCND' policy prevented them from responding. Despite Master Leslie's order that they must provide any documents supporting the existence and terms of such a policy, they failed to provide a single document to support their stance. Instead, they served a statement from a senior cop who asserted the existence of the policy without any supporting evidence. They made an outrageous assertion that to defend the claims could 'potentially endanger life'.

Additionally, if their application to strike out our claim failed, they sought an order releasing them from the standard obligation to disclose other relevant documents to us, such as any reports made by the officers about us. Incredibly, they even applied for an order that *our* identities, as well as those of the officers, must be kept secret. It was clear that the police wanted to prevent the public from hearing or understanding what had gone on.

A hearing was set for November 2013. We had to prepare detailed evidence, not just of all the times they had publicly commented on the officers and the Special Demonstration Squad, including *True Spies*, the 2002 TV series about the unit, but we also had to provide witness statements from Rosa, Alison and me of the evidence we had amassed to prove that our ex-partners were police officers. Our statements and evidence filled two lever arch files and included many of the 'love letters' the men had sent us.

A week before the hearing, after the police had received our extensive evidence, they claimed they had 'devastating' evidence in response and argued for yet another adjournment. We spent ages speculating what it was they might have that was so significant. When the evidence came in December, it was like a damp squib – three self-serving statements from the police asserting they were bound by 'NCND' policy but again not a single document to back up its existence or how it was implemented in practice. A date was set for a hearing to strike out our claim in March 2014.

Lisa
(Officer: Mark Stone)

Royal Courts of Justice, London, 5 November 2013

The three of us with Human Rights Act claims had appealed the James Bond decision of Justice Tugendhat that the cases should be heard by the Investigatory Powers Tribunal and for the common law claims to be stayed pending the outcome of the IPT. After a two-day hearing in October, judgement was handed down on 5 November.

We arrived at court feeling nervous. Sadly, the Court of Appeal upheld the decision that the human rights claims must be heard in the IPT, which was disappointing as that would be likely to happen in secret. However, they did lift the stay on High Court proceedings, allowing us to get on with the common law part of the claims without waiting.

The judgement did contain some findings that we welcomed:

> *The establishing and/or maintaining of an intimate sexual relationship for the covert purpose of obtaining intelligence is a seriously intrusive form of investigatory technique. We do not think that it is in issue that it amounts to an invasion of an individual's common law right to personal security and of a most intimate aspect of the right to privacy under article 8 of the Convention.*

But they also said, 'There is no doubt that, in enacting RIPA, Parliament intended to override fundamental human rights.' So they were saying that, instead of protecting us, RIPA was the framework that gave the police permission to ignore our human rights.

Just the week before, the College of Policing, which sets policing standards across the country, had said that undercover police entering into intimate sexual relationships with those they were spying on was morally reprehensible and should be banned. Yet here was the

Court of Appeal seeming to indicate that RIPA legislation covering these issues was capable of authorising such deceptive relationships.

It was all so contradictory. On the one hand we were hearing that it was authorised behaviour, while on the other hand we were hearing the officers being condemned for their actions. My head was spinning with it all. It felt like the police were willing to use whatever arguments in court that got them out of having to answer our cases even if it was the exact opposite of what they were saying in other forums. I was left in no doubt that the number-one priority of the police as an institution was to protect themselves from criticism. It reminded me of Mark Kennedy's press interviews in which he said whatever he needed to say to shift blame from himself.

Alison

(Officer: Mark Cassidy)

Newsnight, March 2014

By now I'd had to reframe everything I'd believed about my supposedly monogamous relationship with Mark. I'd learnt he'd been married with three young children throughout our five years together. It was time to go to the press. I was interviewed by Allan Little for *Newsnight* and Rob Evans in the *Guardian* about my relationship and the wider scandal.

'So, he really was a police officer, then?' said my father down the phone as I marched along Pall Mall during my lunch break. I was working just off Leicester Square, and had taken to spending my lunch hour walking across St James's Park to sit in a café opposite New Scotland Yard, just in case I might spot Mark. I never did.

'Of course he was a fucking police officer!' I screamed against the noise of the traffic. 'What do you think I've been banging on about for the last ten years?'

My dad chuckled.

I wondered if it was the after-effects of his coma over a decade ago or an indication that he – like so many others – had simply believed me delusional for years.

Helen
(Officer: John Barker)

London, March 2014

For the five of us who could only bring common law claims, the police had refused to plead any defence at all to the facts set out in our claim about the relationships. Instead on 4 March they served legal submissions on us where they argued our case should be thrown out of court altogether, claiming a fair trial was not possible because their NCND policy made it impossible for them to defend the claims. I was outraged at their cheek of claiming they couldn't get a fair trial because of their own so-called policy. To us it seemed clear that they were just using NCND to hide serious wrongdoing. We were all set to argue it out in court.

Two days later, on 6 March, Theresa May, then Home Secretary, announced in parliament that there would be a public inquiry into undercover policing. She said Operation Herne and the Ellison review into police spying on the family and friends of Stephen Lawrence had both unearthed serious failings in undercover policing practices.

That week the *Daily Mail* published a column by Richard Littlejohn attacking the decision to hold a public inquiry. It was clear from his column that he had talked to police sources before writing it, and the rampant misogyny of both him and the police was on display in a section about us:

> *There are currently a number of cases in which an assortment of unwashed dopey birds who slept with undercover officers are seeking compensation, even though no force or coercion was involved. Oh, do grow up. Women often fall for dubious men who pretend to be millionaires, or airline pilots or friends of the Royal Family. That doesn't mean they were assaulted, just duped. What are these officers supposed to do when an obliging madwoman in an anarchist group*

takes a fancy to them, make the old News of the World *excuse and leave? In the paranoid world of criminality, political subversion and terrorism, every action is scrutinised microscopically. One false move and the consequences can be fatal.*

He clearly knew nothing about the details of our relationships, only what some bile-filled cops had told him, but here he was spreading misinformation to the public.

On 14 March, three days after we served our legal submissions which we felt demolished the police application to strike out our case, the police wrote to us saying that in light of the announcement of the public inquiry, they were withdrawing their application to strike out our claim. They said it was *'unsustainable for the MPS [the Metropolitan Police Service] to continue to regard the public interest in maintaining NCND as requiring that the claimants' claims be struck out at the present time'.* The hearing was due to take place at the High Court just four days later. The police proposed we vacate the hearing and that we wait for an unspecified date before there was any further progress.

We pushed back and argued that the hearing date should be kept to set new dates for the various stages of the case to progress, including disclosure of documents. At the hearing on 18 March it became clear that the police were actually still intending to rely on NCND, and withdrawing their application had just been a tactical manoeuvre to delay things yet again. As a result, we were then forced to apply to the court for a decision on whether the police were entitled to rely on NCND to resist pleading details of their case in response to our claims.

Royal Courts of Justice, London, 5–6 June 2014

We had a two-day hearing in June in front of Mr Justice Bean. Outside the court supporters handed out leaflets in the sunshine, explaining what our case was about. Huge banners *'Undercover is No Excuse for Abuse'* and *'Police Spies Out of Lives'* were draped over the railings to catch the attention of passers-by.

Inside the courtroom, the police refused to even say whether they considered undercover officers (UCO) deceiving women into intimate sexual relationships to be a legitimate tactic or not. Eventually the judge lost patience with their evasion and demanded that the police lawyer, Monica Carss-Frisk QC, go away and take instructions from the commissioner. After a short delay, she returned to the courtroom and said, 'I am able to tell you … that if proved that the claimants had long-term relationships with individuals who were undercover operatives the defendant would not consider such relationships justified as a UCO tactic.'

This was a major step forward: until this point, the police had refused to even admit this obvious fact. It seemed they had wanted to keep their options open to continue the practice.

A month later we were relieved when Mr Justice Bean ruled that the police could no longer use a blanket response of NCND to refuse to answer our claims. He ruled there was no legitimate public interest in the Met covering up the existence of such deceptive undercover long-term intimate sexual relationships

We were pleased that his judgement, in contrast to the words of Richard Littlejohn, recognised that such relationships were abusive: *'The Chief Constable conducting the Operation Herne investigation has expressed in trenchant terms the view that if this did happen it was a "gross abuse": I believe that most people would agree with him.'* He then went on to say, *'There can be no public policy reason to permit the police neither to confirm nor deny whether an illegitimate or arguably illegitimate operational method has been used as a tactic in the past.'*

We had won a significant victory for transparency. For us this part of the ruling made total sense; we had argued it was obvious that if officers knew that if they acted unlawfully they might lose the protection of secrecy, this would act as a deterrent to them committing unlawful acts. Whereas if they knew they would keep anonymity whatever happened, this would encourage them to feel protected and emboldened to do whatever they wished, whether it was lawful or not.

In relation to Bob Lambert and Jim Boyling, because their identities had already been publicly confirmed, the judge went on to rule that the police could no longer rely on NCND in relation to them. But because there hadn't been any official confirmation yet about John Dines and Mark Jenner, he allowed the police to continue to hide behind NCND for them. It was so frustrating, especially as he went on to say that it appeared this was probably only delaying the inevitable.

'By a great deal of what may be summarised as detective work of her own, [Alison] has established, in my view, a clear prima facie case that Mark Cassidy was in fact an undercover officer called Mark Jenner.' He added that I was in a similar position in relation to John Barker/Dines.

The Police were given twenty-eight days to amend their defence, with a threatened sanction that if they failed to deal with the issues they were now required to answer, they would be assumed to have admitted them.

The day after this judgement, the Met sought discussions to settle the case with Belinda, Ruth and Rosa, desperate to avoid any public admissions of wrongdoing that would be required by answering our claim. Alison and I were out on a limb. We met our lawyers to discuss whether it was feasible to appeal the part of the judgement relating to Dines and Jenner.

We had legal insurance for our main claim, which protected us against potentially massive costs should we lose. But the company would not extend the insurance to cover the appeal, so we were advised it would be risky to go ahead with an appeal, as we might end up with a massive liability for costs. Alison probably wisely bowed out, worried that her home and family could be put at risk by this potential liability. However, I felt strongly that this was a public interest issue that I wanted to pursue. Dines and Jenner had abused us, so why should they have their actions and identities protected? I decided to go ahead with the appeal on my own, unrepresented. Using my legal experience from the McLibel case, I lodged my grounds of appeal.

London, 14 August 2014

The Metropolitan Police served their amended defence, which formally confirmed the identities of Bob Lambert and Jim Boyling and admitted they had engaged in sexual relationships while undercover. But outrageously, the police then went on to assert that the relationships were based on 'mutual attraction and genuine personal feelings' so they denied any responsibility or liability for the abuse and damage caused.

As expected, the amended defence refused to confirm the identities of John Barker and Mark Cassidy. More bizarrely and showing contempt for us and the judgement of the court, the police defence refused to confirm any details about the existence and operation of the Special Demonstration Squad, despite this having been acknowledged elsewhere in the public domain including reports by Operation Herne.

We felt the police had been pulled, kicking and screaming, to this point in our long battle for justice. It represented a partial victory but entirely lacked any acknowledgement of the harm caused to us and the huge abuse of power these relationships represented. It seemed the police had no remorse. Rather than apologise for the abuse inflicted on us, their attitude towards the litigation was to try to obstruct, delay and create still more stress and upset for us. Their continued attempts evade responsibility and refusal to acknowledge the extreme pain they had caused was aggravating the original violation.

Belinda
(Officer: Bob Robinson)

London, 14 August 2014

I was very upset that the defence suggested that my relationship with Bob Robinson was based on 'mutual attraction and genuine personal feelings'. How can a relationship be genuine when it is based on a massive web of lies? He pretended to be a man with noble ideals and political commitments, when in reality he was a police officer spying on our friendship network. He pretended he was committed to the future when he always knew he would go back to his real job and wife and kids. That doesn't show genuine feelings; it is abuse and I would never have consented to such a relationship had I known. The relationship was a total violation of me and my life.

Helen

(Officer: John Barker)

Crown Prosecution Service announcement, 21 August 2014

Just a week later, the Crown Prosecution Service announced that after reviewing evidence from Operation Herne in relation to four undercover police officers accused of deceiving women into relationships, they had decided there was insufficient evidence to prosecute the officers for rape or sexual assault. They also considered charges of procuring a woman to have sexual intercourse by false pretences, misconduct in public office and breaches of the Official Secrets Act. But again they decided there was 'insufficient evidence for a realistic prospect of conviction for any offences against any of the officers'.

Although the CPS did not publicly declare the identities of the officers who had been investigated, Rosa received official notification of the decision as a result of the interview she gave three years earlier about Boyling's abuse. The CPS statement said, *'There was only one complaint of criminal activity against one of the officers, but a number of other officers were considered as a result of allegations made publicly which investigators had become aware of'*. It seemed clear that since Operation Herne was only investigating SDS officers, this meant the other three investigated had to be Lambert, Dines and Jenner. We were angered that yet again the state was more concerned with protecting the abusers than protecting the public.

Lisa
(Officer: Mark Stone)

London, autumn 2014

When it became obvious the case was going to have to be heard, the police started trying to settle. We wanted our day in court, but the legal system is geared up to make people settle. If the lawyers think you might get more money by going to court, you can have the case heard. But if the lawyers think the settlement money offered is more than you'd get in court, the only way you can carry on is to take the risk of being liable for both sides' expenses, which could be hundreds of thousands of pounds. It meant all the police had to do was offer more than the lawyers could reasonably say they could get us in court, and we wouldn't be able to proceed. I didn't really want to settle – I wanted to get answers – but it looked like this was how it was going to have to end.

The fact that it all came down to money was galling and insulting. I had to sit down with one of the barristers in chambers, to go through the impact Mark had had on my life and couch the damage done in financial terms. She was very sympathetic. She said she knew it was awful and that putting a number on it wasn't the point, but we had to do it.

There's a big thick book that the barristers look through and they say, 'Loss of earnings, that costs this much.' Or if I'd lost a leg, they'd have been able to look that up in a book and say it was worth this much. It was one of the most damaging parts of the whole case, having to list all the things that had been taken from us and think about where our lives would have been if this hadn't been done to us.

The things that had done the most damage to me weren't quantifiable in law. There's nothing in law to compensate someone for losing the chance to have a family. We had to argue to bring that in and keep it in a prominent position. I wanted to talk about how they'd damaged my emotional life, not simply my earning capacity.

We also had to have a psychiatric evaluation back when we were starting the case, to provide evidence of how they'd damaged us psychologically. At that point I hadn't felt strong enough to go and get counselling, so my first experience of talking to somebody about the trauma was sitting in the small, boxy conference room in our lawyers' office with a psychologist they'd appointed. There was no therapy in it. It was just me telling her my damage and then being sent off to deal with it by myself while she wrote a report.

I had to relive it all and then I walked out onto the street in busy central London, having opened it all up but never having had any counselling on how to cope with it. Then I had to cycle home through busy London traffic and try not to fall off my bike. I was still in a state of flashback. I'd be cycling somewhere and when I arrived, I'd realise I'd spent the whole journey in a memory. I was quite easily tipped back into all of that.

Alison

(Officer: Mark Cassidy)

Regent's Park, London, December 2014

Arriving for mediation, we approached an imposing building near Regent's Park, with its white columns and tall Georgian windows. None of us knew what to expect from the process and we were all very conscious of being in an environment usually inhabited by professionals in suits and high heels. We had all made an effort to dress for the occasion, but we still didn't look like the usual types who worked there. We were due to meet senior police to explain how their undercover officers' deceit had impacted on our lives and to negotiate, with the assistance of a legal mediator, an out-of-court settlement. It didn't get much more surreal.

We'd been asked by our legal team to prepare impact statements and write our dream apology from the police. If we had to settle out of court, we had to have an apology; an official admission of wrong-doing. Helen was clear she wouldn't settle without it and we all felt the same. With my background in English and media teaching, I chose to make my impact statement as a video. I had over eight hours of my life with Mark recorded on tape so had plenty to choose from.

Sitting across from senior, uniformed police officers and their lawyers, I was the first to present my impact statement. I watched their faces closely as they studied the projection of moving images filling the large screen: Mark playing guitar in my front room; on holiday with me across the world; at my mother's wedding.

As the strong, articulate women beside me took turns to explain their version of the appalling emotional abuse they had suffered at the hands of the police, I was proud to be one of their number.

Mediation involves parties liaising via a neutral person in separate rooms. We were camped out in a large boardroom, our laptops, notebooks and pencil cases strewn across the vast table. We tweaked my dream apology and after much to-ing and fro-ing of lawyers between rooms, we finally agreed the wording for the official one. It felt like an incredibly powerful statement in which the police admitted to violating our human rights and that the relationships were manipulative, deceitful, abusive and wrong.

At the end of three days of intense negotiation, we were done, and we left the building giggly and exhausted. I remember little about that evening except meandering through central London to find a vegan-friendly restaurant where we laughed and cried and got drunk.

Helen
(Officer: John Barker)

London, January 2015

In December 2014 we'd had the settlement meetings for our claim and after three days of negotiations, the MPS agreed to make an apology and pay damages. But there wasn't time to conclude the settlement process before the Christmas break, so further meetings were to be arranged. My appeal hadn't even been mentioned at the settlement meetings, probably due in part to the fact the lawyers weren't representing me for it, so it wasn't even in their minds, while my mind was all over the place given the stress of the process. At the settlement meetings we had all spoken in front of senior police officers about the impact of the relationships on us and our wish to prevent them happening again to anyone else. It had been an intense and draining experience reliving so many of our painful memories.

The year had only just started when I received a letter from the Court of Appeal advising that on 31 December, I had been granted leave to appeal the NCND ruling on the basis that the judges viewed the point of law raised as a public interest issue. I was really pleased by this news, but within a couple of days the police were haranguing me to drop the appeal. I told them I wanted to continue as I also felt it was a public interest issue – why should a police officer have his identity protected after committing abuses? The police then applied to strike out my appeal claiming I had misled the appeal court by not telling them the case had settled – despite the fact the settlement process hadn't been formally concluded and the courts were shut over Christmas anyway, so I couldn't have told them. And as a litigant in person, I didn't even know I was expected to. The police made dire threats about how much this would cost me, which angered me even more. I was acting on a point of principle, which had been recognised as a public interest issue, and they were trying to bully me into submission. It went to a hearing at which I was mentally exhausted and not on the ball enough; the judges then basically warned that if I didn't win the appeal I was at risk of losing all the damages that had been agreed, and that it would be better for me to challenge the NCND position and pursue the release of the names through the public inquiry, where the financial risk wouldn't exist.

Additionally, in the ongoing settlement discussions the police threatened to pull out of the settlement with all the other women. I wanted to continue with the appeal but all in all felt I had no option but to withdraw.

The police then applied for £10,000 costs, for a hearing that lasted less than an hour. I challenged this and it was reduced to £7,000 but I was livid and refused to pay. Why should I pay a massively over-inflated bill for the police to tell the truth about their employee who abused me while working for them?

Alison

(Officer: Mark Cassidy)

London, March 2015

More women had started to find out that they too had been deceived into relationships with undercover officers and our campaign group Police Spies Out of Lives was growing. Eight of us had set it up with trusted friends at the start of our case. Now our campaigning was reaching new audiences and we were building strong allegiances with other individuals and groups whose lives had been turned upside down by these officers.

Mark Cassidy had joined the construction workers' trade union, UCATT, when we were together, and now the Blacklist Support Group (BSG) had evidence that his intelligence was passed on to the Consulting Association in order to blacklist activists, especially union representatives protecting workers' health and safety. The BSG organised a meeting in a parliamentary committee room to launch Dave Smith and Phil Chamberlain's new book about blacklisting in the construction industry. I was immensely grateful that at the meeting, John McDonnell read out a statement by SDS whistle-blower Peter Francis stating unequivocally that Mark was a member of the Special Demonstration Squad. The façade of 'neither confirm nor deny' was crumbling.

Lisa

(Officer: Mark Stone)

London, June 2015

We had another three days of mediation at this grand building in central London. It was a posh conference facility, and the whole environment was completely outside of our world. The mediations were separated into two events, one back in December for five of the women – although we all attended – and then a few months later for the three of us who'd had relationships with Mark Kennedy. When we arrived in the building for the December negotiations Tony Blair was giving a speech in one of the other rooms. At one point we almost ended up sharing a lift with him, but his security stopped us from getting in. Both times there was a surreal edge to the whole thing.

The police had a room and we had a room, then there was a shared room in the middle. During both the December and the June negotiations, the first day took place in a shared room where we made presentations to the police and their lawyers about what had happened to us. We showed photos, and in Alison's case home videos, and read out letters that the undercover officers had written to us. We tried our best to get across the full impact this had all had on us.

I wanted Mark's cover officer and other people from his unit there, the people who'd been directly responsible for sending him into my life on a daily basis, monitoring me as we spent time together. I felt strongly that they had also been part of my relationship with Mark. They had been present the whole time and had controlled my life without me knowing. I wanted to look those people in the eye and explain what they'd done to me, but I didn't get that chance. It was just the deputy police commissioner and police lawyers, listening to us with stony faces.

Still, it did feel cathartic sitting across from the police officers in uniform and explaining to them how they'd affected my life. It felt like the closest we were going to get to a day in court. They would hear it from us, in our own words. It wasn't public, so it was nowhere near what we wanted, but it was the best we could get.

After that, we spent the remaining days in our separate rooms, with our lawyers going back and forth to meet in the middle. At some point, the compensation offer reached a level where the lawyers said we couldn't go any further without being liable for both sides' costs. It was a really tough decision to settle for compensation out of court. It had never been about the money for us, but it reached a point where we couldn't risk being liable for hundreds of thousands in costs. The only person who didn't have to accept their offer was Kate, as the lawyers advised her there was room for her to push for more, so she would be able to take things further. The rest of us had no choice though.

We made sure that if we accepted the compensation, we would still be allowed to speak publicly about our experiences. The police also agreed to make a public apology. Back in December we had pushed for the apology as it was the only thing we could get that wasn't financial. We had argued back and forth for hours about the specific wording, reaching a compromise that wasn't as much as we wanted them to admit, but was what they would agree to say. We pushed and pushed as much as we could until finally reaching a brick wall. They made it clear that there was no more we could wring out of it this time, and the same apology was extended to everyone (even, eventually Kate at a later date and other women after that). There were no answers to our questions, and no disclosure of files.

In the end it still felt like a massive achievement. The apology meant they admitted it had all happened as we said it had, even if they wouldn't admit to all the details. It was a really important part of getting to the truth and making our story public.

We discussed how we would campaign for the full truth through the public inquiry, as a way to get the answers that we hadn't been able to get through our individual cases. It was a historic moment, but definitely not the end of the road.

After everything was agreed we found ourselves out on the street sharing glasses of fizz with our legal team, Phillippa, Charlotte and Harriet. Not all of the women were there that time, which was a shame. It was an unprecedented case and we'd pushed it as far as we possibly could, and that was worth raising a glass to.

Naomi
(Officer: Mark Stone)

London, June 2015

The legal battle was long and exhausting. By the time the Met closed the final door on us going to the High Court, they had been obscuring, blocking, denying and squirming for so many years that it made me even more convinced that they were hiding much more than we could know. I had had many doubts and questions during the legal process. I wondered if Mark had actually kept silent or lied about us to his bosses – had he covered his tracks on both sides? Was I exposing myself more during the legal process than I had during the seven years I'd known him? At the point where the enforced settlement ended my ability to progress with the legal challenge, the proposed public inquiry seemed to hold out a possibility of speaking out further and discovering more. Or was that complete delusion? Were we crowbarring our way into a room that had already been emptied of any evidence while whole other structures of surveillance were being secretly created elsewhere? However, during the life span of the court case, many more people had realised what they had been exposed to and had joined the fight to find answers. I still didn't have any answers but it felt important to keep going, to keep finding ways to speak out, to not let go of the fight for accountability.

Helen

(Officer: John Barker)

Settlement, London, 20 November 2015

Complications around the settlement process meant that although the apology had been agreed in December 2014, other aspects of the settlement hadn't been resolved so we had to keep the apology secret for almost a whole year. Finding a date to announce the settlement had been a complicated process with eight women, childcare arrangements, and the availability of our lawyers and the assistant commissioner to consider. Finally, a date had been agreed.

Just days before the agreed time, the police notified us that they were no longer prepared to go ahead with reading the apology outside New Scotland Yard as had been agreed. They instead proposed to send us a copy of a recording of the assistant commissioner reading out the apology. We were livid. How could they back out of the agreement now, months after they had signed up to it? As recently as two weeks before they had confirmed that the assistant commissioner would read the apology outside New Scotland Yard. The Met were demonstrating yet again that we couldn't trust a word they said. I wanted us to cancel the settlement announcement until this had been resolved, but some of the women were desperate to get the whole thing over and done with. Trying to resolve this sent our stress levels rocketing. Eventually, given the huge complications in getting everyone together in one place for our press conference, I reluctantly backed down.

We arrived at Doughty Street Chambers for our press conference. I felt nervous and self-conscious lined up in front of national media. The conference began with the broadcast of the apology to us from the Metropolitan Police, read by AC Martin Hewitt:

The Metropolitan Police has recently settled seven claims arising out of the totally unacceptable behaviour of a number of undercover police officers working for the now disbanded Special Demonstration Squad, an undercover unit within Special Branch that existed until 2008 and for the National Public Order Intelligence Unit (NPOIU) an undercover unit which was operational until 2011.

Thanks in large part to the courage and tenacity of these women in bringing these matters to light it has become apparent that some officers, acting undercover while seeking to infiltrate protest groups, entered into long-term intimate sexual relationships with women which were abusive, deceitful, manipulative and wrong.

I acknowledge that these relationships were a violation of the women's human rights, an abuse of police power and caused significant trauma. I unreservedly apologise on behalf of the Metropolitan Police Service. I am aware that money alone cannot compensate the loss of time, their hurt or the feelings of abuse caused by these relationships.

This settlement follows a mediation process in which I heard directly from the women concerned.

I wish to make a number of matters absolutely clear.

Most importantly, relationships like these should never have happened. They were wrong and were a gross violation of personal dignity and integrity.

Let me add these points.

Firstly, none of the women with whom the undercover officers had a relationship brought it on themselves. They were deceived pure and simple. I want to make it clear that the Metropolitan Police does not suggest that any of these women could be in any way criticised for the way in which these relationships developed.

Second, at the mediation process the women spoke of the way in which their privacy had been violated by these relationships. I entirely agree that it was a gross violation and also accept that it may well have reflected attitudes towards women that should have no part in the culture of the Metropolitan Police.

Third, it is apparent that some officers may have preyed on the women's good nature and had manipulated their emotions to a gratuitous extent. This was distressing to hear about and must have been very hard to bear.

Fourth, I recognise that these relationships, the subsequent trauma and the secrecy around them left these women at risk of further abuse and deception by these officers after the deployment had ended.

Fifth, I recognise that these legal proceedings have been painful, distressing and intrusive, and added to the damage and distress. Let me make clear that whether or not genuine feelings were involved on the part of any officers is entirely irrelevant and does not make the conduct acceptable.

One of the concerns which the women strongly expressed was that they wished to ensure that such relationships would not happen in the future. They referred to the risks that children could be conceived through and into such relationships and I understand that.

These matters are already the subject of several investigations including a criminal and misconduct enquiry called Operation Herne; undercover policing is also now subject to a judge-led Public Inquiry which commenced on 28 July 2015. Even before those bodies report, I can state that sexual relationships between undercover police officers and members of the public should not happen. The forming of a sexual relationship by an undercover officer would never be authorised in advance nor indeed used as a tactic of a deployment. If an officer did have a sexual relationship despite this (for example if it was a matter of life or death) then he would be required to report this in order that the circumstances could be investigated for potential criminality and/or misconduct. I can say as a very senior officer of the Metropolitan Police Service that I and the Metropolitan Police are committed to ensuring that this policy is followed by every officer who is deployed in an undercover role.

Finally, the Metropolitan Police recognises that these cases demonstrate that there have been failures of supervision and management. The more we have learned from what the claimants themselves have told us, from the Operation Herne investigation and from the recent HM Inspectorate of Constabulary report, the more we accept that appropriate oversight was lacking. By any standards the level of oversight did not offer protection to the women concerned against abuse. It is of particular concern that abuses were not prevented by the introduction of more stringent supervisory arrangements made by and pursuant to the Regulation of Investigatory Powers Act 2000. The Metropolitan Police recognises that this should never happen again and the necessary steps must be taken to ensure that it does not.

Undercover policing is a lawful and important tactic but it must never be abused.

In light of this settlement, it is hoped that the claimants will now feel able to move on with their lives. The Metropolitan Police believes that they can now do so with their heads held high. The women have conducted themselves throughout this process with integrity and absolute dignity.

Although I hadn't really wanted to settle the case without answers about how the abuse had been allowed to happen, we had at least forced the police to make an unprecedented and powerful public apology acknowledging their responsibility for significant human rights abuses.

I knew from their actions that the police hadn't wanted to give this apology and at least some of them weren't at all sorry about abusing women like us. But we had still won; the public apology meant they and others could no longer claim the relationships didn't happen. And we had it on record to challenge anyone who dared to call us paranoid again.

Just five years previously no one would have believed that state employees would go to such lengths – we had exposed and forced the police to admit a major scandal. We knew there was more to come; more women had already started legal action against the police over relationships they had been deceived into and we also knew of more relationships not yet publicly exposed.

Our press release explained that alongside this comprehensive apology, the Metropolitan Police had made substantial financial settlements to seven of us, meaning we were unable to take our case forward to open court. Only Kate was able to continue and we would support her ongoing fight to obtain disclosure and find out the truth.

It was obvious that the watching press were shocked by the extent of the police admissions, and now they turned to us as we each made a short statement. With an eye on the recently announced public inquiry, I said:

I am glad that the Metropolitan Police have finally admitted that these undercover relationships are abusive and indefensible and I call on them to now come clean about political undercover policing. Through our case alone we know that these relationships spanned a period of nearly twenty-five years, while the vast majority of undercover officers who have been exposed by campaigners are known to have had relationships while undercover.

The public is entitled to know the true extent of these and other human rights abuses committed by undercover political policing units. To that end the police and the public inquiry should now release the cover names of those officers who spied on campaign groups so that those who came into contact with them can make sure the truth is heard by the inquiry.

Alison

(Officer: Mark Cassidy)

London, 20 November 2015

On the day the apology was due to be read out in public, we held a press conference in a basement room in central London. Our support group co-ordinated the whole event brilliantly. They helped out with the sound, managing the media and distributing press releases.

We all sat at a table at the front and showed the apology on a screen behind us. It was surreal, watching Martin Hewitt, the assistant commissioner, read it out. Seeing him in uniform, with all the police logos behind him, I felt vindicated. He was a symbolic embodiment of who we'd been up against and who these men in our lives really were.

After we'd watched the apology, we each gave a statement we'd prepared for the TV, radio and print journalists in the room. It was both exhilarating and nerve-wracking. I was very conscious that Mark and his family would be listening. This was a public message about what had happened to us collectively and the political scandal around that, but it was also an opportunity to get a private message to him.

'I've had my apology from the police,' I said. 'Now I want one from Mark.'

But of course that's never happened.

Still, it felt like a real achievement. There were all these journalists, faces I recognised from the TV news, who were asking us questions and wanted to know more about our story. We were finally getting the word out about what the police had done.

As I sat there looking at the microphones and cameras, I had a vivid memory of whispering to Jude in the back garden fifteen years earlier, saying I thought Mark might be an undercover police officer. I'd felt completely paranoid, reaching into that little dark room of doubt in my head. I'd thought the idea sounded insane, but now I'd gone from whispering about it in the back garden to holding a press conference in front of respected journalists. That was how far we'd come.

Lisa

(Officer: Mark Stone)

London, 20 November 2015

The press conference was the first time I'd been face to face with journalists since the story had broken. It had been an incredibly traumatic time, with the tabloids doorstepping me at my most vulnerable moment, so I was nervous about speaking to them now. Like most of the other women, I still had anonymity, so the cameras had to be angled in such a way that they wouldn't show our faces. I felt very exposed, sitting in front of the press and trusting them to write down what we said but not publish our names or accidentally get our faces in any of the shots.

I had debated with myself about waiving my anonymity, as some of the other women had by that time, but I decided it was important to me to keep my new life, which I'd been working so hard to build from the wreckage of what had happened, separate from all of this. Having a life that felt like my own was an achievement after all the intrusion and destruction of my privacy at the most intimate level. The anonymity could also feel like a 'self-imposed gagging order' sometimes, though, so it was really important that we could all have an equal chance to say our pieces.

I was really pleased that there were so many people there. We'd gone from constantly fighting to stop the case from being thrown out of court, to having a whole roomful of journalists hanging on our every word.

After we'd shown the apology and read out our statements, I felt almost drunk. I was so proud of myself for having faced that fear, and I was very sleep-deprived because we'd been up all night drinking wine and writing our press releases together. I was on an adrenalin high, gabbling away excitedly about our case to one of the journalists. Then he turned round to me and said, 'You don't seem as damaged as the other women.'

I didn't take it in at the time. I just laughed, but afterwards I was really shocked by that. I felt that the journalists wanted us to act like victims, but in that moment I felt triumphant that I'd finally regained some control over my life. We'd had to stay in that place of damage for so long, constantly describing what had happened to us and reliving the experience, but for me the press conference was about what we'd achieved despite all of that. It was a moment to celebrate how we'd fought for that apology and won.

Alison

(Officer: Mark Cassidy)

Birnberg Peirce offices, London, spring 2016

My solicitor Harriet Wistrich explained that a woman had been in touch, wanting to make contact with me.

'Alison, it's Mark's wife.'

I was stunned.

'What did she say?'

Mark Cassidy's/Jenner's wife had been shocked at what the police unit had done and she felt it right that she reach out, having seen all the details in the press.

'Firstly, she wishes for her privacy to be maintained.'

'Of course,' I replied. As far as I was concerned, she was as much a victim in this as I'd been. Mark had deceived us both in the most profound way possible.

'She also wanted you to know that she appreciates you have been through a terrible and abusive experience.' I nodded, but Harriet hadn't finished. 'And she expressed her total respect towards you and your situation.'

My heart went out to her.

Harriet glanced up at me.

'She wants to convey her best wishes to you now, Alison, and for the future.'

Helen
(Officer: John Barker)

Sydney, Australia, early 2016

I hadn't realised the date until afterwards, but on Valentine's Day 2016, something made me search John Dines's name on the internet. To my surprise and, after years of finding nothing, a document popped up with his signature on the bottom. It was the first proof I'd had in over twenty years that he was still alive. John was working at a leading graduate police college – Charles Sturt University – in Sydney, as a course director. The document was about a programme he was involved in to provide training to Indian police officers. When I dug a little deeper, I was concerned that the training included a section on tackling so-called left-wing extremism – a term that is never properly defined and seems to include anyone who challenges the status quo. I was worried John might be teaching the newly discredited tactics that he and others in the SDS had used on us. I couldn't bear the thought that Indian women might also be put at risk as a result. These same tactics had now been acknowledged to be human rights abuses, and I wanted to ensure they didn't get passed on to other police forces internationally. If I had to travel halfway across the world to alert people and prevent it from happening to anyone else, then I would.

It was all very short notice, so initially I'd planned to travel to Australia alone. But our solicitor, Harriet Wistrich, told me the emotional impact might be huge and to take someone with me. I followed her advice and, along with my friend, Jax, flew to Sydney just three weeks after I'd found the document.

To be honest, I had no real plan, only the idea I wanted to make sure people knew who John was, what he'd done and not to allow him to continue under the radar.

On our first day in Australia, I went to speak to a journalist who wrote for the *Guardian* and to a Green MP, David Shoebridge, who said he would raise the issue in parliament. He was also concerned about the potential for human rights abuses. I arranged to meet them both again the following week.

Initially I'd thought of holding a protest outside the college where John taught, but checking a map I realised it was right out of town at the end of a peninsula where there would be no one passing – no one would even know we were there. I had to think of something else.

The next day was Saturday and Jax and I wandered into the city to check out other university addresses for a potential picket. There was nowhere suitable, but later we stumbled across the Sydney Mardi Gras, enjoyed ourselves for a while in the carnival atmosphere, but then lost each other in the crowd. We made our way back to the B&B independently. Then, suffering from jet lag, we promptly fell asleep with no plan in place.

Aside from university addresses, the only detail we knew about the training was the arrival time of the flight of Indian police officers on Sunday morning.

We'd toyed with the idea of holding a protest at the airport, but decided it was too risky given the heavy security. I awoke early the following morning, looked at my watch, and realised that Jax was also awake.

'The flight will be landing soon,' I remarked.

Jax sat up in bed.

'Do you know, Helen, we've woken up so early that I think it's fate. We should travel to the airport to see if we can spot him.'

I decided she was right and threw off the duvet.

'Come on, let's go.'

In my head, I half-expected John to be on the flight from India, but I didn't really have a clue. By the time we'd reached Sydney's Kingsford Smith Airport, the arrivals board told us the plane had just landed. We knew it would take a while for them to walk through the terminal, so we found a position where we could see all the travellers coming down the arrivals ramp.

'What does he look like?' Jax suddenly asked.

My nerves were shot as I tried to explain the John I remembered from twenty-four years ago. It seemed fruitless – like looking for a needle in a haystack. I wasn't sure I'd recognise him after all these years, let alone Jax, who'd never met him. My eyes were desperately scanning the crowds for sign of a group of delegates from India, when Jax ran over. She jangled with a mixture of jet lag and nervous excitement.

'Helen, I think I've just seen him.'

My breath caught inside my chest.

She couldn't have. She doesn't even know what he looks like.

'Where?'

I didn't want to take my eyes away from the new arrivals in case I missed him.

'Over there, come on, I'll show you,' she said, grabbing my arm.

Deep down, I didn't hold out much hope. I was certain she'd spotted someone of a similar description, but who wasn't John. I was more concerned I'd miss him, wasting time on a wild goose chase.

'Where?' I asked impatiently, my eyes scouring the crowd of people.

'Over there!' She motioned with a discreet nod of her head.

And that's when I saw him – his dark brown hair had faded to a silver white, but there was no mistaking him. His confident demeanour among a crowd of Indian officers, giving them directions.

'Oh my God!' I said, clamping a hand against my mouth. 'It's him!'

It was the first time I'd seen John in almost a quarter of a century; the man I'd loved, the man who had deceived me.

'You go, in case he sees you,' Jax suggested. 'We don't want him to know we're here. You follow the Indian police officers. I'll get some photos of him.'

I followed a group of Indian police officers outside and away from the terminal and watched as they boarded a fleet of coaches.

There was a nearby bench, so I sat down to make myself less conspicuous. I waited for John and Jax to reappear. As time dragged by, my mind began to wander. I'd had no intention of confronting John; I'd come to terms with the fact he'd been a professional liar, so there was little point in asking questions because I wouldn't be able to trust his answers. But as the minutes ticked by, I grew more and more anxious.

It's twenty-four years since I last saw him; why the hell did I just walk away?

My stomach churned with uncertainty and I cursed myself.

I can't believe I just did that. I've blown my only chance to confront him.

It felt like an eternity, but out of nowhere, Jax reappeared.

'Where is he?' I asked.

'He's coming. He's just waiting for a few stragglers, but I managed to get a few photos.'

Jax showed me, but our nerves were on edge and all of her pictures had been affected by camera shake. I realised that getting a decent photo of him was now a priority.

I approached the terminal exit. As I did, I spotted John, who was walking towards me. Initially, he was a little distance away so I used my zoom lens. However, I realised photos would be much sharper without it so I continued as he grew closer. It suddenly struck me that he must have seen me. John was only fifteen feet away but, just like Bob outside the TUC headquarters, he was acting as though I wasn't there. With nothing else for it, I grabbed my mobile phone, held it up, pressed record and began to film. John immediately grabbed an old lady's luggage trolley as if to help her. He was still doing it – acting out a part, using the woman as a shield. With the old woman now in shot, I stopped filming and waited to see what he'd do next. As he reached the parked coaches, he let go of the woman's trolley and turned towards the Indian officers. Determined but feeling sick with nerves, I approached. Jax realised I was about to confront John so she got out her mobile and began to film it all. I was in a daze as I stood in front of him; I hadn't planned or thought through the encounter, but it was now or never.

'You owe me an apology,' I said.

John looked at me; all those years of trying to piece the clues together, but here it was – the final piece of the jigsaw. I'd waited a long time for this moment and this time there was no escape. He couldn't run, not any more.

'Apologies,' John replied.

After twenty-four years, was that all he had to say?

My brain felt like cotton wool. I spoke again. 'A big apology,' I added.

'Big apologies,' he replied.

His words were devoid of emotion and they left me stumped. I didn't know what I'd expected, maybe a heartfelt apology, maybe more excuses, more lies, anything but this. I struggled for words and tried to think of something to buy more time.

'We need to talk.'

At this, John looked straight at me.

'Okay, I just need to get all these people on the coaches, then I'll speak to you.'

'Okay.'

I went over to Jax. She whispered she'd captured the entire thing on film and we discussed what to do next.

'I think you should go, in case they decide to arrest us,' I insisted.

Two nearby armed police officers had watched the entire exchange with interest and I didn't want to drag Jax into trouble. Not only that, but I didn't want the police seizing and disposing of vital film footage.

Jax left as I sat down on a nearby bench, watching John to make sure he didn't disappear again. I tried to run questions I wanted to ask him through my mind, but the stress of the situation prevented me from thinking clearly. When the coach doors finally closed, I got up and moved towards him.

'Okay, where shall we go?' I asked. 'Somewhere quiet, preferably.'

John looked a little surprised.

'Sometimes busy places are more private,' he said cryptically before leading me to a fairly bustling café inside the terminal.

I hadn't rehearsed our confrontation but with plenty of questions buzzing around inside my head, I began to fire them at him, one by one. As he answered, I was certain he was still lying at some but not when he answered others. Then I asked John the most important question.

'Why did you have a relationship with me?'

He glanced up from his coffee and looked me directly in the eye. There was a slight pause before he answered.

'What did I have? All I had was a van …'

At first, I wondered what he meant, then I realised; he was saying he'd used me as his prop – his way into the group and the close-knit community of activism. He was saying he hadn't done it for love.

A lone man arriving out of the blue might cause suspicion, but a man with an activist girlfriend? That was the perfect cover.

Was that true? Who knows. I wasn't sure I believed this, as we didn't start our relationship until three years into his deployment, by which time most people already trusted him. Clearly, though, this is how he had justified it to himself.

I wasn't finished.

'After you'd left and you knew how worried I was about you, why didn't you get in touch to stop the torment I was going through?'

John glanced down at his coffee.

'I'm sorry, I had a really shit time too. It – the whole thing – messed my head up and I just wanted to put it behind me and make a new start.'

The more I listened, the more my emotions swung from one extreme to the other. On one hand I burnt with rage at how he had treated me; on the other, there were moments when I found myself feeling a bit sorry for him. Then I remembered all the tears and lies he'd acted out in the past and I found myself struggling to know what to make of any of it. I was emotionally exhausted.

'I can't think of any more questions right now, but I'm sure that as soon as I leave, I'll think of more. If I do, would you be willing to talk again sometime this week? I'm only here for a week.'

John nodded in agreement.

'Yeah, sure. You can get in contact via my work email or phone. The end of the week is better for me.'

Back at the B&B I checked my messages and discovered friends in London asking for an update on when we were going ahead with the picket. They told me before I left the UK that they planned to do a solidarity picket outside Scotland Yard on the same day. I felt a pang of guilt, in spite of what John had done to me. I knew he had a wife and children, and I didn't want to intrude on their lives. I didn't feel like doing a picket any more, so I texted my friends and told them not to worry about it.

But a short while later, they replied saying they wanted to go ahead. I was stuck.

I wasn't ready to tell anyone that I'd spoken to John because I didn't know how I felt about it myself. So how could I tell them why I didn't want to go ahead? Although I felt massively conflicted, I decided I couldn't let my friends down after they'd put themselves out for me, so I suggested the end of the week to buy myself more time to think.

Later that day, I emailed John and asked him to meet me on Monday or Tuesday.

He didn't reply.

As arranged, I met the *Guardian* journalist the following day for an interview.

'Are you going to confront John Dines?' he asked.

I paused, unsure if I wanted to tell anyone yet, least of all the media.

I realised then that I had to see this through – I had to put my feelings to one side and expose John Dines for what he was and what he'd done.

'I already have. I did it yesterday. I have phone footage. I'll send it over.'

The journalist wrote up the story and tied the whole piece up with questions raised in the New South Wales Parliament a couple of days after my interview. Then he emailed John to ask if he had any comment. In contrast to his lack of reply to me, John replied to the journalist within a couple of hours. And that's when it really sank in – John didn't give a shit about me; he never had. I'd just been a prop – a bit part – in his cover story, just like his van.

UCPI Announcement, 20 December 2016

Five years after we had started our case against the police, a year after the police apology and nine months after I had confronted John at Sydney Airport and he later admitted to the *Guardian* that he had been a police officer who deceived me into a relationship, the Undercover Policing Public Inquiry finally confirmed publicly that John had been a police officer! Until that point, both the police and the public inquiry had refused to confirm it.

It was just before Christmas, a time when people wouldn't be paying much attention, and I was in New Zealand visiting family, facts I'm sure were taken into account when making the decision on the timing of the announcement.

I was given twenty-four hours' notice, so I spent a day of my holiday writing a statement for the press and our campaign website:

While I welcome the official admission that my former partner John Dines was an undercover policeman in the Special Demonstration Squad, it is a travesty that the police have been allowed to take this long to confirm what I and others exposed years ago. Even after they issued a public apology for serious human rights abuses to myself and six other women who had been deceived into relationships with undercover policemen, the police still argued they could not confirm the identity of my abuser. To date, despite that apology, they have also refused to confirm the identity of Mark Jenner who deceived 'Alison' into a five-year relationship. We and other women similarly deceived have had no disclosure at all about how these abusive relationships were allowed to happen, instead we have been subjected to intrusive demands for evidence of the effects of the abuse. None of those responsible for this abuse have been held to account – even those still employed by the police have kept their jobs.

It is an insult to the many victims of political undercover policing that the police who are responsible for serious human rights abuses have been allowed to cover up the truth and withhold information from those they abused. The public inquiry should release as a matter of urgency the cover names of all these political police and also the files they compiled on campaigners, so that those spied on are able to understand what happened and give relevant evidence to the inquiry.

We know that over a thousand campaign groups have been spied upon by these political undercover policing units. This represents a significant interference with the right to political freedom of thought and the right to protest. Ultimately it is a means for those who hold power to preserve the status quo and prevent social change. For this reason it is in the public interest for the cover names of all the political undercover police to be released, along with the files they compiled so that those who have abused their power can be held to account, the public learns the true extent of this political spying in this country and further human rights abuses by such units can be prevented.

London, August 2017

In August the following year, I got a letter from the Met solicitors demanding I respond in fourteen days with my proposals to pay the £7,000 costs of the NCND appeal back in 2015. I couldn't believe they had the gall to demand I pay them for their efforts to suppress the name of my abuser. I tweeted a photo of the letter and was surprised and cheered by the reaction. So many people were outraged by the police's conduct. Quite a few people messaged me to say they would fundraise or donate, but I didn't want other people to pay it, I wanted the Met to abandon their demands in light of the fact they were clearly in the wrong on this. Green Party politicians Caroline Lucas and Jenny Jones retweeted it, and Jenny wrote to the commissioner to urge her to 'not press this outrageous demand'. The police backed down.

London, March 2018

The Undercover Policing Inquiry released the SDS Tradecraft Manual from 1995 that provided guidance to undercover officers. A section headed 'Sexual liaisons' noted, 'The thorny issue of romantic entanglements during a tour is the cause of much soul-searching and concern. In the past, emotional ties to the opposition have happened and caused all sorts of difficulties, including divorce, deception and disciplinary charges. While it is not my place to moralise, one should try to avoid the opposite sex for as long as possible.'

The document also advised, 'If you have no other option but to become involved with a weary [activist], you should try to have fleeting, disastrous relationships with individuals who are not important to your sources of information. One cannot be involved with a weary [activist] in a relationship for any period of time without risking serious consequences.' There was no mention of the consequences for women deceived by officers, and it seemed to us that this document was proof that SDS management had known about their officers engaging in deceptive relationships and had done little or nothing to stop them.

London, November 2020

After repeated delays and a series of preliminary hearings, the Public Inquiry into Undercover Policing finally got formally underway with a series of opening speeches charting the development of secret political policing since the 1960s, on behalf of both those who did the spying and those who were spied upon. The inquiry was supposed to end and report in 2018; instead it is expected to continue until well beyond 2023. For our part we have still had no disclosure from the police and it feels like their endless demands for secrecy relating to both officers' identities and decades-old documents are an attempt to delay the inevitable until most of the officers are retired and they can claim these appalling events are 'historic'. They want to pretend that there's nothing to see here. Justice delayed is justice denied, and we are forced to fight on to expose the truth.

Impact

Belinda

To this day, I have no clue of the reason why I was deceived by this man. What on earth gave the police the idea it was acceptable for me to be used in this way? I've asked the Met for any information at all but nothing has been forthcoming.

I sincerely hope that one day they will fully internalise how inappropriate and cruel it was to play with emotions and interfere with the life chances of those of us directly affected, including myself. I do not feel the police have given me a full and frank disclosure. This represents a lack of respect towards us all.

Alison

It's over twenty years since I believed Mark was working for the British state, and it's an experience that has shaped much of my adult life. Thankfully, life has moved on but like any trauma, it's something I've carried with me. Something I've had to explain to new friends and colleagues; something I had to live with for years, watching people's sceptical gaze as I explained what I thought had happened to Mark and why. It was obvious many thought me a drama queen, others paranoid and delusional.

Our stories illustrate, in the most concrete way, the feminist adage: the personal is political. While it's our personal stories that have generated the most public awareness of the Metropolitan Police's actions, it's essential to us that their political dimension is not lost. What happened to women like us is central to how the police functioned. The exploitation and abuse of women was fundamental to the undercover officers' success in the field. We hope the public inquiry into undercover policing that is currently underway will, in its final report, make a finding of institutional sexism in the police.

The experiences of women like us span nearly five decades, yet their significance will only fully be understood many years from now. Not only have we been directly impacted by the actions of these officers and their managers but so too have our children: those born as a result of the operations, those who grew up knowing these men in their fake personas, and those other children born to women affected – I include the ex-wives of these officers.

When I first embarked on the legal case in 2011, our son was seven and our daughter four. One day, a few years later, I freaked out at our then eleven-year-old son for lying to me about something trivial because – as I tried to make him understand without being able to fully explain – I couldn't handle lies. My husband stepped in and said we had to tell him why. The intergenerational trauma resulting from these police deployments is something yet to be fully explored.

In spite of the horrendous nature of what's happened, I'm buoyed by the camaraderie and comradeship I've had the opportunity to experience as a consequence of it all. Groups and individuals from different backgrounds and political traditions have succeeded in working together to expose this wrongdoing. Together, we are a formidable force and I hope that fact gives these officers and their managers regular nightmares.

Yet, one thing remains: despite the compensation, the apology and the ongoing inquiry, I still have no answers from Mark or his employers as to why, for five years, this officer was entwined in my most intimate and personal life. And I'm not sure I ever will.

Naomi

I began to question everything. The police had been gathering information on how a community and a network worked, how people come together and organise civil disobedience and how people campaign. They wanted insight into people's lives.

Slowly, Mark built himself a giant web that then became his safety net. If I doubted him, then I doubted myself, my friends and my community.

We hadn't agreed to these relationships – there had been no informed consent – because we didn't know who we were in a relationship with. I'd willingly had a relationship with Mark Stone, but he didn't exist – his identity had been fabricated by the police, paid for by the police, and backed up by a police team and equipment. I hadn't consented to that. Mark had been trained with public money and was one of many.

I'd been having a relationship with the state and I didn't even know it.

I never *ever* would have consented to that intimate relationship if I had known who he really was, what he was doing and for whom.

It was in 2011, sitting in a room of other women as stunned as I was by what had happened, that I first heard the term 'mirroring' and heard in their stories versions of what had happened with Mark: like the other undercover cops, he'd been taught to mimic and reflect back to us our own interests and desires to create that feeling of connection and intimacy. They'd been mirroring each and every one of us. All the things Mark had said and done were things he'd learnt in his training to make people feel as though they were special and that he somehow 'got them'. Everything, even his involvement in open relationships, had been a form of mirroring. Mark was mirroring Lisa's relationship with someone else by being with me. There's no anger or blame in that; I hold nothing but warmth for all my friends who were in open relationships and the genuine way that we lived our lives back then. But I believe Mark was mirroring Lisa's open relationship by having one with me because I was a close friend. By doing it this way, he was very visible. By mirroring, these officers made it feel like there was a connection; that we'd not only found someone who was compatible, but someone who was warm and kind and seemed to like everything we did. Mark had pulled this off with great success because I'd believed him, and so had everyone else.

Many, many people had also been close friends with Mark so, while discussing the relationships he had, we mustn't forget the friendships these officers also betrayed. When I first met Mark, I thought we had many friends in common. It would be over a decade before I learnt that his understanding of that community, and those friendships and connections, was prior knowledge gained from other undercover cops spying on social justice networks. Spying simply for the sake of spying, to infiltrate our lives to observe us. The extent to which he would betray every one of those friendships was completely undreamt of. It seems impossible to unimagine that betrayal now, to go back to a time before that knowledge seeped into my bones, but it really never ever occurred to me then that Mark Stone was anything other than my friend.

Recently, I thought about my brother's wedding day. When I looked over photos from that day, I noticed that in all the pictures taken by the professional photographer, Mark was turning away, hiding behind me, wearing shades. It left me cold. What he seemed to have forgotten was all the snapshots people had taken. Here, he was laughing with me, smiling, sharing a joke, dancing. Here was the person I thought I was at the wedding with. A decade later, I still cannot reconcile those two different people, caught up in one man.

Lisa

Ten years later, this story still haunts me, and in some ways feels more present than ever now with the public inquiry into undercover policing and hearings in the Investigatory Powers Tribunal. It's become a campaign for me now. I'm still fighting to keep the story in the public eye so they can't get away with doing this to someone else. At least now, people will be aware of what could happen, and so they'd be more likely to spot it happening than I was. I feel like I have a chance to show the systematic, institutional nature of what we all went through. To show people that this also happens in the UK and it isn't just something that the Stasi in East Germany would have done. They were trying to crush opposition and dissent, prevent people from protesting effectively by insidious psychological means. We think our system is so democratic, but it's far from it.

All the other forms of activism I used to be involved with have melted away. I don't go on demos or protests any more. I don't get inspired to campaign for the environmental and social justice issues I used to be so passionate about. I miss that part of me, but if I'm really honest with myself about why I can't face it, it's more than just the deep discomfort I have around the police now. It's a cynicism. This cynicism comes from having poured my heart and soul into trying to build a better world and having been so shattered by the personal costs. Is it worth it? In the face of what they did to us, can we expect to still make a difference? Did we ever really make a difference? I saw how the wider political and social scene around me was devastated by all of this and I haven't found the energy to put into re-imagining it.

When I see and hear of new activities and campaigns now though, I do feel lifted. I'm so happy to see people out there on the streets, shouting about how things need to be better. Lots of new young faces, and even some of my contemporaries carrying on regardless. I am so elated that they can move on without the mistrust and cynicism, because it's more important now than ever.

The personal effects of all of this on me are also still very evident. I've built so much to be proud of in my new life, but I'm still single. No one has used a lover's terms of endearment towards me since. I'm bruised by the experience, and unable to open myself up to intimacy and love from someone new. Although I really would like to be able to meet someone, I can't imagine placing my trust in someone else's feelings for me and, if I'm honest, I'm still not convinced I'm deserving of love like that. I hope someday I can brave deep feelings again.

I've received incredible love from my friends and family so, in many ways, I feel blessed, but my ability to love in that way was so damaged that I fear it is irreparable.

I never will know if the decision not to start my own family was truly my decision, or one made while influenced by Mark Kennedy, who already had his own family. Did I make that decision under my own free will? I'll never really know the answer to that. I made my life decisions based on being with someone who didn't even exist.

I'm forty-seven now, and I met Mark when I was twenty-nine. I'd been in the prime of my life, but the police stole those years from me, and all the subsequent years spent fighting for justice that I'll also never get back.

There are still so many unanswered questions that I've had to learn to live with. I still need to know how much the police knew about our relationship, how much I was targeted for surveillance, and how much of our relationship was his own idea. Were they listening in to our phone calls and reading our text and email exchanges? Did they come with us on holidays, did they observe and follow us the whole time we were together? Was it all planned and watched by men in a back office somewhere? How many of my private intimacies were actually public with other officers? Did they see pictures of me naked? Did they follow him to my father's funeral? Did they discuss why it was so important for him to attend, and why he was in the official mourner's car? How much of it was authorised?

How was he allowed to keep the same undercover identity and contacts while going on to work for the private company Global Open after leaving the police? It amounts to effectively selling information about us. Was that a common practice? How much of my private life did they get to see? Who is looking into how companies spy on protest movements and how can we hold them to account when they can simply fold like Global Open has?

As a police officer, Mark's handler knew where he was the entire time, and I refuse to believe they didn't know their officers were involved in long-term relationships. I doubt we'll ever get a definitive answer to who knew what, as it may not be in the paperwork. So much of it may have been agreed with a 'nod and a wink'. We do still have to continue to ask these questions, even if I despair of how much we'll ever find out. The more we make this public and the louder we shout about everything they've done, the less chance they can get away with it today. Sadly, I don't believe for a second that they've stopped spying on people and getting so deeply involved in their most private moments. They will have just learnt how to do it differently, and how to not get caught.

During an in-depth interview given to Victoria Derbyshire on the radio in 2012, Mark was still referring to himself in the third person.

He told her: 'I enjoyed the life Mark Stone led, but I enjoyed the job Mark Kennedy had.'

When asked, 'You say you loved her, but how could you deceive her like this?'

He replied, 'Mark Stone never lied to her.'

He didn't know who he was by the end, and it has been quite a journey since for me to discover just who I am. After all, I spent six years with a fictional character, so who did that make me? I'd been so shattered by the experience that I needed to rebuild myself from the fragments. It's a work in progress.

Helen

It has been a painful process writing this book, as indeed was fighting the case: learning the similarities of the other women's stories, raking over old memories, reading through letters, diaries and notes that I hadn't looked at in years. I'd loved other partners before, but John was the first person I had ever 'fallen in love with' and wanted to spend my life with. When he disappeared, I worried for him, thinking he was a tortured soul alone in the world with no family left and no close relationships, but I know now he was in fact married and all his family were alive. That gives a very different perspective on what he wrote in those letters, especially when it is clear that he knew the worry and distress he was causing me. The more I read, the more I could see a pattern where my emotions were deliberately abused – initially to draw me closer to him and into a relationship so he could use me, but, later, I can only think it was about trying to leave me in pieces in the hope that I would be unable to function and continue to be politically active. Realising the gratuitous nature of the prolonged abuse to which he subjected me, it became clear that playing with my feelings was either a hilarious game to him and the unit or it was a deliberate attempt to destroy my sanity. It hurts to realise that someone can choose to be that abusive.

I was twenty-two when I met John, twenty-four when we became intimate. John knew the entire relationship was false, that he never wanted nor intended to have children with me or grow old together, that his deployment would end within a few years. Later, he put me through endless unnecessary worry about his mental state, and even if some of that was real distress as a result of his dual identity, he knew that should never have been my responsibility.

For years, the photo of me and John on the beach in Scotland was a treasured memory of our seemingly blissful relationship, but looking at it again after learning the truth about who he was and what he was doing in my life, I feel sick. I wonder what thoughts were going through his head at the moment it was taken. He's looking at the camera as though everything is fine and we are in an equal, happy partnership. But he wasn't a friend and lover with shared values and hopes for a future together; he was a policeman using me to try to undermine the movements of which I was part.

John knew that if I understood the truth about who he was I would never have entered into a relationship with him and would never have consented to sex with him. He knew all that, but he chose to ignore my right to bodily autonomy and instead use me for his cover and/or for sex. Just as Lambert, Boyling, Jenner, Kennedy and so many other men used the women they deceived.

They all exploited our bodies and lives for their own gratification, and they exploited our emotions, deliberately manipulating our feelings with false stories about personal traumas and their need for support, wasting our time and energy. They invaded our personal, moral and physical integrity.

How could these officers do this to women? How could they have so little regard for our feelings, sanity and rights? It's part of a long continuum of males being socialised to view women as not fully human nor deserving of equal rights. There is an expectation that our freedom and autonomy is secondary to men's wants; our purpose is to service their desires. Overtly, probably few men would recognise such thoughts as their own beliefs, but the frequency with which women are subjected to unsolicited comments about their appearance, demands for a 'smile', cat calls, sexual harassment and assault, indecent exposure and its modern counterpart dick pics, rape jokes and objectification in advertising and porn – it all shows a widespread culture of contempt for women.

These attitudes have their origins in the fact that for centuries women were legally considered the property of men, obliged to do as their fathers, brothers or husbands required, 'given away' in marriage from father to husband. Although laws have changed, it takes longer for habits to alter; attitudes are passed down from generation to generation. Given the prevalence of such views towards women, it's not so surprising they are also found within the police force. It is appalling, however, that the institution itself took no steps to challenge these sexist attitudes, nor to prevent them from translating into deeply harmful abuse of women. Instead, the canteen culture in a predominantly male workplace allowed such sexist attitudes to be amplified.

These attitudes weren't limited to the police either. When we began to expose the relationships, politicians and commentators tried to trivialise and justify them on the basis that the work the unit was doing was important, or that we deserved it in some way – even though there was no law that said if a police officer suspected someone of a crime they were entitled to sleep with them to find out.

The Crown Prosecution Service decided not to charge the men, claiming we had consented to the relationships, despite the fact the men had denied us the ability to meaningfully consent. It is obvious there is no way anybody would agree to a relationship with somebody if they knew that everything about that person was fake and if they knew that they were there to spy on them. They knew our consent had been fraudulently obtained.

Even in the courts, the judges, when considering setting legal precedent on the issue of deception vitiating consent, seemed more worried about the consequences of such change for men caught lying about their age or occupation than they were about protecting women from deception by men. They repeatedly pontificated on how to draw the line between preventing the kind of deep deception committed by the officers against us, and avoiding ensnaring a man who exaggerated his accomplishments or knocked a few years off his age on his dating profile. In doing so, they were imagining themselves in the shoes of men who lie, rather than women robbed of our autonomy. They tied themselves in knots over this issue, when the question that should have been asked was not the difficult one of distinguishing between degrees of deception, but the question of motivation. What motivation does a man have for lying to a woman – why does he do it? The reality is that if a man lies about himself in order to cover up something he knows might make a material difference to whether a woman wants to have sex or a relationship with him, he is trying to remove that woman's autonomy; he knows or fears that the woman would decline sex if she knew the truth and he is trying to circumvent that. Therein lies the violation.

So this is what institutional sexism looks like – male-dominated institutions judging the world through the male lens and failing to give equal consideration to how women might be adversely or differently affected to men by the actions (or inaction) of those institutions. The assumption that, as a woman, you don't deserve the right to make a fully informed decision about who you want a relationship with or to have sex with; and that your autonomy is secondary to what men, or the state, want to use you for. Failing to consider the likelihood of disproportionate harm to women resulting from a male-dominated unit having the power to deceive and play God with people's lives, particularly in light of the fact that social pressures encourage women to defer to men. Failing to consider women's specific disadvantages in relation to both risks of pregnancy and also limited childbearing years as compared to men.

The impact on me and most of the other deceived women was immense. I have only had two intimate relationships since John's disappearance in 1992. The first lasted a couple of weeks and ended after I couldn't handle the thought that my new partner might not be being totally honest with me. The second was not until I was thirty-nine. It was with someone I had known for many years (hence I could mostly assume he was a real person) and was heavily influenced by the fact I wanted to have children and time was running out. In fact, time had run out. I had seven miscarriages, caused by trisomies, which become much more likely the older a woman is. The last of these occurred in January 2011, just as the scandal of the undercover relationships was breaking. The heartbreak combined with the emotional toll of reliving the deception was too great to continue to try.

The other significant impact was from burying my emotions. I kept quiet about my concerns about who John might be, fearing that the police might prevent me finding out the truth, with the result that I cut myself off from my emotions and became an actor myself, acting as if everything was okay when actually I frequently wanted to crumble and break down inside. Such deadening of emotions has a long-term emotional impact, stunting our ability to experience not only the lows but also the highs in life.

We brought the case to expose the police use of these abusive relationships and to prevent them happening to more women. It is not acceptable for undercover officers to engage in sexual relationships with the people they are infiltrating, ever. It was a massive step forward to force the police to acknowledge this in their apology to us, but we cannot relax. As a society we have to make sure that these abuses never happen again.

The feeling of violation is still raw. I still don't know what personal and intimate information was discussed in the back office or put down on my record for anyone to see in the future. The permanent culture of secrecy that has been granted to these political policing units allows and actually encourages the abuse of state power. There should be an automatic right for people subjected to state surveillance to be allowed to see any files kept on them after a period of five years (subject to limited exceptions if they are part of an ongoing live investigation into a serious crime). This would act as at least a partial brake on police wrongdoing, since they could no longer assume that no one will ever find out what they did. The police are fond of saying 'if you have nothing to hide, you have nothing to fear'. Why shouldn't this sentiment apply to them too? They are a publicly funded body, supposedly acting in the public interest. Shouldn't the public have the right to find out if they have acted with integrity?

We women, for our part, wanted to make the world a better place, a fairer place. We didn't deserve this. Our lives were derailed – for what? So that the police could prevent change, undermine democracy and prop up the interests of the wealthy and powerful in our society.

Our story is one that needs to be told because there is widespread misunderstanding about the nature and impact of these abusive relationships, but our story is also part of a wider one about the nature and extent of secret political policing in the UK. We now know that over a thousand groups in the UK have been spied on by these units. We didn't have the space to tackle the wider issues in this book, but we encourage everyone to read up and oppose secret political policing because it represents an unjustified interference with efforts to challenge injustices and improve society for all.

For further information, please see:

Police Spies Out of Lives
    policespiesoutoflives.org.uk
Campaign Opposing Police Surveillance
    campaignopposingpolicesurveillance.com
Undercover Research Group
    undercoverresearch.net

At least sixty women.

Hundreds of true stories.

Almost fifty years of deception.

Tens of thousands of lies by undercover police spies.

Scores of survivors yet to be heard.

Are you one of them?

Acknowledgements

From us all

As well as Harriet Wistrich, to whom this book is dedicated, we want to thank Phillippa Kaufmann and Charlotte Kilroy for their impressive and unrelenting legal work and support; and to Gareth Peirce, Kate Thomas and all at Birnberg Pierce for pushing forward the fight for justice for so many years. Thanks also to Rob Evans and Paul Lewis at the *Guardian*, for helping to blow the story out into the open.

Our appreciation goes to everyone who has enabled us to tell our story including Veronique Baxter at David Higham, Veronica Clark, and to Lorna Russell, Claire Collins, Bethany Wright and all at Penguin Random House.

And thank you to those who have supported PSOOL to raise awareness, support survivors and battle to expose the truth – not least to the formidable women with whom we first set out on this legal fight for justice. So much love to you. We've achieved so much, and it's not over yet.

Alison

Thanks to my friends and family who put up with me obsessing about Mark's disappearance, listened to my endless theories, and who read and re-read my various accounts of the experience – you know who you are. Love and thanks to my husband, who helped me to rebuild my life.

Belinda

My friend Simon, who passed away in 2016, was strongly affected by the discovery of Bob's deceit. He gave his full permission for the story of Bob's pointless and unjustified betrayal of his trust to be told.

Helen

Thanks to the friends and family who listened to and endured my pain when John disappeared and supported me during my long search for the truth and then justice afterwards. Eternal thanks to Rosa for finally providing the certainty about who John was and for the insights you shared. And to Jax for accompanying me on a stressful and emotional journey, and for switching your camera on at the right moment!

Lisa

Thanks to all the amazing friends and family that stood by me as my world turned upside down, particularly to those who helped me confront Mark, for stepping up when I most needed them. Also, thanks to B, my business partner and dear friend for offering a way to build a new life with purpose, and for all the patience she's shown for the role this epic, endless fight for justice still has to play after all these years.

Naomi

D, Y and all the friends who held me up when we first found out and have sustained me in the years since. To the five people who did what needed to be done that night in October 2010 and faced the moment as they have faced so much of their lives, with honesty and integrity regardless of the risk to self. Finally to FB, who has been through it all with me and given so much. For your calm integrity and your steadfast commitment to what is right and true you have all my love and respect, always.

Timeline of undercover police relationships

Chronological list of undercover police spies known or reported to have deceived women into intimate relationships or had sexual contact, plus three female officers who deceived men. Officers' cover names are given in quote marks. The names of the eight women who brought the original case and the officers who deceived them in bold.

Period	Officer	Number of civilians
1970s	HN302 (unnamed)	1
1974–76	HN300 'Jim Pickford'	1
1974–76	HN354 'Vince Miller'/ Harvey	4
1975–76	HN297 'Rick Gibson'	Mary, +3
1977–82	HN126 Paul 'Gray'	1
1979–83	HN106 'Barry Tompkins'	1
1979–84	HN155 'Phil Cooper'	2 or 3
Late 1970s–1980s	HN21 (unnamed)	2
1982–85	HN67 'Alan Bond'	1 (may have fathered a child undercover)
1982–85	HN12 'Mike Hartley'	2
1983–87	HN11 Mike 'Blake'/ Chitty	Lizzie +1
1984–88	HN10 **Bob 'Robinson'/ Lambert**	CTS, Jacqui, RLC, **Belinda**
1987–90	HN87 'John Lipscomb'	4
1987–91	HN5 John **'Barker'/ Dines**	**Helen**
1991–95	HN2 Andy 'Davey'/Coles	Jessica +1
1991–95	HN78 'Anthony Lewis' / Trevor Morris	Bea, Jenny

1992–96	HN1 'Matt Rayner'	Denise, +1
1993–97	HN43 Pete 'Daley' / 'Black'/ Francis	2
1994–99	HN26 Christine Green	1 man
1995–2000	HN14 **Jim 'Sutton'/ Boyling**	Monica, **Ruth, Rosa**
1995–2000	HN15 **Mark 'Cassidy'/ Jenner**	**Alison**
1997–2002	HN16 James 'Straven' / Thomson / Kevin Crossland	Sara, Ellie
2000–05	HN77 'Jackie Anderson'	Sexual contact with men
2000–06	HN104 Carlo 'Neri' / Soracchi	Lindsey, Donna McLean, +1
2003–08	EN34 'Lynne Watson'	1 man
2003–2010	**Mark 'Stone' / Kennedy**	**Kate Wilson, Lisa,** Eleanor Fairbraider, Sarah, **Naomi**, C, +5
2004–07	HN18 'Rob Harrison'	Maya, +1
2004–09	EN1 'Marco Jacobs'	AJA, ARB
Late 2000s	HN91 (unnamed)	1

The numbers given here represent only the examples we know about. We believe they are likely to be the tip of the iceberg.

- Number of undercover officers – 139 (66% of those who applied to the public inquiry for anonymity were granted it; 71 cover names released).
- Number of groups spied on – over 1,000.
- Number of women deceived into intimate relationships with undercover officers – over 60.*

* Not all women affected are core participants in the public inquiry

- Number of male undercover officers known to have deceived women into intimate relationships – 26.*
- Number of deceased children who had their identities stolen – 42.
- Number of justice campaigns spied on – 26.
- Number of elected politicians spied on – 10.
- Number of blacklisted workers, trade unions and political activists spied on – 59.†

* Three female undercover officers are known to have had intimate relationships with male activists. Two of these were brief sexual encounters, one was a lengthy relationship.

† Figure expected to be much higher than this as many files were destroyed before the Information Commissioners Raid in 2009. Source: www.spycops.co.uk & https://www.ucpi.org.uk/about-the-inquiry/#stats

Timeline of Legal Fightback

March 2011, Birnberg Peirce offices, London

Lisa and Helen Steel visit lawyer Gareth Peirce at Birnberg Peirce & Partners (BPP) solicitors to explore the possibility of suing the Metropolitan Police. Gareth says she wants to take the case forward and will speak with solicitors at BPP who specialise in civil and human rights law.

June 2011, Birnberg Peirce offices

Helen, Lisa, Alison, Rosa and Ruth all meet together for the first time with Gareth Peirce and Harriet Wistrich, solicitor at BPP, who agrees to take on the case.

December 2011, letter before action

Letter before action sent to Metropolitan Police on behalf of eight women deceived into relationships by undercover police: Lisa, Naomi, Kate, Rosa, Ruth, Alison, Helen Steel and Belinda. Letter sets out the basis for claims against the police commissioner arising from the collective experiences of all eight women and requests disclosure. The women make claims under common law for deceit, assault, misfeasance in public office and negligence, and also for breaches in the European Convention on Human Rights, including Article 3 and Article 8. Lisa, Naomi and Kate also make claims under the Human Rights Acts, the other women being unable to bring claims under this act as the relationships took place before it came into force in October 2000.

February 2012, Met Police confirm Kennedy was UCO

Reply from Metropolitan Police confirming that Mark Kennedy had been employed by the Metropolitan Police to infiltrate campaigns from July 2003 to February 2010.

April 2012, Particulars of Claim (three women)

Particulars of Claim served for three women able to make human rights claims as well as common law claims.

June 2012, Met Police response

Six months after the letter before action, the Metropolitan Police respond, claiming for the first time that they can 'neither confirm nor deny' whether any of the men had been undercover police officers. They also seek to have the High Court claims put on hold to await the outcome of the IPT cases.

August 2012, Police Spies Out of Lives

We establish Police Spies Out of Lives to raise awareness of the abusive relationships, provide support to women affected and to campaign on the issue of consent, institutional sexism and disclosure of police files. We create an online presence (policespiesoutoflives.org.uk) to reach both the general public and other women who may have been targeted by the Metropolitan Police. An additional SpyCops website (spycops.co.uk) is created in 2019, offering an overview of the policing scandal.

November 2012, High Court

Three-day hearing in High Court over police application for human rights claims to be heard in the IPT and for a stay of the common law claims until the outcome of the IPT.

December 2012, Department of Professional Standards

Alison and Belinda meet senior officers from the Metropolitan Police Department of Professional Standards to discuss making a formal complaint about Mark and Bob. The Police refuse to confirm or deny the men as employees of the Metropolitan Police present or in the past.

17 January 2013, High Court

High Court rules that human rights claims must be heard by the IPT. The common law claims are put on hold pending that outcome.

5 February 2013, Home Affairs Select Committee

Lisa, Alison and Helen give oral evidence before the Home Affairs Select Committee about being deceived into relationships with undercover police officers.

March 2013, Particulars of Claim (five women)

Particulars of Claim served for the five women who are only able to bring common law claims.

May 2013, Met Police formal defence

The Metropolitan Police serve formal defence of 'neither confirm nor deny' (NCND) – asserting they cannot be expected to defend the claims as it would mean revealing operational undercover details.

June 2013, *Undercover* book and *Dispatches* documentary

Undercover: The True Story of Britain's Undercover Police by Rob Evans and Paul Lewis is published.

Channel 4's *Dispatches* programme covers the story. Police whistle-blower Peter Francis reveals he was ordered to spy on the family of murder victim Stephen Lawrence as part of a 'smear campaign' against them. Helen Steel, Belinda and another woman called 'Jacqui' also take part.

August 2013, High Court

First High Court hearing of the case of five women. Police ordered to provide disclosure or make their long-threatened strike-out application within a month.

August 2013, Home Affairs Select Committee

Government rejects Home Affairs Select Committee finding that there is a compelling case for overhauling the legislative framework governing undercover policing.

September 2013, Met Police application to strike out

The Metropolitan Police apply to have the common law claims thrown out, asserting they cannot defend the claim due to 'neither confirm nor deny' (NCND) policy and therefore should be released from disclosure of evidence rules.

5 November 2013, Court of Appeal (three women)

Court of Appeal dismisses Lisa, Naomi and Kate's appeal against decision that IPT had exclusive jurisdiction to hear Human Rights Acts claims, but lifts stay of execution (temporary suspension) on the common law claims saying these can now proceed in the High Court.

Hearing for police application to strike out the other five women's claims is postponed to March after the women serve substantial evidence contradicting the police claims relating to NCND.

March 2014

Andrew Clarke and Geoff Sheppard, who were convicted in 1988 of planting incendiary devices in Debenhams stores that sold fur, lodge appeals against their convictions. The principal ground of their appeals is the role that Bob Lambert played as an undercover officer in these events. The appeal is now on hold at the Court of Appeal, pending the outcome of the Undercover Policing Public Inquiry.

6 March 2014, Public Inquiry announced

The Home Secretary, Theresa May, orders a public inquiry into undercover policing in England and Wales, after an independent inquiry confirms that Scotland Yard had spied on the family of Stephen Lawrence.

The Home Secretary brands the revelations 'profoundly shocking and disturbing', adding 'policing stands [are] damaged today'. She warns that the 'full truth' has yet to emerge.

N81 – the officer sent to spy on the Lawrences – monitored them during an inquiry into the Met's bungled handling of the investigation into their son's murder. N81 gathered personal details about Stephen's parents – Doreen and Neville Lawrence – in a move said to have given the Met a 'secret advantage' over the family during the inquiry.

N81 worked in the Met's controversial undercover Special Demonstration Squad (SDS), along with Peter Francis, who also spied on the Lawrence family when they were trying to bring the racist killers of their son to justice.

18 March 2014, High Court

High Court hearing of police application to strike out the five women's claims on the basis of NCND is aborted in light of the announcement of the Public Inquiry. However, the women argue that the courts set new dates for the next stages to prevent the Met creating endless delays.

July 2014, High Court

High Court rules the Metropolitan Police cannot rely on a blanket 'neither confirm nor deny' policy to have the case thrown out. However, it allows them to rely on NCND for John Dines/Barker and Mark Jenner/Cassidy.

August 2014, Lambert and Boyling confirmed as UCOs

The Met serve an amended defence that formally confirms the identities of Bob Lambert and Jim Boyling and admits that they engaged in sexual relationships while undercover. They go on to assert that the relationships were based on 'mutual attraction and genuine personal feelings', thereby rejecting any responsibility or liability for the abuse and damage caused. They refuse to confirm the identities of John Barker and Mark Cassidy.

August 2014, Crown Prosecution Service

Crown Prosecution Service (CPS) makes a public announcement that, after reviewing evidence from Operation Herne in relation to four undercover police officers accused of deceiving women into relationships, they had decided there was insufficient evidence to prosecute the officers for rape or sexual assault, procuring a woman to have sexual intercourse by false pretences, misconduct in public office or breaches of the Official Secrets Act. They assert there was 'insufficient evidence for a realistic prospect of conviction for any offences against any of the officers'.

A spokesperson for the Metropolitan Police tells the press: 'Following the CPS's decision the MPS is now considering if misconduct proceedings are appropriate. We are not prepared to discuss the identity of these officers.'

December 2014, mediation, London

Mediation meetings held. Alison, Helen, Belinda, Rosa and Ruth, agree in principle to settle claims with the Metropolitan Police after securing an unprecedented apology and damages. Lisa, Kate and Naomi also present at the mediation to negotiate the apology, which is made public in November 2015.

June 2015, mediation, London

In further mediation meetings Lisa and Naomi reach a settlement with the MPS. Kate is the only one of the eight women who is legally advised to refuse the settlement offer and so is able to fight on.

The public inquiry is established. Inquiry findings are due to be delivered to the Home Secretary by July 2018.

July 2015, High Court, Global Open

A woman with the pseudonym 'C' sues Global Open. She says Mark Kennedy pursued her to start a relationship with him while he worked for Global Open when he returned to activists using the same undercover identity he had used while employed by the police.

21 October 2015, Undercover Policing Public Inquiry

All eight women are designated core participants in the Undercover Policing Public Inquiry (UCPI). The Inquiry opened on 28 July 2015 but does not begin to hear evidence until November 2020. The Inquiry received applications from over 380 individuals, groups and organisations.

20 November 2015, MPS apology made public, London

The Metropolitan Police issues a public apology to seven of the women. It is read out by Martin Hewitt, assistant commissioner of the Metropolitan Police, and published on the Met website. The women are not allowed to be in the same place while he reads it and instead are forced to watch it on a large television screen at Doughty Street Chambers, where they hold a press conference.

January 2016, High Court

The son of Bob Lambert and 'Jacqui', another activist he deceived into a relationship, sues the Metropolitan Police for damages.

March 2016, Sydney Airport, Australia

Helen Steel confronts John Dines at Sydney Airport after discovering he is responsible for training police officers.

December 2016, UCPI confirms Dines was a UCO

Helen finally receives official confirmation that John Dines was an undercover police officer, in a letter from the Inquiry.

January 2017, Kate's case

Kate settles her common-law claim by accepting an earlier offer from the police, meaning that she is not bound by the same settlement agreement as the other women, and can take her case to the IPT.

April 2017, UCPI confirms Jenner was UCO

Alison finally receives confirmation from the Inquiry, and then sometime later from the Metropolitan Police, that Mark Jenner was an undercover police officer.

May 2018, Boyling found guilty of gross misconduct and sacked

DC Jim Boyling is found guilty of gross misconduct and sacked from the police following a hearing based on Rosa's evidence. Sutton had infiltrated the campaign group Reclaim the Streets and had relationships with three women. The Met calls his actions 'unacceptable'. A panel hears allegations that Boyling had begun a sexual relationship with Rosa 'without authorisation and without a policing purpose' and rules it amounted to gross misconduct. It further rules the officer had failed to disclose the relationship to his superiors and he broke strict police rules by admitting to Rosa he was an undercover officer. Rosa learns from the panel that Boyling had been submitting Special Branch files on her, both before she moved into his flat at his behest and also in the heyday of their relationship.

The Public Inquiry chairman states the final report won't be ready until the end of 2023 – five years late.

June 2018, Lush campaign on spycops

High-profile publicity campaign about undercover relationships launched by Lush in partnership with Police Spies Out of Lives.

September 2018, Met Police admit Article 3 breaches

The Metropolitan Police admit Mark Kennedy's sexual relationship with Kate while he was undercover was a violation of her fundamental right not to be subjected to torture or inhumane or degrading treatment.

Postscript

November 2020, UCPI opening speeches

As we finish drafting this book, opening speeches and evidential hearings of the Undercover Policing Public Inquiry begin remotely due to COVID restrictions.

2–19 November 2020, UCPI Tranche 1 (Phase 1)

Evidence concerning undercover officers deployed between July 1968 and the end of 1972 is heard

21 April–13 May 2021, UCPI Tranche 1 (Phase 2)

Hearings covering SDS undercover officers whose deployments started between 1970 and 1979.

30 September 2021, Kate wins IPT case

Kate wins her case in the Investigatory Powers Tribunal, the secret court that we initially all fought to keep our cases out of but that ironically has provided the most disclosure of relevant files so far, not only for Kate but for Lisa as well. Lisa was prevented from also taking her case there by the terms of the settlement agreement, but provided a crucial witness statement and supporting evidence. This was the culmination of the legal meetings that began with all eight women in 2011.

The IPT ruled that the undercover policing operations against protest movements were 'unlawful and sexist'. It identified a '*formidable list*' of breaches by the Metropolitan Police of fundamental human rights, including:

- Article 3 – prohibition of torture and cruel, inhuman and degrading treatment.
- Article 8 – right to respect for private and family life.
- Article 10 – freedom of expression.

- Article 11 – freedom of assembly and association.
- Article 14 – freedom from discrimination against women.

It concluded that the failures of the Metropolitan Police had a disproportionate impact on women in terms of the number of women affected and the greater impact on their lives through the risk of pregnancy or interference with their childbearing years.

October 2021, UCPI announces further delays

The Undercover Policing Public Inquiry announces further delays to Inquiry hearings. Now the second tranche (covering 1982–92) will not be heard until 2024, and later tranches not until many years after that. There is no end in sight and the women have still not received any disclosure or answers from the police about the contents of personal files held on them or who knew of the relationships.

9–20 May 2022, Tranche 1 (Phase 3)

Hearings primarily covering SDS managers between 1968–82, including oral testimony from seven former SDS managers.

Additionally, five former SDS undercover police officers from the Tranche 1 era gave evidence at closed hearings from which all non-state core participants were excluded. Of these, two – HN21 and HN302 – are known to have had sexual contact while undercover.

September 2022, UCPI releases the name of additional officers found to have had intimate, sexual relationships

The UCPI releases the name of the officer known as Vince Miller, real name Vince Harvey, an officer who rose through the ranks of the Met to become Tactical Services Director of the UK National Crime Intelligence Services. He admitted to having a sexual relationship with 'Madeleine' and that she would not have slept with someone she knew to be an undercover police officer.

November 2022, UCPI reveals further officers' real names

Special Demonstration Squad officer James 'Straven' has his real name, James Thomson, added to the UCPI website. Thomson initially applied for, and was granted, anonymity over his cover and real names, until it was discovered that he had lied about not having sexual relationships in his cover identity. He had two relationships, with 'Sara' and 'Ellie', and maintained a friendship with 'Ellie' that lasted for 18 years until she discovered his true identity.

June 2023, UCPI publish Interim Report on SDS

This damning Interim Report from the UCPI states the unit had a 'perennial feature' of undercover officers forming sexual relationships with women activists.

Covering the formation of the Squad in 1968–82, it finds that the SDS unit should have been disbanded in the 1970s and that its activity was a waste of time, and its intrusiveness would have caused outrage if revealed.

It records that while the main justification for the unit was said to be for public order purposes, "it is a striking feature of the reporting of almost all SDS undercover officers that it contained extensive details about individuals – their political views, personality, working life, relationships with others, and family and private life" and that "this was not an accidental by-product of reporting on public order issues."

The Inquiry Chair, Sir John Mitting, said in his view that only three groups were ever 'a legitimate target' for undercover policing of any kind. In his report, Sir John wrote that these issues 'should have been addressed at the highest level within the MPS and within the Home Office.'

He concluded:

'The question is whether or not the end justified the means [...] I have come to the firm conclusion that, for a unit of a police force, it did not; and that had the use of these means been publicly known at the time, the SDS would have been brought to a rapid end.'

The report does not assign blame, but finds that there were four crucial issues which should have alerted the Metropolitan Police and the Home Office to serious problems:

- long-term intrusive relationships by undercover officers.
- the legality of entering private homes without a warrant or just cause.
- the theft of deceased children's identities by officers.
- undercovers taking on positions of responsibility in the groups they were targeting and using that to report on personal details of people engaged in legitimate activities.

Campaigners welcome these findings but continue to press for long-standing demands: for the release of all personal files, the cover names of all the spycops, and a complete list of all groups targeted, so that the full extent and nature of secret political policing in the UK is exposed.

July 2023, Police disciplinary tribunal highly critical of SDS guidance and culture

A tribunal investigating Jim Boyling, who had an intimate sexual relationship with three women, finds him guilty of gross misconduct but mitigated by systemic failure of the SDS. To date, Boyling is the only undercover officer to have ever been disciplined for sexual misconduct.

July 2024, UCPI Tranche 2 begins (1983–92)

The next phase of the public inquiry (UCPI) reconvenes for live evidential hearings. It is beset by problems caused by the prolonged delay of disclosure to non-state core participants, including Belinda and Helen. It is criticised by women for failures and unfairness, including the delays to disclosure seemingly to protect police privacy and state secrecy, but leaving insufficient time for non-state witnesses to review documents and properly prepare for hearings.

Met police opening speeches apologise again for actions of SDS

Counsel for the Met police state: 'at least nine undercover officers in Tranche 2 engaged in deceitful sexual relationships whilst they were deployed. This was completely unacceptable. So too was the failure of their managers to identify and prevent those relationships from happening. The MPS apologises to the women affected, and to the public, for these failings and for the wider culture of sexism and misogyny which allowed them to happen.'

October 2024, Tranche 2 (phase 2)

In his opening speech, Counsel to the Inquiry (CTI) sets out that Belinda is deeply hurt by Bob Lambert's deceit and feels angry and violated, and that evidence shows that Lambert is known to have entered into at least four deceitful sexual relationships and to have fathered a child while undercover.

He says that John Dines has provided a witness statement admitting his sexual relationship with Helen, but has refused to give live evidence to the Inquiry: 'On our reading of his witness statement, he is stating that he used her to maintain his cover and obtain intelligence. In other words, cold, calculating emotional and sexual exploitation'. Dines' statement asserts that his managers knew about his sexual relationship with Helen.

CTI also refers to Helen's protracted searches for 'John Barker' in the 1990s and 2000s and acknowledges 'considerable steps were taken by the Metropolitan Police Service to try and prevent Steel from finding Dines. They included relocating Dines, at one point, at very significant public expense'.

As a consequence of the extensive delays to disclosure and the emotional impact of reading this, Helen's evidence relating to Dines is postponed to Tranche 3. However, she gives evidence in Tranche 2 in relation to Lambert's actions and reporting.

November 2024, Belinda gives evidence to UCPI

At the time of writing the first edition of this book, Belinda did not feel able to disclose that Bob had told her, prior to the Debenhams incendiary device incident in 1987, that he was going to take part. She believes it is important to be completely transparent in her evidence to the Public Inquiry so explains what he told her about his involvement in this incident. In this evidence, she also explains that she accompanied Bob when he visited Geoff in prison on at least two occasions.

Spring 2025, Documentary series to be broadcast based on this book

As part of the women's aim to ensure this never happens to others again, a documentary series is broadcast raising awareness of this state-sponsored abuse and the culture of misogyny that the police and security services have normalised. Campaigning continues for a transparent and robust Inquiry that is currently committed to publishing its final report by the end of 2026, by which time it will have run for over a decade. The women also continue to campaign for decision makers to reverse the current legislation that places undercover officers completely beyond the law.